Also by Agnes Newton Keith

Before the Blossoms Fall

Before the Blossoms Fall:

Life and Death in Japan

by Agnes Newton Keith

AN ATLANTIC MONTHLY PRESS BOOK

Little, Brown and Company·Boston·Toronto

FIRST EDITION

T 9/75

Library of Congress Cataloging in Publication Data

Keith, Agnes Newton.
  Before the blossoms fall.

  "An Atlantic Monthly Press book."
  Includes index.
  1. Japan—Social life and customs. 2. National characteristics, Japanese. I. Title.
DS822.5K4   952   75-12880
ISBN 0-316-48630-2

ATLANTIC—LITTLE, BROWN BOOKS
ARE PUBLISHED BY
LITTLE, BROWN AND COMPANY
IN ASSOCIATION WITH
THE ATLANTIC MONTHLY PRESS

Designed by D. Christine Benders

*Published simultaneously in Canada
by Little, Brown & Company (Canada) Limited*

PRINTED IN THE UNITED STATES OF AMERICA

For my husband — without whom this book
would not be — my gratitude and love.

Acknowledgment

I wish to thank the Japan Foundation for making this, my fourth visit to Japan, possible. I am most grateful for their generous financial arrangements. Even more, I appreciate their unfailing assistance, always graciously given, in locating people, places and projects. Each member of the foundation whom I met quietly contributed toward the making of this book.

I also thank various members of the International Hospitality and Conference Association, which functions under the planning section of the Foreign Affairs Ministry, for making my travel arrangements.

I acknowledge with awe the incomparable assistance of the very fine Japanese daily press.

And I thank every Japanese whom I met and talked with because the sum of these meetings adds up to the total of this book. They are the source of the warmth, respect and affection which I feel in my heart for these fragile islands and their enduring people, who live on a troubled earth in hostile seas — and prosper.

Author's Note

Japan is a more endearing country in human terms than any stranger coming from the Western world will imagine before he arrives. It is a place where a paradoxical people live, love, work and attempt to be happy more or less as we do at home.

For forty years now these extraordinary people of very considerable genius have played a part in my own personal life in its most critical periods. Now, after knowing the Japanese in war and peace, in poverty and prosperity, I ask myself, How can I know the truth about a people whom I love — and do not fully trust? Who contradict themselves, who are emotionally extravagant, who are unsurpassed for energy and diligence, and who can face an ugly death gracefully when they cannot face life? This book is an attempt to arrive at a little understanding of a very contradictory, controversial people of great ability, high intelligence, and genius.

The Japanese inhabit five completely indefensible islands, with no place to hide. They are about two hundred miles from the Russian mainland, a stone's throw from the Russian-occupied islands of Sakhalin and the Kuriles, one hundred miles from Korea, and five hundred miles from China. Japan's total land area is less than that of the State of California, with three quarters of it too mountainous to cultivate. The Japanese are not self-sufficient in food or in energy — except human energy. They are controlled by an ancient code of human obligations, yet they control by modern means their own population growth. They live for their jobs, not for pleasure, and they are exquisite craftsmen. They ignore happiness, they welcome suffering. They outstrip the world in modern production, and their rate of growth is the fastest in the world. They worship being Japanese.

Japanese women have walked many paces behind men for centuries. Today they walk abreast. Does this mean liberation? Or merely longer legs? Or a new kind of woman?

These remarkable people rode the crest of the wave of prosperity in 1973. A year later, they swim in its trough. But they are the same people with the same handicaps — and the same genius. Their seas are wicked, their islands shake, their trees are crippled, their earth slides into the sea, and the people survive.

A. N. K.

December, 1974

Before the Blossoms Fall

1

∽∽∽∽∽∽∽∽∽∽∽∽∽∽∽∽∽∽∽∽∽∽∽∽∽

L OVING THE ORIENT is a state of mind, not body, and I was thrilled to be back in Tokyo in the staccato clatter of small, fast-running feet. Even its musty smells and smoky smog were welcome after the sterile cold winds of a Canada winter.

We were met at the Haneda Airport that February night by a handsome young Japanese wearing the Western Establishment uniform of a smart black business suit with a pastel pink shirt and a wide, bright-striped tie. This was Mr. Kimura of the Fujo Travel Service, and he seemed to know all about Harry and me. He had been sent by the Foreign Affairs Ministry, he said, to help us through customs and immigration, and to escort us to our hotel. He spoke English well, though he didn't always understand it. We had no problems with our passports or luggage, but when we went to the exchange office to buy yen we found the U.S. dollar just starting a fatal downward plunge which proved disastrous to tourists. As we were only allowed to change a very limited number of dollars, we were glad to know that Mr. Kimura was nearby.

We explained to him that we had made reservations by

cable from Canada to stay at the Hotel Maranouchi where we had lodged in times past. He assured us he would deliver us safely. Then, dashing recklessly into the passing traffic, he forcibly captured a taxi into which he loaded our bags and us, and gave quick directions to the driver.

The route from Tokyo Bay to the city follows the rusty, now-abandoned monorail line which was built for Expo '67, and is presently interlaced with Freeway No. 1. On the freeway a clanking, metallic serpent of motorcars and buses stopped and started with reluctant obedience to some distant signal miles ahead. Mr. Kimura mentioned that there was a strike on of trains and buses, with some two and a half million workers out. I tried to imagine how two and a half million more people could possibly get onto these crowded roads.

Looking beyond Mr. Kimura's broad shoulders, which wedged me down between himself and Harry, I saw that physically this Tokyo of 1973 bore little resemblance to the city I remembered from eighteen years before. I had to admit that the lure of the Orient seemed dead — or noisily dying. Here in its place were Chicago, Pittsburgh, Detroit, New York, Los Angeles, et al. . . . Here was a destructive dynamo of unleashed twentieth-century industrial energy pouring its force through the steel frames and human bodies of modern slaves to the Gross National Product. God bless America! We had given Japan the atom bomb; now we were giving them the subway rush and ulcers.

I had made no attempt to follow Mr. Kimura's directions to the hotel. When we drove up to a large, imposing entrance to a luxurious looking hostel which had nothing in common with the old Maranouchi I remembered, it didn't surprise me. This handsome exterior was only a part of the renovated picture of general Japanese affluence, I supposed.

We stood silently at the registration desk while Mr. Kimura dealt with the clerks in Japanese, expertly but unnecessarily as they all spoke English. I looked about at the quietly handsome lobby, the paneled walls, the elegant crystal chandeliers, the large, live juniper tree which was growing in a man-made pond in the center of the lobby. This hotel was obviously first-class, and what impressed me most was that it was filled with Japanese. Twenty years ago there would have been foreigners only. Obviously the remodeled Maranouchi was prospering, and so were the Japanese.

Thanking Mr. Kimura, we signed the register and received our keys and told him goodbye, never to see him again. Official Tokyo is full of people whom one sees once and never again. Then we were ushered to our room by a smiling young man who continued to smile when, following desk instructions, we did not tip him. In years past we had been told that the good performance of a Japanese subordinate is taken for granted and not to be bought with cash. We had wondered if this had changed with the new prosperity, and we were happy to find that it hadn't. One of the greatest terrors of foreign travel in many countries is not knowing how much to tip without insulting somebody or being made a fool of.

Our room was large, handsome, pleasantly warm. We called room service for sandwiches, which arrived promptly, were freshly made and good. Then we fell into two crisp, white, luxurious, beautiful beds and slept.

The next morning I noticed the name Hotel Okura embossed on the bath mat. When the waiter brought our coffee, I showed him the mat and asked, "Why does this mat say Hotel Okura?"

"Because this is Hotel Okura, madame," he said.

The Brazilian coffee was strong, hot, savory and served in a silver thermos pot. "This coffee is so good," Harry said, "I don't care what hotel this is."

Later when we went down to the desk we asked the clerk what price we were paying for our room, and who had made reservations for us. "Foreign Affairs Ministry made your reservations," he said, "At a special low rate," and he named a price which horrified us by its extravagance.

"But we had reservations at the Hotel Maranouchi," I said faintly.

"I don't think so, madame," the clerk said, "But I'll call there." He did so, and the Maranouchi assured him they had no reservations for the Keiths. Obviously Foreign Affairs knew best.

"Think of that wonderful coffee!" Harry said philosophically.

Our first duty in Tokyo was to call on the Japan Foundation, whose invited guest I was. This we located in the new Daito Building, Kasumigaseki, Chiyoda-ku. There we met Mr. Kichimasa Soda, who was expecting us, as he is the head of the Exchange of Persons Department. He seemed a very nice person, gentle in manner, somewhat Europeanized in speech, as he has been in Paris for some years with UNESCO. He introduced Mr. Tatsuo Noguchi, head of the Dispatching Division, also in his late forties. Then Mr. Fumitomo Horiuchi was called for and introduced, a young man with a bad cold and sore eyes who seemed to do the legwork for the others. All were wearing neat black suits with white shirts, wide bright ties and well-cut jackets.

Mr. Soda asked if we were pleased with our hotel accommodations. I told him we were — except that the Okura was really too expensive for us as we had expected to go to the old Maranouchi. He then said rather rebukingly that obviously the

Foreign Affairs Ministry would not wish to book visiting strangers in a second-class hotel. In any case, I would find that the special rate we were booked at was as low as I would pay at an inferior hotel at a regular rate. I saw his point. From then on we accepted that Foreign Affairs always knew best.

Even more important, Mr. Soda told me that the foundation was allowing me a per diem while in Japan. They would also supply a motorcar and a driver for my use while we were in Tokyo, and an interpreter when I wished one. Train fares would be paid for me to any destination in Japan, but outside of Tokyo I myself would have to pay for an interpreter, and his hotel expenses. They asked me to estimate my probable length of stay in Japan, as they proposed to pay my total per diem in advance. This was a lifesaver, as the value of my U.S. dollars was shriveling hourly. As to the length of our stay, Mr. Shigiei, who represented the Japan Foundation in Washington, had once suggested to me a ten-day visit, which I had said was ridiculous. Now I told Mr. Soda that six weeks was the very least I could do anything in — and he agreed.

He asked in what way the foundation could assist in my work. I told him that from my point of view, my work was to meet and understand the Japanese people as I found them today. From the foundation's point of view, my work was to write something which would promote friendship and sympathy between our two countries. I believed the two objectives complemented each other.

I told Mr. Soda that I would need assistance in locating certain people whom we had known in the past but with whom we had lost touch, and others whom I did not know but believed could help me to assess the new Japan. I gave him a list, which we had previously prepared, of fifty names, accompanied by addresses where possible, of persons I hoped to meet. The name of Mr. Hidemi Kon, president of the Japan Foundation, came first, apropos of my advice from Mr. Shigiei to call promptly on Mr. Kon.

Mr. Soda passed my list to young Mr. Horiuchi, who asked me when I had last seen these friends. When I said in 1955 he clucked his tongue and shook his head and said they were probably all dead by now. I agreed that this was possibly so, but not necessarily so, as we ourselves were still alive. Mr. Horiuchi, being under thirty, was probably surprised that we were not dead. Then all three gentlemen said that it was very difficult to locate anybody in Japan without having the person's telephone number, as street names and numbers had been reshuffled so many times during and since the Occupation days. However, they would do their best for me.

Then I suggested that today I might call on Mr. Kon, president of the foundation. Mr. Horiuchi hastily disappeared to telephone Mr. Kon's secretary. He returned to say that Mr. Kon was not available at present — possibly out of town — possibly not well — possibly . . . well, possibly . . . Mr. Soda then said the obvious — that I had better see Mr. Kon another day. I assume my rank and status had not yet been determined by Mr. Kon.

Mr. Horiuchi then made an appointment for me to meet Mr. Kikuo Nishida, secretary general of the national commission of UNESCO, the next day. One name out of fifty was located.

I asked Mr. Horiuchi to obtain for me the recent issues of the *Japan P.E.N. News,* journals which are printed in English and cover contemporary Japanese literature. He agreed to do so.

By this time the less important individuals in the rear of the offices could be seen at their desks consuming their midday rice with chopsticks from small bowls held under their chins. We got up and said goodbye. We left the foundation feeling

8

much impressed with the pleasing personalities and the co-operative attitudes of the men we had just met, but with the realization that nobody could help us but ourselves. My picture of new Japan was already changing; they were a wonderful people with a miraculous GNP — but they were no more efficient man for man than we in the West. They just worked harder.

2

෴෴෴෴෴෴෴෴෴෴෴෴෴෴෴෴෴

W HEN THE JAPANESE STEAMER *Asama Maru* slid gracefully into Yokohama Port on our honeymoon journey
one October forty years ago, we were together on the deck and
rejoicing at the Asian world before us. We were welcomed by
five splendidly dressed Japanese gentlemen hurrying up the
gangway. Approaching with shining smiles, correctly measured
bows, and formal greetings, they were, it seemed, Harry's
friends who managed timber and rubber estates in British
North Borneo, where he had been living for the last ten years,
and was taking me now as his bride.

The leader of the delegation, Mr. Hamasaki, a gentle-
spoken, fragile man, promptly presented us with a typed, hour-
by-hour itinerary for our activities during a proposed five-day-
and-night tour of Japan escorted by the five gentlemen. The
tour was scheduled to start immediately, Mr. Hamasaki said,
and transportation was awaiting us now on the dock. The gentlemen were smiling hospitably and obviously anticipating our
happy acceptance.

I waited for Harry to speak, feeling certain that he would politely refuse the invitation in favor of our solitude. Instead I heard him answer with obvious pleasure that we would be ready to go in five minutes. As he hustled me off to our stateroom I asked anxiously, "Do you mean it? What shall I take?"

"Oh, anything, anything — just anything! You're lucky, dear. You'll see a Japan with them that you'd never see on your own. I've done it all before — but this is your first visit." Harry dragged his suitcase out from under the berth, dumped out its contents, and started throwing in gray flannels and shirts, saying, "Hurry up, dear. We mustn't keep them waiting. Just toss in a few things."

In desperation I "tossed in" my red satin slippers and my best plaid taffeta dress from Hollywood, a couple of sports blouses, and several pairs of white sharkskin shorts. These last Harry hastily threw out, saying, "You'll never wear shorts in Japan! Better just wear your tweed suit and forget the rest. Ready?"

I wasn't ready, but I was resigned; my new life had started.

Five days later I knew that for better or worse Japan had entered my life to stay. Not that the experience was always comfortable; our hosts worked on day and night shifts, while we had to be alert at all times. Harry solved his problem by going to bed one night and missing a geisha party — although he insisted that I must go in order not to disappoint our friends. I put on my red plaid dress and went with the five gentlemen and came home filled with sake and admiration for geisha girls. No Japanese wife would have gone to a geisha party, I realized later, but our friends probably assumed that American women would do anything — and it was one of the few times when Harry cultivated my Americanism.

We wore off our feet to the ankle bones touring museums, climbing steps to temples, hobbling over pebbled roads to view shrines, squatting on our heels, and scuffling our shoes off and on. I was almost ready to jump over Kegon Falls in despair after we had walked for an hour in a cold fall wind through dripping, rainy forests over soggy moss to view Kegon's icy, glistening stream which had inspired so many suicides, an action with which I temporarily sympathized. When our escorts saw me shivering, we went to a teahouse and they sent for a bottle of Suntory whiskey to warm me, and I was too ignorant of Japanese etiquette to appreciate what I was doing by drinking whiskey at teatime. After that I was usually offered Suntory, which I refused, instead of tea. Meanwhile I kept reminding myself that I would enjoy it all in retrospect.

Back in Tokyo we went to the *Kabuki* theater and ate and drank our way through its remarkable daylong program of dancing, gesturing, singing and miming, which we in the audience accompanied with eating and drinking. Although at times the spectators, when not munching and sipping, appeared to be half asleep, they never failed to rally with enthusiastic bursts of applause for every familiar, well-loved and well-known dramatic crisis.

An event of almost equal importance to me was the purchase of a genuine long-sleeved Japanese bridal kimono, black decorated with white chrysanthemums. On the advice of our Japanese friends we bought this at a large department store where, as I tried on various kimonos, my Western height stopped passers-by.

Mr. Hamasaki even arranged for "Bebe-chan," the young Japanese daughter of an associate, to go about with us for several days so that I should have female companionship. Bebe-chan proved to be adorable and surprisingly adaptable, and when she shared a cocktail with us one evening she shocked her Japanese chaperones — but enjoyed herself. By now I felt that I had never met more kindly and courteous people than our Japanese friends.

And dutiful and nature-loving too, for there wasn't a beauty spot we missed if they could help it. As it rained all the time, the leaves of forests, pines, junipers, and orchards dripped with crystals, the crimson tiled roofs of temples glittered, the Golden Pavilion shimmered, and Buddhas of jade, gold or bronze were at their jewel-like, most impressive best. The miniature beauty of peaked mountains, twisted trees, tiny, fertile, dung-fed farms, clear flowing streams, polished pebble gardens, carefully combed sand plots, all shone in the autumn rain in a lacquered landscape. I was a Californian and not used to country like this — never monotonous, always sculpted and tortured, sea and land woven into a tapestry, rocky coasts with a furious beauty, deep valleys, wild gorges, and wind-torn trees filled with ancient magic — a land of natural beauty in miniature, all framed and delivered before my eyes. Its delicate loveliness entranced me, and has stayed with me ever since.

When the day's work, and it was work, was done and we all relaxed together in some inn, sitting around a charcoal-burning *hibachi* to warm our feet, we talked of our homes and families. Our Japanese friends' homes, with paper walls and sliding doors and scant furniture, were not materially like our own; and when we exchanged snapshots of our families we saw that their family faces were wide and flat, with high cheek-bones, and narrow, dark-brown eyes set slantingly, and straight black hair. But one thing we found we all had in common — our homes were the physical core of our lives, and our families were the emotional and spiritual centers. Both home and family were indestructible, we would have said then.

I had left the *Asama Maru* with strangers, but I returned to it with friends — one of whom, Mr. Hamasaki, was to remain so to the end of his life twenty years later. Harry had been right when he said we could never have seen Japan on our own as we saw it with them. Perhaps the growth of friendship depends on the climate about it, and in 1934 the emotional climate was good. I fell in love with the Japanese.

For the first time in my life I forgot about the angle of their eyes, and thought of them in the same way I thought of us. They were small compared to Westerners, but well put together, energetic, vital, polite, determined and seemingly very gentle. They were carefully literate in their English speech. To them, beauty was its own reason for being, and not always to be priced. This was an exciting thought to one from the Western hemisphere.

Each had a closely guarded core of sentiment for his family. Each may have loved his wife, but such a statement would never be made. They could be flirted with, amused, diverted, and they could offer genuine admiration. Each one I met was equally surprised, I think, that I was basically the same human flesh as he — despite the level of my eyes. It was a great and moving discovery to me that this previously unmet world of the Orient was filled with the flesh, blood and feelings of people not unlike ourselves. So much more intriguing, I thought, than if they had been like the people in *The Tale of Genji* (which of course they were, inside).

With the exception of Bebe-chan, I didn't meet any Japanese women. This also was a comment on this era in Japan. Most nice wives and girls were naturally at home. I admit I didn't miss them or think too much about them. They were beautiful, Harry said, and very gracious and charming — but he had been here before — without me. I could only judge what I saw on the streets — and the girls either looked quite delicious or decidedly drab.

Perhaps none of this explains completely my sudden emotional involvement with the Japanese — unless one adds that it was our honeymoon.

We rejoined our ship at Kobe and then sailed through the Inland Sea which is really a chain of five seas linked together by channels. I thought it was the most beautiful stretch of water in the world. I still think it is — but today many areas of the Inland Sea are poisoned.

There are several thousand islands in *Seto-Naikai*, as the Japanese call the Inland Sea, and these have always been the source of much of Japan's food. The busy fishing villages gave testimony to this, as did the sturdy, well-muscled fishermen for whom fishing was then a lifetime career. From many of the island shores there arose tiered rice fields, vegetable gardens, and fruit orchards where peasant farmers, grateful to inherit any tiny patch of soil, worked long and hard without questioning their destiny. In those days there was an ancient, unwritten pact between the people and their natural island resources, an understanding of mutual need.

That was a long time ago — forty years. The wives of those farmers and fishermen didn't play golf or bowl; their sons didn't commit suicide because they failed their exams; their daughters didn't abandon their unwanted babies in trash cans in stations. All wives were in the fields or kitchens then, all sons were needed at home, and all babies were wanted.

Today the pollution in some areas of the Inland Sea is growing deadly. The situation is reported to be five times worse than it was three years ago. Japanese industry itself is now dependent on heavy chemical industries, all of which discharge pollutants, while waste waters and oil flow into the sea from paper pulp mills and metal industries. The poisonous products released by the Red Tide organisms, a periodic natural phenomenon not confined to Japan, brings death to much marine life. Oil dumping and the release of waste oil by metal indus-

15

tries has contributed to death-dealing conditions. Many fishery resources in the Sea of Harima are now ruined, and those in Osaka Bay have been damaged by organic mercury and cadmium-polluted waste waters flowing into the bay. These are, perhaps, but a few examples of the damage being inflicted on the marine environment.

The most notorious example of pollution is that which resulted recently in the Minamata Disease caused by organic mercury poisoning. This mercury came from Chisso Corporation industrial waste, which emptied into Minamata Bay in Kumamoto Prefecture on Kyushu Island. The disease, which paralyzes the nervous system, has so far resulted in some sixty-three deaths, and thousands of cases of serious illness. The case against the Chisso Corporation had been fought in the courts for some time, and the final verdict has just been given that Chisso must pay a total of some $13 million to the victims of the illness.

Not only the Inland Sea but many farmlands have been damaged by the use of certain farm chemicals, and cadmium soil poisoning in farm and rice lands results in double destruction by washing into the sea, where it is rendering oysters unfit for human consumption.

However, today the Japanese government is taking a new, strong stand against pollution and in favor of conservation of the environment at all costs. In 1971 the Environmental Agency was established, and provision of adequate funds for research and environmental control are now being provided.

I next saw Japan in 1939 when the temper of the world was raw and frayed with war. We had been home on leave and were waiting to go to Oxford for Harry to attend a three-months refresher course in forestry, when the fateful day came, September third, 1939, and the British Empire was at war. We were ordered to return to British Borneo by the first trans-Pacific steamer sailing from Vancouver, and we had no time to get visas for Japan before sailing. But being filled with friendly feelings and happy memories of Japan, we anticipated no trouble in landing at Yokohama. However, when we asked to go ashore at this port we were escorted to the Water Police Headquarters and held there in custody throughout the ship's brief stay — a very different reception from that of our honeymoon visit. We realized afterward that this was the beginning of our war.

Being young and reckless, and not believing what we saw if it didn't suit us, when the steamer proceeded to Nagasaki to coal we tried again to land. This time it worked — with the aid of a good many cigarettes. At Nagasaki dockyards, behind high mat screens, there was then under construction the largest and most heavily armed ship-of-war in the world, we were told. We believed it. By this time we also believed in the war. And as our unborn son was now kicking forcefully, we believed in him too. That was a long time ago in a different world.

Our next contact with the Japanese was in January, 1942, when their victorious army entered Sandakan Bay in British North Borneo as an occupying force just a year and nine months after our son George was born. Our friend, Mr. Hamasaki, who was in Borneo managing a rubber estate, tried to help us, but he was as helpless as we against the Japanese military forces. A few weeks later as the result of Japanese interrogations I lost an unborn second son. I couldn't believe such behavior was possible from the gentle Japanese. Shortly after this we were confined in prison camps in Borneo, our two-year-old son George and I being imprisoned together, and Harry held separately. We were incarcerated thus as prisoners of the Japanese for almost four years, until September 11, 1945.

During this time starvation was our worst and most enduring enemy. Starvation is not hunger; hunger is healthy, starvation is deathly. Starvation approached us week by week, and day by day, and in the end we almost died of it.

In 1944, while being interrogated in camp by our captors, we both received serious physical injuries. Throughout those four years I kept asking myself, how could these brutal jailers be of the same blood and race as the gentle, sensitive friends of my first visit to Japan? Yet in the end we believe that Harry's life was saved by the intervention of the Japanese camp commandant, Colonel Tatsuji Suga. That was a long, long time ago — the longest time of all — in a different world from now, thank God.

While a prisoner of the Japanese I had kept secret notes about those four years in captivity. Ultimately these became the nucleus of a book, *Three Came Home,* published in 1947. Oddly enough, the book became a best-seller in Japan.

When my royalties were blocked in postwar Occupied Japan, my publishers warned me that the only way I could use them was to spend them in that country. Harry said NO! He never wanted to see the blank blank country again, or the so-and-so bastards!

But I had an incurable desire to put together those contradictory persons whom I had experienced in such extremes of living, and try to get a whole man out of them. I had to find the reality. So in 1955 we went to Japan to spend our yen, going, I admit, with some uncertainty, antagonism and even revulsion.

I already knew that our Japanese prison camp commandant, Colonel Tatsuji Suga, had left a widow, for after my book was published she had written to me and said she wished to meet me. I knew she had a son and two daughters, but I did not then feel able to meet these people in person. Even ten years after the war, my skin still crept at certain memories.

I wanted to forget my personal part in the violent past. I didn't wish to be sinned against — nor to sin; I didn't want to be pitied — nor to pity. The only friend we wished to meet was Mr. Hamasaki, who had written to us long before, asking us to come to see him. Except for him, we just wanted to be strangers on a holiday in Japan.

But we couldn't holiday with what we found. We saw a country in which not only the armed forces but every civilian had suffered almost mortally. Except for Mr. Hamasaki, our old friends were dead. Mr. Hamasaki was like a skeleton from prolonged malnutrition and his struggle against a fatal illness. Shortly after we left Japan he died. His wife wrote to us then saying that it had made him happy to see us again, and to know that we parted as friends.

We learned that all over the Japanese archipelago men, women and children, infants and old folks, had died of starvation, many of sheer misery and desperation as the war hung on. Thousands of others were killed under saturation bombing. We saw the entire stretch from Yokohama to Tokyo, once solid housing, now flattened by bombs and scorched black by fire. Tokyo itself was half destroyed, and every street corner was haunted by silent, gaunt, blind or mutilated veterans. We didn't have the heart to go to Nagasaki, or to Hiroshima to look for the family of our camp commandant, Colonel Suga — after what we saw.

This was the first time I had thought of the Japanese as suffering as much or more than ourselves; the first time I had not thought of *us* as the aggrieved persons. Now gradually my feeling became one of sympathy and pity for *all* of us caught in the slavery and stupidity of war.

In wartime all suffer: this we had accepted mentally long

before. But we learned it emotionally in Japan in 1955 — ten years after being freed from a Japanese prison camp. That was a long time ago in a very different world.

Nine years later, we retired to our home in Canada.

This was the second spring of the war in Vietnam. In the United States a President had been elected by the mothers of America in a vote for peace. Another candidate had been defeated by his stand for war. The first two United States Marine combat divisions had landed in Vietnam. Our son George, survivor of a prison camp childhood, was one of those U.S. Marines.

Time passes. Ultimately it was the ninth year of the war in Vietnam, and the people of the United States had had enough. Although people continued to be killed out there, villages were ruined and raped, women and children ran from death and were overtaken, soldiers stood fast or ran — but they weren't *our* soldiers anymore. Suddenly, it almost didn't matter to us in the U.S.A. — for somehow we had found our way out of the bloody slime. Ultimately, our prisoners came home, our fighting men came. Our son was home. Most of us never knew what the war had been about — except that it was too far away and too damned long.

I have a private world and a public one. My private world is my family, and until this one is moderately in order I can't concentrate on the other one. All through the Vietnam war there was something terribly wrong with both worlds, with a son in the combat zone. When George came home to his wife and children, for us as individuals the war was done.

Then I began to concentrate on what I wanted more than anything else — a final trip to a suddenly wealthy, to-be-envied Japan. I had known the Japanese in war and in poverty; now I wanted to meet them in peace and prosperity.

My editor and my publishers thought the trip was a good idea, as did my family, friends and associates — but nobody knew how to pay for it — including me. It was at this crucial moment early in 1973 that I first heard the voice of Mr. Shigiei over the telephone from Washington, D.C.

"Can you go to Japan for the Japan Foundation, Mrs. Keith?" asked the unknown Asian voice speaking across the North American continent.

"When?" I asked.

"Now — in a week or so," the voice said.

"Make it two weeks," I compromised.

Ultimately, our trip was arranged entirely by long distance telephone via the Japanese Embassy in Washington, because of the Canadian mail strike. First, I had to renew my U.S. passport, and the passport officer in Vancouver was away on holiday. When he returned, my new passport was sealed into an on-strike mail box. When I asked the Japanese consulate to give me a visa good for two months they countered with the offer of a ten-day tourist permit. I explained that I was going to Japan at the request of the Japan Foundation to study, and I needed at least two months. They said they had never heard of the Japan Foundation, and requested a letter from their embassy in Washington to authorize my visa. I called Mr. Shigiei in Washington and asked him to telephone Vancouver. The telephones went on strike. This was followed by a long weekend off for embassies. Ultimately I went to Vancouver and filled out a number of forms at the Japanese consulate. Their handsome, overheated office had counters and tables stacked with pictorial pamphlets inviting everybody except me to visit Japan. A charming little lady helped me with the forms while a retiring little gentleman inspected me from behind a half-open door, and between them they ended by giving me the number of days I asked for.

In filling out the forms, the tiny lady advised me not to say that the purpose of my visit was to study. Instead, she suggested that I say I was going to visit the president of the Japan Foundation, Mr. Hidemi Kon, whose name appeared on the foundation letterhead. This I did, and a week later we left for Tokyo to visit Mr. Kon, who had never heard of us.

Early February is the worst possible time of year to visit Japan. No cherry blossoms, chrysanthemums, festivals, weddings — only burials, abandoned babies, dead grass and hara-kiri. But having been to Japan many times before, the month didn't really matter to us. It was the change in the Japanese people we were going to see, not the change in seasons.

Once settled on the groaning, monstrous plane headed for Tokyo, I had time to remember the personal reasons why I, an old woman now, was determined to make this one final trip back to a country I hated — and loved.

3

MR. KUNITERO NISHIBERI called on us the day after we
arrived, bringing with him Mr. Hiroshi Yoshida. Both
gentlemen were dressed in best executive-style costumes with
smart black suits, snow-white shirts, and very wide, striped
satin ties. Neat and svelte, with shining black hair, high cheek-
bones and Tokyo tans, they looked exactly as they should for
what they proved to be, representatives of the Foreign Affairs
Ministry.

Our visitors presented their cards, a helpful habit without
which I would never have caught up with their full titles which
were, respectively, Chief of Administration Section, Internal
Operations Division, Ministry of Foreign Affairs, and Director
of Planning Office, Foreign Affairs. Both represent the International Hospitality and Conference Association. They explained that the Foreign Affairs Ministry has a special planning section solely devoted to arranging programs for various
foundation and cultural exchange visitors, who number into
the thousands in Japan, and who, like me, hope to benefit both
Japan and themselves by their visits. I was about to be planned-
for, my visitors said.

Mr. Nishiberi is a charming man of possibly thirty-five, with intense brown eyes, a responsive smile, instantaneous reactions, and slender fingers darkly nicotine-stained. That he will wear himself out by forty-five, was my guess. He was never without a smoldering Japanese cigarette, whose reeking smoke circled about his head and into my eyes. He insisted on giving me one of his cigarettes to try, and it tasted bitter and moldy. He is a very dynamic person, and of the people whom I have met so far this visit, he is my favorite.

After several cups of Brazilian coffee we came to the purpose of his call, which was to give us advice about our travel itinerary, including what trains to take, sights to see, and inns to patronize. We told him that we had already made an outline of where we wished to go, and we hoped to follow it — but we did need train schedules, hotel reservations, and so on. Mr. Nishiberi said he would return in a day or so with the practical details worked out, especially costs. His only comment on our proposed schedule was that it looked like hard work, and he hoped we were strong enough for it. So did we.

Indeed he did return, the following afternoon. With great personal zest, he had been busy remodeling our own outline of where we wished to go. I didn't really see what advantage his ideas had over ours, but he did — and he was confident and determined.

"You must stay at Takamatsu," he said firmly, "That is my hometown. My father lives there, and you may stay at his house overnight."

"You are too kind," I said, picturing mentally the dismay that two foreign visitors would precipitate on a small Japanese home.

"Takamatsu is on the island of Shikoku where you have not yet been. I insist that you stay several days with my father."

24

"That would be much too kind. We could not accept it." I said, hastily.

"Your father would disinherit you!" said Harry.

At that Mr. Nishiberi broke into sudden laughter and said philosophically, "Yes, probably he would. Never mind, there is a hotel there, the Takamatsu Kokusai, where we shall arrange for you to stay."

"Don't forget Hiroshima in your plan. We have a friend to look up there."

"Yes indeed, Hiroshima . . . I have taken many people to Hiroshima. All tourists go there, but not all have a proper sensitive attitude. One lady I took to the hospital there to visit patients who were still ill from radiation. We entered the room of one patient who was very ill and badly disfigured. This heartless visitor just glanced at the patient, then turned her eyes away from him and hurried outside. This was not proper behavior. Why could she not just touch him gently, perhaps place a fresh flower on his chest, and say, 'I shall pray for your recovery'? Why not show him some sympathetic feeling?"

I saw Mr. Nishiberi's point — also that of the visitor who might have been *too* distressed to stay, and I also saw how easy it is to be misunderstood by an intensely emotional people like the Japanese — and how important the gift of a few flowers could be in this flower-mad, beauty-worshiping country.

"You are a confusing people," I said, "You like flowers and sympathy, and you weep for your dead, and do nothing for your old folks who are still alive. I don't understand you."

"We don't understand ourselves," he said proudly.

"Is that why you leave it to foreigners to write about you and explain you to each other — probably incorrectly?" I asked, for I have been impressed by shelves full of publications by non-Japanese writers purporting to explain how and why the Japanese behave as they do.

He smiled noncommittally; the Japanese are excellent at not committing themselves.

"Now I am beginning to understand," I said, "why Ruth Benedict was able to write the best-ever book about Japan by staying at home in the U.S. and reading about your country and never coming here. It's less confusing. It's you Japanese who confuse us!"

"Oh, you mean *The Chrysanthemum and The Sword*," he said with instant interest. "Yes, *she* understood us."

Maybe I should have stayed at home to write my book. I shall carry fresh flowers with me in the future.

Every time Mr. Nishiberi visits us we end up with political and philosophical discussions. Although very earnest, he has a keen sense of humor — a not unusual combination in these people. He says that he is worried because Socialism and Communism are very much on the rise in Japan, and he sees them both as threatening to and alien to the Japanese code. He says that the Chinese are individualists — and so are the Americans. I try to follow his course of reasoning here, but just then he says he must go.

Before he leaves he says, "I shall take you to visit my family in Tokyo this Sunday." Then (is it a warning?), "We Japanese have two faces; one to show the world, and one for our family."

Does he read Robert Browning, I wonder?

> God be thanked, the meanest of his creatures
> Boasts two soul-sides, one to face the world with
> One to show a woman when he loves her!
> —Browning

This evening on television we watched bowling and the roller derby, and a "Lesson in Modern English," illustrated by a tantalizing Japanese girl. She demonstrated the phrases

"That's the way the ball bounces," and "That's the way the cookie crumbles." Both phrases essential to proper English, I assume.

Mr. Nishiberi's comment on the rise of Communism in Japan set me off on a witchhunt for facts, but I soon found that people were wary of committing themselves. If you were not a Communist you shunned comment for fear of getting involved with the bogey man. If you were a Communist — well, I hadn't met any avowed ones so far. Although it was obvious from their increasing numbers in the Diet that they must be around.

Today we kept our appointment with Dr. Kikuo Nishida, secretary general of the Japanese National Commission for UNESCO, Ministry of Education. A pleasant, good-looking, middle-aged man, he has an impressive manner and perfect fluency in English. When we return from our travels in the country he proposes to arrange a meeting for us with some university students, girls and men. There are so many different political factions represented among the young people, he says, that it will be difficult to choose any of them without the choice being seen as favoring one political group above another. The universities are all political hotbeds, and some have very hard cores of young revolutionaries quite ready to murder for their fanatic creed.

This fact was proved in the recent Lod Airport massacre at Tel Aviv, which was almost certainly the work of the *Rengo Sekigun*, or United Red Army — as are many of the Palestine Liberation Organization atrocities. The United Red Army has never had a large popular following, as it is the most extreme of eighteen radical student groups. At the same time, its excessive violence has attracted secret admiration from many young Japanese who recognize the death urge in it, and who see death in the pursuit of any objective as being the path to glory.

An adolescent romanticism is obvious in the swashbuckling manner in which the Red Army commits atrocities, and at least a half dozen policemen have been killed in struggles with them. Generally, the worst of these brutalities take place outside of Japan in order to avoid offending the extreme moral codes of the members' parents and homeland. The Red Army purges its own ranks without pity, and at least fourteen members have been tortured to death for crimes which range from a waning revolutionary enthusiasm to taking too much pleasure with women.

At Waseda University the *Kakumaruha*, or Student Revolutionary Marxists, have been the cause of violent riots in factional clashes with the *anti-Kakumaruha* group. Wearing helmets and armed with steel pipes, both sides have inflicted many injuries, some of which proved mortal both for each other and the police. The *Kakumaruha* lynched one student who opposed them. Waseda University itself appears to ignore the violence — perhaps having no other choice.

The large Yasuda Auditorium at the University of Tokyo also has been the scene of violent fighting among student factions, and the auditorium was once set on fire.

With this background of youthful bloodshedding, we asked Mr. Nishida if he could attribute its quality of vicious violence to any special cause. And also, what was the reason for the turning against their elders of young people today.

He answered that today in urban living a man's home was completely separate from the place where he made his living. Sons saw little of their fathers, and knew even less about the parents' work. Consequently, sons could not benefit as in the old days by a father's good example. A farmer used to show his son by his own example that he worked hard and was a kind and decent man. What a father *does* is more important than what a father *says* when he comes home late at night, tired out and cross.

After the Second World War, Mr. Nishida said, the new generation lost confidence in their elders, whom they held responsible for the miserable state of affairs in the world. Blinded by their own innocence, idealism, and ignorance of the world and its problems, the young people refused to make any allowances for the older generation.

Mr. Nishida confirmed that the suicide peak in Japan comes between the ages of twenty and twenty-five, then drops lower through the middle years, but with old age it increases again. No one can explain satisfactorily the reasons for the peak with young people. Some say that failure in their entrance exams, or overworking to try to pass the exams may contribute. Hanging seems to be one of the most popular methods of taking one's life, to judge by press reports — a rope being within the means of everyone.

4

IN THE AFTERNOON we drove to the Museum of Modern Art, and found a building which is simple, statuesque, and architecturally pleasing. Here we met the curator, Mr. Timon Miki, hospitable, cultured and sophisticated. A man of middle years, he spoke correct English with considerable effort, a fact which made me apologetic for not speaking Japanese. He conducted us through the museum, first enlisting his young lady assistant to accompany us, as her English was more fluent than his. A slender, pleasant young person, she proved to be extremely knowledgeable about the various exhibits, and the two of them stayed with us for almost two hours. During this time we saw only two other visitors in the whole museum.

Most of the oils dated from 1910 to 1960, and showed a strong European influence, especially those painted after the Second World War, when the goal of most Japanese painters was to study and work in Paris. Several famous painters were represented in the museum by their latest works, whose gaudy oils and bold, crude colors almost stunned my eyes — especially when they were hung beside earlier traditional paintings.

Although these modern oils were less to my taste, Mr. Miki assured me that in the Japanese art world they are greatly admired. For me, they had lost their Oriental validity.

The base of traditional Japanese art, Mr. Miki told us, is in an accumulated Chinese art culture, an Oriental legacy which is itself an intrinsic part of the Japanese people. I think Japanese works of art resemble their creators — they are better when they are being themselves than when they are trying to adapt to Western concepts. Their own art is born from a unique awareness of nature and beauty, sensitive attributes which most Japanese have, and which do not mix well with stark realism. It does not suit the Japanese nature to see only the warts on the face of his model, for he paints (or works) with love.

The irrational, uninhibited but imaginative arrangements of material objects into works of art, as portrayed by the surrealist artists Salvador Dali and Miró, were greatly admired in Japan and attracted many followers who ultimately developed their own school of surrealistic painting. A school of which Masao Tsuruoka was one of the most popular artists.

Abstractionism, once a worldwide fad, gained disciples here also. Most of them, however, managed to imprint a decidedly Japanese pattern on their works. One of the best-known is Kenzo Okada, who now lives in the United States. Before we left the oils, Mr. Miki said that he felt that the best of the modern school of painting combined the vitality of the Western world with the painstaking delicacy of the Orient.

We also saw and admired some exquisite silk screens which were mostly made in the first decade of this century in the traditional Asian style.

In the place of honor in the main floor entrance gallery, there was a magnificent exhibit by the famous wood sculptor, Denchu Hirakushi — who had just celebrated his one hundredth birthday, and is still carving. His realism seems touched by a spiritual power which makes it unique. Materially, his work had a warm, living quality which made me want to touch and stroke it. Unfortunately, most people reacted in this same manner, and there was a large sign asking people to resist the impulse, and *not* to touch.

Before we left the museum I had collected all the pictorial catalogues in sight even though I couldn't read them. It was maddening not to know what was said about these artists by critics who went beyond their own personal reactions. When we said goodbye to Mr. Miki he gave us tickets to go to the Yamatane Museum to see an exhibit of contemporary Japanese style paintings. We shall go tomorrow.

The day we arrived in Japan the U.S. dollar dropped from Yen 303 per dollar to Yen 260, or close to a 17 percent devaluation. In all my years of traveling in foreign countries, I have never before had to ask to have my U.S. dollars changed into foreign currency, *as a favor to me*. A salutory experience, I suppose. I am now trying to adopt a new attitude in which I anticipate a loss in everything I do, and only ask by how much? Prices here are so high regardless of exchange that a bit higher adds little to the fantasy. I have stopped translating yen into dollars; we just select our dishes from the right-hand side of the menu. And no matter how modest an item we choose, we are always treated with courtesy.

A tall, very slim young Japanese, with skin-tight checked pants, a white turtleneck sweater, and a sun-lamp tan, had come to our hotel room to deliver my per diem allowance in yen from the Japan Foundation. Like all our young visitors, he was pleased to stop long enough for a cup of good coffee and to practice his English. And like all Japanese business visits, this one did not start with business.

"Suichiro Ogino is my name," he volunteered with a cheerful smile, "But they called me The Freak at Sophia University. I was their first hippie! But I didn't do anything bad, of course — like taking drugs, or marijuana or glue sniffing. But I had this long hair and these pants and this sweater . . ."

Suichiro has a look of immaculate cleanliness, which includes his long, jet-black hair, which reminds me of a Japanese doll's wig as it falls from the center of his head down over his eyes. I can't imagine him with a crew cut, for the black shock of wild hair flapping about his animated face is part of his personality. I'm sure he uncovered a new self when he let his hair grow long like this.

"What does your father say to your long hair?" Harry asked.

"He protested at first . . . then he gave up. But he knows I am not bad. My mother too . . . She always understands me."

"Did many students use drugs at the university when you were there?"

"Oh, no! We couldn't get drugs. The government is very strict about drugs. Perhaps some of the boys sniffed a little glue — but nothing else."

"How did you happen to get involved with the foundation? Most of them seem rather conservative."

"I studied anthropology at Sophia, and when I graduated I didn't wish to go into business. I heard about the Japan Foundation and I applied and got the job. It is an opportunity for me to go to primitive countries like the South Sea Islands, and Canada and the United States, as the foundation intends to open up offices all over the world. At one time I had the ambition to be an anthropologist — but now I think travel with the foundation will enable me to study primitive people just as well. I wrote a paper once about French and British Canadians."

"As examples of primitive peoples?" suggested Harry.

33

Suichiro looked at him rebukingly, uncertain how much he was being teased.

"We went to the Museum of Modern Art yesterday," I said. "The building is dignified and beautiful. We saw some exquisite silk screens from the nineteenth century. I prefer your own traditional, more delicate and subtle art style to that of your twentieth-century Japanese artists who studied in Paris and paint with heavy, lurid oils and follow European art forms. What do you think?"

"We don't like the word 'traditional' used in art," he said earnestly. "It is a backward concept. Japanese feeling should be expressed in any art form we wish."

"What do you think of Japanese society today?" Harry asked. "Are you satisfied with it?"

"No. We young people are all very dissatisfied with it."

"What are you going to do about it?"

"We don't know — but we shall change it. I must go now. I have brought your per diem from the foundation. Please sign here." He handed me an envelope, stood up, bowed very correctly, old style, and went to the door. He turned to us, stood there smiling and said, "Suichiro is my name — but please call me Su. My friends all do." He bowed again, stepped out and closed the door. I thought him one of the most attractive young men I have met.

We learned later that Su is twenty-three years old, a graduate of Sophia University where he took high scholastic honors. He commutes daily between his job in Tokyo and his home in Yokohama, an hour's train trip, and also tutors a grade-fourteen Chinese lad three times a week in social sciences.

I look forward to meeting Su again — perhaps even in my own primitive country sometime!

Just before Su got up to leave, Isoko Hatsumi arrived. She is one of the persons with whom we have been trying to get in touch ever since our arrival. Finally, we sent a telegram to her address asking her to telephone to us. This she did, but we were still trying to communicate by telephone in different languages. Nevertheless, she managed to understand enough to come to call on us at our hotel. Before she left we had arranged to meet her and her sister Chiyo here at the Okura for dinner after we returned from our travels.

Dr. Kazuo Minami's first home in Tokyo was destroyed by bombing and fire in the war. His present home is in Shinjuku, in the vicinity of Waseda University where he holds a professorship. His son and his son's wife and baby occupy the ground floor of a three-story house, and Dr. Minami and his wife live independently on the third floor. A woman comes once a week to clean the house. Dr. Minami says it is now almost impossible to get live-in household servants as all the girls want outside work. The senior Minamis eat their meals out at a restaurant, as it is not worthwhile, the professor says, for his wife to cook just for two of them — Japanese food preparation being the elaborate process it is. This is an unusual attitude in a man of the professor's era and age, sixty-six years. The traditional Japanese attitude has always been that the more time a wife spent in the kitchen the better. I think the professor's standards of wifely behavior have been affected by his years in the United States when he taught for some time at the University of California in Berkeley. He is a graduate of the Massachusetts Institute of Technology, and Professor of Architectural Engineering and Soil Mechanics at Waseda. He is sophisticated, gentle, charming and speaks excellent idiomatic English. He has traveled widely in Europe and given professional consultations for UNESCO as a world expert in earthquake-resistant construction. We first met him some years ago in El Marj, Cyrenaica, Libya, when most of the little mud-brick town of El Marj had fallen down during a severe earthquake. Dr. Minami had been called in as an expert in his line for UNESCO.

He tells us that professors are the lowest paid of all Japanese professional people, and promotion is entirely by tenure of service. The result is that everybody waits hopefully for his superior to die prematurely, as otherwise the seniors may hang on until they are seventy years, at which age they can retire and draw the university pension. Professor Minami is hanging on himself, he says.

Another oddity in the educational setup is that a professor may not disagree about anything, even an incorrect scientific statement, if it issues from his senior in line. I think this must make it difficult for truth to triumph, and if it does it must be by a circuitous route.

We asked him what he thought was responsible for the rebellious attitude of so many young Japanese as demonstrated by the student riots of recent years, especially those at Waseda University. He answered that Japan's defeat in the war was partially responsible for destroying the confidence of the young generation in its elders. I suggested that although the U.S. had won the same war of which he spoke, our young generation was also in rebellion. In our case, it was probably not a reaction against losing a war, but against fighting another war in which we did not believe — in Vietnam.

Basically, Dr. Minami said, he thought the youth rebellion in Japan was caused by too-permissive upbringing and lack of parental control. However, most signs of rebellion disappeared by the end of the third university year, and by the last year most students were quite content to accept the appropriate and traditional positions offered to them, and behave thereafter in a disciplined manner.

Only one out of ten who apply for university admission and

36

take the entrance exams is admitted, and sitting for these exams is a crisis in the young person's life. He works very hard to prepare himself, and then if he passes he usually settles back and does as little scholastically as possible for a year or so. This gives him spare time for rioting, bull sessions, et cetera — maybe for exploring a few girls — but not the campus girls. Then comes the final year and he forswears his riotous past and lines up in the proper vertical structure for making his living, and guaranteeing his lifetime security. Dr. M. said that some of his best students were girls, and that the high level of their studies was more consistent throughout the four years than that of the men.

"What about arranged marriages?" I asked.

"Almost all marriages are still arranged by go-betweens," he agreed. "Respectable girls don't usually have any other opportunities to get to know young men. Even in the university, there is little mixed social life and almost no give and take between the sexes. Most girls graduate from the university without ever having been kissed. A go-between is merely a practical way of helping eligible young people to meet. If a girl does not like the prospective suitor brought to her she does not need to marry him, or even continue the friendship."

Here in the hotel lobby and restaurant we have watched a number of go-betweens functioning, as the *omiai*, or matchmaking interview, is usually quite obvious. The father and mother and possibly the grandparents of both boy and girl are present with the two young people, and of course the go-between, usually a very respectable looking elderly lady. The young man is always much slicked up and adopts a rather sophisticated air, while the girl is sure to be at her prettiest, but her manner is shy and touched with a pretense of indifference. The finances of both young people and their families will have been discussed previously, and now at the *omiai* only polite conversation ensues between the sets of relatives and the go-between, while the youngsters watch each other warily from the corners of their eyes. Ultimately the girl will get up and disappear — ostensibly to powder her nose. Finally she returns, and then if the parents hint to them to do so, the two young people may make their excuses to leave the group together and go off and get acquainted. This *may* be the beginning of a betrothal — but it is not obligatory that it be so.

Before we said goodbye to Dr. Minami we asked him if he thought the new, taller, so-called earthquake-proof buildings in Tokyo and other Japanese cities would stand up through an earthquake. He smiled and said, "We must wait and see."

Although he has traveled so widely, Dr. M. assured us he would not consider living anywhere other than Japan. He is sophisticated on the surface, but in his inner being I am certain he would never wish to be anything but Japanese. This is one of the great strengths of this people. They *wish* to be Japanese. This is an elitist nation, and the Japanese are the elite.

Before he left us our friend produced from his *furoshiki* (a decorative square of material) a gift for me of a handsome crystal pelican wrapped by Mitsukoshi. This beautiful and felicitous creature would be happy in our Canadian home, to which it ultimately traveled wrapped up inside my hat, which Harry was about to throw away.

5

~~~~~~

THE NISEI AND SANSEI are respectively the second- and third-generation offspring born abroad of Japanese immigrants. In California and Hawaii the Nisei have not had an easy time, nor did they grow up without experiencing prejudice against themselves. But they did have an opportunity to survive and to gain an education. In the end, many of them fought courageously for the country of their birth and adoption; both in the Second World War and in Vietnam. Today the senator from Hawaii, Daniel K. Inouye, is a Nisei who fought with distinguished bravery in the Second World War and lost his right arm doing so. The House of Representatives boasts two other Nisei, the talented architect Minoru Yamasaki, and S. I. Hayakawa, the brave little former president of San Francisco State College, who refused to be intimidated by rioters.

Quite by accident, while we were waiting for a friend in the Foreign Correspondents Club in Tokyo, we met a young man whom I shall call Robert Kawasaki. His features were pure Japanese, but his husky build and American mannerisms marked him as being from the States — just as my Americanisms probably marked me — as we fell into casual conversation.

In my present role of inquiring reporter, one which I dislike, I force myself to ask questions on subjects which I would otherwise just wonder about. So I said, "I think you are a Nisei?"

He smiled and said, "I am! And you too are certainly American."

"Then you must feel at home in Japan?"

"I don't. Being a Nisei is more alienating than if I were a *gaijin* — you know — a foreigner. Japanese don't particularly like us. They seem to resent us, and make us feel we are not wanted."

"I read an article about that in a newspaper — published by this club, I believe. But I don't entirely understand why you should feel that way."

"I suppose we don't fit in here. They like to say that our parents left because they couldn't make it in Japan. Well — even if that's true it's no disgrace. Our old people worked for everything they ever got in the States — and it wasn't easy. I was born in a relocation camp during the Pacific war in 1944. But after the war we settled in San Jose and I went to school there and grew up with white Americans. And after all — I'm American."

"I expect you really represent a mixture of Japanese and American culture?"

"No, I don't think so. That might be desirable — but it's impossible. You have to be one — or the other. I am American."

"What are you doing now in Tokyo? Are you staying long?"

"Only long enough to find out what I need to know. You see . . . I am writing a book about how the Japanese look to us Nisei and Sansei. Of course, our parents, the Issei, have unhappy memories of their early struggles in America — but they also have unhappy memories of Japan. And they know that today in the States they can be sure of getting Social Security and welfare payments sufficient to live on — if necessary. Here in Japan, old people can't even buy enough food with the payments they receive."

"I envy you because you speak Japanese — that opens the door for you."

"It doesn't, really. My Japanese isn't good enough for them. If I were white and spoke Japanese this well they'd be telling me how good I was. But because I am Nisei they think I should speak perfectly."

"Are you married?"

"Yes, to another Nisei. She was born in the same relocation camp and we've always known each other. We have a son, Michael, a Sansei, ten years old. That's why I didn't bring my wife with me. I don't want to interrupt Michael's education at home."

"But don't you feel that he ought to know something about the homeland of his people?"

"America is our homeland. When Michael is older he can come to Japan if he wants to — but meanwhile it is best for him to understand that he is American. They say it takes five years for a Nisei to make a friend in Japan, and I believe it. They call it a vertical society: I call it a closed society — one you must be born into. I know there are some Nisei in the States that yearn for Japan — but let them come and try it!"

"I think I remember that in San Jose where you live your mayor is a Nisei, Norman Mineta?"

"True. And he was elected by a tremendous majority of voters, almost all white. Japanese-Americans there are only one in forty."

"I can't help but feel that you are not doing justice to Japan.

If you thought of yourself as a complete foreigner here you wouldn't find Japan any more difficult to feel at home in than any other foreign country. Possibly you expect too much!"

He smiled and said, "You may be right. Well — as I said before — if you have two cultures in your blood you are going to be confused, at least until you choose one or the other . . . Pardon me . . . that's my man . . . I'll see you around."

Although I always believe that I have blunted any reasonable ache at returning to Japan, I am never quite certain what my instinctive reaction will be when I see the Japanese on their own good earth again. I know I have never hated them; I have hated war, which makes all of us brutal and stupid, doing terrible things for exalted reasons. But sweetly reasonable though my intellectual attitude is, my flesh still cringes at my memories.

But no need to worry! The war is over and forgotten here. If you speak of it, young people do not listen, or answer rebukingly, "We have forgotten!" and older people grow deaf to you. And if its shadow lurks in some gray heads, those are not the heads who lead Japan today. The entire nation is launched on something more timely than its past — on growing rich! Never was less nostalgia visible in any country than here. Japan is living in her future.

Not everything is rosy. The symbiotic relationship of years ago between the people and their natural island environment has altered. The rhythm of the seasons, of the rise and fall of sap, of natural needs and their natural fulfillment is being halted. In its place the air throbs with an artificial tempo stamped out by flying feet pursuing a jet-age goal.

What happened to destroy that ancient relationship? What uprooted the farmers from their lands and sent their children running to the cities? Who poisoned the fish in the seas? Who silenced the words of Buddha with worship of the Gross National Product? Who folded away the kimonos and dressed the girls in mini-skirts and pants suits? Who built box-like skyscrapers, tenement houses and factories in Tokyo so that the countryside for miles around is buried under cement and steel?

Who put a network of steel rails and highways above the earth, and tunneled into it? What brought that gray essence, smog, to Tokyo to smother its ugly skyline? Its horizon is stenciled by tall buildings topped by long-necked cranes which break through the gray haze as they wait impatiently to build higher and higher. What happened?

The war happened. The war that "we have forgotten" left a proud, defeated nation conscious of its own ignominy, with a great need to prove itself and make a conquest by other means than war. As this other means it chose Big Business in collusion with Government.

In another way, one can say that the Japanese did this to themselves by being a people who cannot accept being second best. They are elitist by nature and they have a priceless quality, the willingness to work hard for what they want — a quality that the Western world is losing, taken from us by the welfare state. I don't particularly admire the goal of wealth and a huge GNP, but I admire the Japanese determination to get what they go for, even while I regret what they are giving up to get it. They have beaten the West at its own game, just as the Western world is asking if the game is worth the price.

Pollution of sea and air is nothing new in Japan. The government has for decades held its nose in favor of industrial growth, and both mine-waste contamination and people pollution have existed. But industrial growth has never before been the nation's *prime* target. That is the difference between then and now.

Throughout Japanese history the heroes have been scholars, statesmen, royalty, gods, artists and artisans, holy men, aristocrats and warriors. In the seventeenth and eighteenth centuries the feudal Samurai warriors who worshiped their swords became dominant, as did their tales of heroic warfare. But by mid-nineteenth century a wealthy merchant capitalist class had emerged to control the nation's economic life. Then in the early twentieth century the civil government was again effectually ruled by the military and did what it was ordered to do. Before the Second World War the Japanese people found themselves under the fanatic military regime of frenzied militarists, a tryanny which left them no choice but to become nationalistic and militaristic. This iron regime continued with almost complete domination over the emperor, the government and the people, until the annihilation of the navy and the collapse of Japan in surrender to the Allies on August 14, 1945.

Throughout Japanese modern history its millionaire merchant families have had a strong indirect influence, by collusion and corruption, on Japanese government. But never until recently have national and international financial success been acknowledged as the concentrated objectives of the nation, its government and its people.

Prewar Japanese worshiped different gods at different shrines from those of the new generation. Today young people visit shrines as educated sightseers and not as believers. To them the forty-seven Ronin, the mandala, flower arrangements, Zen Buddhism, geishas, Japanese baths, an appetite for rice and sake . . . and the GNP . . . are all equally Japanese. But the GNP brings home the cash. They have lived too long without comforts, not to mention luxuries. They are tough and resilient by nature — but human. Money speaks louder than the voice of a Samurai.

Does any of it make sense? The nomadic Bedouin lives on

44

his desert in poverty. When brought to the city he asks, What is there to do here? He returns content to his life of privation. The jungle folk of Borneo who no longer have heads to hunt ask what to do? . . . and return to their jungle to die out as warriors, or to live and play politics. In years past we North Americans have crossed our continent, climbed our mountains, fished our lakes, swum our seas. What is left today is people who live on wheels, eat food from supermarkets, cook vegetables prewashed and packaged, buy meat without bones and bread without wheat. Is it too late for us to ask what to do? Even should we ask, who is to answer?

So the yen is now too high and the dollar too low, and there is every reason for serious depression. But I cannot be downcast long in Tokyo. This city is filled with high-voltage energy and unlimited faith in its ability to carry on at the pace that kills without being killed. Its streets are filled with young to middle-aged people all running or trotting, not walking; with hurrying crowds, with miraculous taxi drivers, with solid streams of Toyotas, Toyapets, Datsuns, Mazdas, most looking new and shiny and few, if any, banged-up. In the very hub of this traffic tangle lies the serene presence of the dignified Imperial Palace which houses the beloved, if no longer deified, imperial family. The palace grounds are surrounded by an ageless example of stone masonry, the hand-laid moat wall, a reminder that the Japanese have long been able to work miracles; their problem is to choose which miracle to perform.

"But where are the old people?" I asked young Mr. Horiuchi. "I never see any old folks on the streets. Your statistics show that you Japanese, who used to have a short lifespan, now have one of the longest lifespans in the world. I think it is seventy-five years of age for women, and seventy-three years for men. Where are these aged people?"

"They're at home . . . watching television!" said Mr. Horiuchi with a laugh.

"Then God pity them!" I said. "Your TV programs are even worse than ours." But I knew what he meant was that it didn't matter *where* they were; after age fifty-five in Tokyo they were old and out of circulation.

Unless, of course, they were very rich and at the upper levels of some powerful association, combine or company. In which case a man might remain active until he was seventy, eighty or ninety years of age, for by tradition he retained his company powers and prerogatives until death removed *him* but never his powers. But these men were not to be seen on the streets of Tokyo. They were driven about almost invisibly sunk in the rear seat of a glass-plated showcase of a large, imported, left-hand-drive American car. Such a car sometimes swooped up to the hotel entrance, taking preference over all the waiting cars while it gently disgorged its diminutive, old and precious load of a solid gold man. Then we knew that old folks did in fact exist here.

We spent several hours at the Yasakuni Shrine today, where a long strip of tree-lined park in the very center of Tokyo City is entered through a boulevard of huge *torii*. Yasakuni is the home of the Shinto deities whose shrines are dedicated to the spirits of all who have died for their country. It is famous as the place to which the ashes of soldiers killed fighting abroad are always returned — symbolically, if not physically. Walking there under the tall, brooding *torii*, the tall gateways to Shinto shrines, I found myself thinking of the dead warriors of my own country and of the brutal, senseless waste of all those brave young men from both countries who had slaughtered each other in the name of patriotism. Brave young men . . . forgotten today both in Japan and the United States . . . and we seem to have learned nothing from them. Perhaps the children and young lovers who play and stroll here, holding each other's hands under the trees and beneath the *torii*, bring more comfort to the spirits of the dead soldiers than do tears. I think the dead are bored with tears by now.

There is a patriotic song which once swept the Japanese nation and was sung by thousands of young men in the 1940s as they left their homes to go to the war —

> Going out to sea
> A water-logged corpse I'll be
> Going up the mountains
> A moss-covered corpse I'll be
> Beside my sovereign do I wish to die
> Never will I
> From my duty turn.

These were the same young men whose heavy boots slogged up the hill road past Government House when they occupied Sandakan, North Borneo, in January 1942; who bargained for my wristwatch as they dragged it from my wrist; who kicked, slugged and shot unarmed civilians; who tortured prisoners when told to do so; and who ultimately died and left their decomposing flesh and bones in unnamed graves in Borneo.

These were the heroes whose symbolic ashes went home to the Yasakuni Shrine, where under shadowing trees today their spirits are honored in communion with young lovers, whose hands touch gently while their youthful voices shout, "We have forgotten the war!" For Japan, these were its heroes; for us, they were the villains.

Harry and I stopped before one of the shrines to toss a few coins into the offering box and, following the orthodox custom, we clapped our hands to attract the attention of the god within, then folded our hands together, bowed our heads in prayer, and made a wish. As we turned away from the shrine we came face to face with a young man whom I had previously noticed as we walked up and down the boulevard under the *torii*. Glancing at him then I had felt certain that he had been educated in the United States, or at least spent some time there. His dress, although not at all hippie, was more expensively casual than the strict black attire of the successful young Japanese businessman of his age — perhaps thirty years — and it included what looked to me like a Brooks Brothers sports jacket.

As we turned from the shrine his eyes met ours and he said with a most un-Japanese directness, "Pardon me . . . but I see you know our Shinto custom. But you are . . . American?"

"I am Canadian . . . my wife is American," Harry said rather stiffly.

"Canadian? Yes, that explains it. You do not look American . . . your manner is not American, but not quite English."

"You have lived in the United States?" I asked.

"Yes, I spent three years studying at Columbia University."

"Did you enjoy it there?"

"Well . . . I was not always happy. But now . . . I am not too happy here. I miss the freedom from convention of the States. Talking to you like this is not at all Japanese, you know . . . but I enjoy talking with Westerners . . ."

That was the beginning of our friendship with Jiro Endo. Occasionally you meet someone who attracts you tremendously and at the same time has the capacity to annoy you terribly. Jiro turned out to be like that. Physically he was finely built with small, strong bones which were far from fragile. Being a Japanese it is almost superfluous to describe his coloring, but his eyes were different. They were liquid and expressive . . . not brittle and glittering and flat like some Asian eyes; not closed off, secluding, a wall to hide behind . . . but eyes that invited you to talk with him, to trust him, to sympathize with him. And, even if he didn't always deserve it, you sympathized.

We walked to the nearest bar and had beer together, but before we parted we told him we would soon be leaving Tokyo for several weeks and meanwhile we gave him our Okura Hotel address and asked him to get in touch with us there.

He agreed with apparent enthusiasm to do so and we felt sure he would. It was a pleasant change to have somebody anxious to make contact with us instead of our trying to connect with them.

It is difficult for me to find the link between the Japanese I used to know and those I see about me today — the link between generalities I have formed from past observations and the facts I find to be true today. The link between those I see but do not *know* and the few persons that I do now know. I think Jiro Endo can help me.

I have always thought of the Japanese as an ornamental people, and now they are more so than ever before. From the Western point of view their greatest physical defect has been disproportionately short legs. In the new generation this has been partially remedied thanks to a different life-style. Young Japanese today have spent less time on their bent knees than their parents did, they eat a better diet and take different forms of exercise. In one generation they have literally changed the shape of their own legs. Elongated and more shapely, this adds new dignity to the still small but nicely built males, while the girls, with skins like camellia petals and eyes like polished jewels, are transformed by these added inches into some of the loveliest women in Asia.

Freed from the limitations of kimonos which they now reserve for weddings and parties, dressed in pants suits or skintight sweaters without bras, or the briefest of mini-skirts and pantyhose, wearing ridiculous high heeled sandals, these girls step out with the confident, challenging stride which is typical of youth everywhere. When they fold up their kimonos and put on mini-skirts they seem to change their personalities.

But let them once return to that flower-sprinkled garment for a party and surround themselves with other twittering girls, all kimono-clad and blooming with painted blossoms, their faces tinted pale pastel pink, and the modern miss has gone. She has become again a giggling creature, lilting voiced and pigeon-toed (which she must be to shuffle along in a kimono) with hands like fluttering butterflies and a helpless, appealing look in her lovely eyes.

But don't believe appearances. This modern girl is clever. She has her feet planted in two worlds now and is struggling to keep her balance. Is she "liberated"? Is she able to handle the new situation? Who knows? Young females are today lined up on one side . . . and centuries of tradition on the other.

Nothing is yes or no, white or black in this country. If Japanese girls are really as confident and capable as they appear to be, why are they still jumping over Kegon Falls in the final gesture of non-confidence? Why do I read in the news that a boy and girl of sixteen years have hanged themselves in the park . . . that two teenagers tied their wrists together and jumped over a cliff . . . that a girl of eighteen threw herself in front of the Tokaido Express . . . that girls are still unwillingly pregnant . . . that unmarried mothers abandon their infants in shopping bags? Why?

Here in Japan nothing is what it appears to be. Every group of young people I talk with or see in villages or cities, on streets or in homes, in schools, offices, shops and trains, is laughing, joking, apparently happy and gay. And yet the next day one of them will be swinging limply from a tree in a park. For Japan has the highest suicide rate in the world among its young people of fifteen to twenty-five years. Now in this confusing country I feel that I am learning some of the questions ... but who has the answers?

6

~~~~~~

MOST OF THE PEOPLE we see in the hotel lobbies are businessmen, half of them Japanese and the others foreign and generally of Jewish origin. The Americans look overfed and undergroomed compared to the Japanese, who are slender, neatly dressed and well-groomed. The European commercial representatives are chiefly Germanic, huge of stature and clad in ultra-conservative, funereal black suits. Everyone regardless of nationality carries a neat, shiny, new, black attaché case. It is obvious that a wealthy Japan now has the whole world waiting, either to sell her something or to snatch something from her. The smell of money pervades the air.

It is also obvious that dining is very important to business. Our hotel has five restaurants. At the top, to serve drinks and sandwiches, is the Skylight Roof, from which one looks out over Tokyo smog. On the tenth floor is The Continental with fine European dishes of every sort, and always crowded with the expense-account clientele despite its exorbitant prices. Lower down on the fifth floor mezzanine an excellent Chinese restaurant lurks, where its shockingly high tariff does not seem to discourage gourmet diners, mostly Japanese. A Japanese dining room on the fourth floor mezzanine is equally good and equally costly and a favorite place for tourists. On the ground floor is The Terrace which smells of rancid frying fat and has little to recommend it — not even low prices.

But on the fifth floor is the French Orchid Room, our favorite and also that of many Japanese. The table linen is delicate and crisp, the cutlery is heavy and handsome, the china is thin, fine and gold-rimmed, and the food is unfailingly good and graciously served. The French bread alone is worth coming for, and there is a choice of good wines. The cheaper items on the menu are fish, chicken and omelette and any one of these, accompanied by a bottle of good wine and French bread in the atmosphere of the Orchid Room, is as good as a feast.

I have been told that very few foreigners stay at a Tokyo hotel longer than three days. By the fourth day we were being warmly greeted by the dining room staff, in spite of our economical orders, as Mr. and Mrs. Canadian.

The many wealthy Japanese families who eat in the Orchid Room are usually celebrating a birthday or some other special event. They arrive in whole families which include everyone from babes in arms, small children and adolescents to grandparents and other antediluvian relatives, and everyone is obviously enjoying himself. The older women are elegantly dressed in exquisite and appropriately tinted kimonos, the children are in latest model Western styles, the men and boys in spotless, knife-pressed black suits, except for an occasional patriarch in a crested, rustling black kimono, and the teenage girls are in mini-skirts. They all arrive in large motorcars with self-important, dignified drivers who appropriate first place at the hotel entrance while the ancients are delivered with care, their fans gently wafting, their silk garments rustling, their bald heads gleaming. I expect they will not be seen again in public until the next anniversary . . . if they make it. Then once again we will know that old folks, if rich enough, do exist in Tokyo.

The host usually orders the table d'hôte meal with beef at 4,000 yen (about $16) per head, plus local Japanese wine which is quite good. After the meal is served the infants spend their time clawing at the napery and trying to climb on top of the table or throwing buns on the floor. The ambulatory children, having first satisfied their appetites, run from table to table to see what other people are eating, while their seniors laugh and talk and toast each other and smile indulgently at their gamboling offspring. The hotel waiters remain unbelievably good-tempered, smiling tolerantly on the playing children around whom they must dodge. These Japanese youngsters are the most beautiful and charming children in the world — to look at. If they weren't they couldn't possibly get by with their hotel behavior. I have seldom seen a crying child here; they have nothing to cry for. One can tell from observing Japanese family parties that they do not go in for babysitters.

Most teenagers, however, behave quite decorously in public, probably because there is a cutoff age to permissiveness at home. When this stage comes too abruptly the youngsters have difficulty in adjusting to the stern aspect of a tougher world than the one their mothers made for them. Insecurity and depression may follow when the adolescent goes out into a real universe which is blind to his mother's love and admiration for him. This critical macrocosm demands that he give proof of himself as a man when he probably feels more like a mouse. But it is in the rules for masculine behavior that insecurity must be hidden and there is nothing but gay self-confidence apparent among the handsome, black-haired, creamy-skinned, pink-cheeked young boys we see about us in the Orchid Room.

When the sweets are placed on the party table everyone will

gather at the host's side. Now the dining room lights are dimmed and the waiters with lighted tapers all group around the gala board and sing . . . what else but "Happy birthday, dear Miko" (or whoever), "Happy birthday to you!" At this moment the maitre d' wheels in from the kitchen a beautiful cake surrounded by real pink carnations and flickering with the proper number of candles. By now everyone in the dining room has joined in singing "Happy birthday, dear Miko" in an atmosphere of sentimental good feeling and friendship. Harry is the only one who stays aloof at this ceremony. He mutters to me, "I'd die if they did that to me!"

We watched this happy-birthday episode taking place several times a week during our stay at the hotel. One American custom at least has been retained from the Occupation days.

When we were here in 1934 the country moved in a controlled rhythm and life was lived at the tempo of a tea ceremony. Today it is more like a coffee break, for Japan belongs to the young, vigorous and vital. Everybody hurries and, although they sometimes gasp a bit, they smile and never question. They have grown tired of their elders' living in bygone times. The young have no past. It is only as one grows older that the past seems important. There is more of it.

Today, the present is exhilarating and worth working for, and the future belongs to the young alone . . . and they know it. No one of my approximate age, except another touring American, is to be seen on the streets, in the shops or in the hotel lobbies, unless perhaps it is some ancient scrubwoman, too long employed to be fired and too underpaid to make it worthwhile. We have seen no black people in Tokyo. There are numbers of Southeast Asians, Koreans, Filipinos, Malayasians and Middle Easterners.

Most American girls here look like refugees dressed in cast-off clothing collected by the Salvation Army for the victims of a disaster. The Japanese girls look much neater, their bodies being smaller and less blowsy, and what passes as a ragbag assortment on a large-boned Western girl may look amusingly bizarre on a dainty Oriental. One thing the Japanese girls here universally fall for is the new mode in shoes, with three- to six-inch-high platform soles and even higher heels. The remarkable thing is that they can run, trot and gallop in these monstrosities, the wearing of which *should* break their little necks.

Pants suits look wonderful on them now that their legs are a bit longer, plus also the addition of platform soles. Mini-skirts are unbelievable in their minuteness and are maddeningly attractive. One involuntarily waits for a girl to bend over . . . but when she bends it's with her knees.

I think the obvious differences between us and the Asian world are no longer differences of race or of culture, but differences of generation, of economic status, of professions and of commercial interests. There is an international youth culture, and young people behave much alike wherever we see them. More can be conveyed to young Japanese through our modern rock and jazz than by books. More can be understood by them about our Western youth by our music than by stories or even films. Disk jockeys are now worldwide conveyors of culture. Rich Japanese probably have more in common now with rich Americans than they have with impoverished Japanese. Big business and great commercial kingdoms are international bed companions all over the world. Violence is worldwide, crime has no nationality, kidnapping and highjacking recognize no boundaries and no national loyalties, and even abandoned babies are now a world phenomenon.

We went to Charles Tuttle's book shop on Jimbo-cho this afternoon, window-shopping along the streets, entering shop after shop that sold secondhand books. Two of them had the nastiest magazine displays I have ever seen in the English language, accompanied by equally nasty photographic illustrations. One sample was titled *Black Fuck*. A number of young Japanese men stood there browsing.

Many of the shops were exhibiting nude paintings and photographs but none of these was obscene or pornographic. Perhaps one nude alone is art, and two nudes together is pornography? I suppose the answer must be an individual one. The shops were filled with young people standing and reading from the shelves. The shopkeepers sat at the rear of the store huddled over their *hibachi*s or oil stoves, chafing their hands and sipping tea and reading, seemingly uninterested in making sales. If you wished actually to buy a book, you selected it and took it to the back and paid for it.

In seeing how voracious the new generation in Japan is to read, the thought has occurred to me that a young Japanese woman and not I should be writing this book.

Later we went to Maruzen Book Shop to buy a 1972 *Japan Almanac*, but found they were sold out. We searched the shelves for books by Japanese writers about the young generation and couldn't find any in English translation. We asked the clerk to show us what young people were reading, in either Japanese or English. He pointed out the usual Japanese classics. This wasn't what we meant, we said. He looked at us with perplexity. Who could ask for anything better than the classics!

But young Japanese must want fact and fiction that deal with life as it is today, and not as it was under the Shoguns, or the Samurai, or even the war generation before themselves. They must wish to know what people of their own age are dreaming, thinking, doing, hoping for in this new, rich Japan. Or do they? Presumably someone does, as the *Japan Times* regularly publishes a column, *Weekly Best Sellers*, consisting of books published in the Japanese language.

I asked the clerk for Shintaro Ishihara's *Season of Violence*, the story of the violent doings of teenagers of the infamous Sun Tribe, the *Taiyozoku*. He said it was sold out in the three languages — English, French, and Japanese. Perhaps this answered my question as to what young people wanted .o read. Many stories of youth must, and do, exist here in Japan, but are not translated into English.

The clerk then volunteered the fact that a book about young students was to be published posthumously in the autumn. He gave us the Japanese title and then explained that it was a collection of the diaries and memoranda of Etsuko Takana, a twenty-year-old campus activist who committed suicide in 1969 during a campus dispute at Ritsumeikan University in Kyoto. This would be the writer's second posthumously published book. The coming book was sure to be a best-seller, he said.

We asked about *The Japanese and the Jews* by Isaiah Ben-Dasan, who claims to be a Jew born in Kobe. Many Japanese feel that he must be Japanese because he is so sensitive to undertones of the Japanese national character. The narrative is presented in Japanese essay form. Ben-Dasan writes that the Japanese are political geniuses, while the Jews are politically naive. We were not surprised to find that this book was not available. We had already purchased a hardcover edition from the hotel book shop, where the front shelves are stocked with respectable and expensive current novels, travel guides, and illustrated books about Japanese gardens and flower arrangement. The shelves in the back of the shop are lined with paperbacks detailing assorted erotic activities, especially created for the travel-worn *gaijin* salesman when the hotel-provided Gideon Bible ceases to hold his attention.

The Ecstatic One by Sawako Ariyoshi was sold out. This story of the aged has sold over a million copies, an unheard-of Japanese sale. Today in Japan how to care for the aged is the most vital problem, even as it is in Western countries. In Japan

58

the average wage earner is being retired at fifty-five years, while the average life span has been prolonged to seventy-three years. These last eighteen bleak, jobless years stare him in the face.

To make matters worse, city housing has suffered extensive war destruction, while city populations have greatly increased. Many people of working age live in tiny, newly built apartments too small to accommodate their parents. The traditional refuge of the elderly in the homes of their children is almost nonexistent among working classes in the cities. Nursing homes for the aged are pathetically inadequate and insufficient for the oversupply of old people. In any case such homes as there are usually do not have adequate operating funds, food, beds, baths or nurses. In them, the aged exist in wretched suspension while awaiting death without dignity.

The Maruzen shelves were filled with copies, both paperback and hardcover, of Yukio Mishima's famous books, all of which I have at home. I saw only two of Jiro Osaragi's novels, *Homecoming* and *The Journey*, both of which I have. They are written in muted tones, yet full of action, and the theme of the sinfulness of greed runs through them. Both are, I think, symbolic. *Homecoming* dwells on the impossibility of settling down at home after years of foreign exile. *The Journey* tells of the American impact on Japan at the end of the Occupation. The title refers to life as a journey without destination.

There were a number of titles by Yasunari Kawabata, who won the Nobel Prize for literature in 1968. These included his famous novels *Snow Country* and *Thousand Cranes*. The theme of the latter is based on the existence of hidden forces beyond human understanding. I saw numerous editions of *Tales of Genji* by Lady Shikibu Murasaki, and, of course, *The Pillow Book* by Sei Shonagon, both of which chronicle life during the Heian Period — A.D. 794 to 1192. I asked for

Black Rain by Masuji Ibuse, but it was out. I was particularly anxious to own this book; I had read it and thought it the most touching, pathetic and frightening story of the atom bomb and its aftermath in Hiroshima that I had ever read.

Literary critics who know infinitely more than I do about the subject, and with whom I am glad to agree, all say that the literary quality of Japanese writing is extremely high, both in book form as well as in their excellent magazines, journals and newspapers. Certainly the *Japan Times* ranks with the world's best newspapers. The Japanese are, in fact, a wonderfully literate people.

Yet most of the books I have read, except for *Black Rain*, *The Ecstatic One*, and *Woman in the Dunes*, give an unrealistic picture, or no picture at all, of present-day life in Japan as most people are living it. A large part of Honshu Island is now a dismal jungle of smoking factories, grimy homes, speeding trains, overhead wires, screeching cars and hurrying workers gasping for breath. It is a scene that demands to be painted, a story waiting to be told. Yet the most frequent themes in Japanese writing are abstract or symbolic ones, often of death and loneliness and of man's isolation. Born alone, he goes through life alone, and ultimately dies alone; it is this basic feeling of aloneness which makes him cling to tribalism, as the Japanese are wont to do. They accept death as the reasonable, normal outcome of life, rather than denying death and fighting it as we do. For them, the pursuit of happiness is not a goal, and their novels seldom have happy endings . . . unless oblivion and death are happy.

It is not surprising that science fiction with its out-of-this-world solutions is popular, and so also are "Monster" stories, both being escapes from familiar reality. Equally popular are health improvement books, as no one is more anxious to develop his muscles, jog his liver, unplug his bowels, clear his skin, brighten his eyes and improve his posture than the Japanese male.

After leaving Maruzen's we returned to the Kanda district where the streets are lined with book shops. The sidewalks are alive with young students all engrossed in themselves, their conversations seemingly filled with goodwill and confidence. The bespectacled, diffident, rather anxious looking young student of twenty years ago has almost totally disappeared. Today there is a confident, long-haired young man, in turtleneck sweater or leather jacket, tight jeans and tall boots, and his glasses may be contact lenses. He strides with the same self-confident swagger as his young Western counterpart. He can smile beautifully, but he can't laugh at himself.

On Sunday we walked from the hotel on the outskirts of Tokyo down into the city, which suddenly struck me as being grotesquely ugly and without any allure. Uglier because the shops were closed and many of the windows shuttered for Sunday. Why Sunday, I wondered, in this Shinto-Buddhist nation. Good business practice, I suppose. The few pale-faced people on the streets had relaxed their normal fast pace to a rather tired, aimless amble, as if the motive for life was lost, as I suppose it was what with no job to go to, no money to be made this day. On Monday they will accelerate again, secure in the ethic of work, proud that they are needed, hoping to be indispensable . . . for there is always somebody's hot breath against their sweaty necks. At least the Sunday slowdown proved they were human.

On this quiet day of empty streets we became especially conscious that many of the large new city buildings are designed without imagination, just great rectangular cement blockhouses. One exception is the Kasumigaseki Building, a highly polished edifice which stands thirty-five stories high with all the dignity and class of a handsome, once beautiful, jet-bejeweled widow. Its shimmering ebony surface can be seen all over Tokyo when smog allows.

It seems sad to me that although some of the loveliest and most utilitarian city buildings in North America have been designed by Japanese architects, Tokyo itself settles for the outrage of these great unbeautiful hunks of office space. Both Seattle and Vancouver have fine examples of what Japanese designers can do by using fountains and running water and gardens with tall, transplanted trees in the street entrances to give a feeling of space and air. This banishes the sensation of being swallowed up and engulfed which comes over you when you step directly from the street into the closing doors of some monstrous building.

In justice to Japanese buildings I must comment on an incredible glass edifice which we passed later on in our travels . . . on the outskirts of Osaka, I think it was. In this building the entire ground floor area is given over to tall transplanted trees which grow from the ground floor upward to the equivalent height of six floors. The office area commences with the seventh floor. Looking at this glass structure from the outside one sees a solid forest of trees from which a glittering building seems to arise. Whoever imagined this dream building might well get to work in Tokyo. Or is it possible that imported Western architects are responsible for the Tokyo monstrosities?

Mr. Honma has now taken us in charge and, with any luck, we will soon get out of Tokyo. The last thing we wish is to sit in a deluxe hotel in the city when I want to write about peasant and proletariat of the country.

Office work hours here baffle me. The Planning Commission is attached to the Foreign Affairs Ministry and the closing hour is theoretically 5:30 P.M. But Mr. Honma invariably visits us on business between seven and ten in the evening. If we commiserate with him on working overtime he laughs and tells us that he hasn't finished at the office even now . . . or that he is due at the airport at midnight to meet some new arrival. He never seems aggrieved at working late; rather he is proud to be needed . . . to be, he hopes, indispensable. And then after fifteen hours of office work he has an hour on the subway to reach his bachelor apartment.

This attitude toward work is universal here. Starting with the porters and waiters who are always smiling and anxious to serve, this desire to please goes all the way to the top. There are some very rich people in Japan and, obviously, they aren't rich because they are lucky but because they work at it.

This afternoon Mr. Honma brought us a list of total estimated expenses for our travels. These constantly rose higher, and today they included the $30 per day, salary alone, for the Japanese interpreter while traveling with us. The shock of the total daily expenses was shared by Mr. Honma himself. His immediate suggestion to reduce it was to cut down on the cost of living of the Japanese interpreter who would be with us. This we vetoed as impossible. We couldn't possibly sit down to a good meal at the end of a hard day's travel and say to our companion, Just cold rice for you! Finally Harry said to Mr. Honma, "Just tell us what it will cost. We are going, no matter what!" That settled it.

Sitting with cups of coffee we asked him if the Japanese in general were racially prejudiced against black people. His answer was, "Frankly, we do not feel comfortable with them. But as individuals I can like them. I learned English from a black American professor and I liked him very much." I thought that Mr. Honma's phrase about "not feeling comfortable" with blacks expressed very well both the interracial and the intercultural problem.

Before he left us he promised that he would come back the

next day, bringing all our train tickets and reservations, and would also bring our future interpreter to meet us. But we don't expect him to . . . not tomorrow, anyway!

Meanwhile I do hope that Jiro Endo, the pleasant, rather enigmatic young man whom we met at the Yasakuni Shrine, looks us up here at the hotel before we leave Tokyo. I think he will. He seemed to wish to continue his Western contacts.

7

~~~~~~

A TALL, well-built, pleasant-faced man, obviously English, was standing at the lobby desk to meet us as we stepped out of the elevator. He had an engaging, rather diffident manner, which, we discovered over a drink, hid his sometimes flamboyant but very real knowledge of Japan. He knew, or knew about, everybody of interest in this country.

Lewis Bush had come to Japan as a very young man before World War II as a lecturer in English language and literature at Hirosaki and Yamagata Higher Schools in North Japan. He married a charming and cultured Japanese girl, Kaneko, shortly afterward, a marriage of love for both of them and one which lasted for many years in spite of the obstacles which exist in every mixed marriage. This happy yet often touching story is sympathetically told by Lewis in his book, *The Road to Inamura*. Perhaps because of his marriage, which has enabled him to see two points of view, there are few Europeans today who know and understand both old and modern Japan as Lewis Bush does.

His name had been given to me by Eleanor Hardie, a friend

who lives near us on Vancouver Island. She and her husband Harold were for a period in the same Hong Kong prison camp as Lewis, who later was transferred to a military camp, the story of which he ultimately told in *The Clutch of Circumstance.*

As Eleanor was uncertain of his address I had asked my Foreign Affairs helper to locate him, a task which turned out to be simple, as Lewis writes a weekly column in the *Japan Times,* and broadcasts on national radio three times a week. His home is at Kamakura, about fifty-five miles from Tokyo, fifty-five minutes by rail, on the Miura Peninsula, a favorite beauty spot and the home of many artists and writers as well as the Great Buddha. Lewis, with his second Japanese wife and their five-year-old son, lives there and comes to Tokyo by train almost every weekday. Today we were meeting for the first time for lunch at our hotel.

The real tragedy of his own war, Lewis told us, was the personal one of his first wife Kaneko. She had become a British subject by her marriage to him and had thereby incurred the distrust of both sides in the war. At the beginning she had been interrogated in Hong Kong and confined there by the British as a suspect enemy espionage agent. Later she was returned to Japan, where she was held under guard by the Japanese as an enemy alien. Suffering from the worst of two worlds, separated from her husband and isolated from her own countrymen, she emerged at the end of the war physically and emotionally ill, a condition from which she never fully recovered. She died some years ago as an indirect result of her imprisonment.

Lewis is now married to a young Japanese schoolteacher and they have a son of five years. "A new experience for me," is how he describes being a father. He and his wife are devoted to the boy and plan for him to go to England when he is ten to study at Blue Coat School, in which he is already enrolled.

Meanwhile Mrs. Bush and the small boy leave home at seven every morning to go by train to Yokohama, where he attends the International School where teaching is in English. When the day's study is over they return by train to Kamakura. I asked whether the boy considered himself to be Japanese or English and Lewis answered, "English, of course!"

The Bushes own two homes in Kamakura and they expect in time to sell one to help pay for the boy's education. They do not plan to live indefinitely in Japan, although Lewis says he will never retire. I asked him what he was writing at present and he said he was fed up with writing about Japan and wanted a new field to deal with. This being so, I felt no guilt in profiting by his experiences.

He agrees with us that the position of women has improved considerably as a result of the American Occupation, but there is little if any change in regard to permanent land reform. This latter was one of the principal Occupation goals and one which General MacArthur believed he had achieved. Many large firms are now buying up land wherever they can find it in Japanese islands or territory, and the island of Okinawa, just recently returned to Japan, has already been partially subdivided.

I asked what had happened to the illegitimate mixed-blood children of the Occupation Forces. He told us of the Elizabeth Saunders Institute, which had been set up years ago to look after some of these children after General MacArthur had apparently refused to do anything about them. He mentioned a very successful boxing champion in Tokyo now as being the offspring of a black American soldier and a Japanese girl.

We asked him about the *Burakumin*, or the *Eta*. He said they still exist today and live in certain limited areas, one being Hiroshima and another the Island of Kyushu. The term *Eta* means unclean, and indicates that in times past these people were outcasts. In 1922 a movement was begun to abolish legal discrimination against them and they are now referred to as *Shin-heimin,* or new citizens. But prejudice still exists, especially in regard to employment and marriage. A man of the *Eta* may escape from his environment and appear to be the same as any other Japanese . . . until for some reason publicity focuses on him. Then if his *Eta* origin is exposed, prejudice will hound him and he may lose his job or even his betrothed wife, for no more just reason than the taint of his birth.

All of this didn't come through at our first meeting with Lewis Bush; I acquired some of it later by reading his own books, all of which have an authentic Japanese background and are factually fascinating. As is true of many people who write, the real Lewis Bush is more persuasive in what he writes than in his spoken words and his physical presence. From reading his books I have formed a real respect and liking for him, which might surprise him as it goes far beyond the bounds of our limited social meetings.

Meanwhile, I must learn more about the *Eta,* and *why* they became social outcasts.

He looked us up! Our young friend Jiro Endo whom we met at Yasakuni called on us a few days ago. We are finding him a wonderful source of information as well as an amusing companion. He loves to talk!

He was telling us yesterday that he himself sometimes prays at a Buddhist temple, sometimes worships at a Shinto shrine, other times he may attend Christian church services on a Sunday, all this without qualms . . . and yet he still describes himself as being in reality an atheist! He says there is no conflict of logic in this because Buddhism is for the future and Shintoism is for the past. He didn't say where Christianity came in. He thinks the Japanese know us Occidentals better than we know them because we talk more but they listen better. (Not Jiro, I thought!)

I asked him how vital ancestor worship was among people of his own generation . . . say, thirty years of age.

"Of course," he said, "we no longer actually 'worship' the dead of our families. Today we feel great respect for them and we feel an intimate bond with those elder members of our family who can still be remembered by the eldest *living* members of the family. For instance, my father's father, who lives with us, actually remembers his own grandfather, who is my own great, great grandfather . . . and so almost a living part of my family.

"It is all so different here in Japan from the United States," he continued. "Here we believe there is time enough . . . both for the living and the dead. We aren't afraid of being dead. Death impresses us much less than it does you. We can face it with complete resignation, almost a masochistic pleasure. Some Japanese experience a sensual ecstacy which satisfies our strong urge to martyrdom. But you Occidentals never really believe in death . . . until it happens to you! For instance, in Japan suicide is not just an act of despair. It is a positive statement about dying *for* something . . . an act of glory.

"Some Japanese say," he continued, "that we support the cause of peace . . . with violence. But remember . . . you must never ridicule us . . . we really do prefer death to ridicule. And hopeless causes . . . we have an unfortunate aptitude to kill people for hopeless causes . . . and then to die for them ourselves! You Americans play games for fun but we Japanese play games to win. That is why we can even accept treachery if it helps us to win."

"No wonder the Japanese surrender in 1945 was such a traumatic experience!" I said.

He smiled. "Didn't you know that we Japanese never say that we surrendered in 1945? We merely say that we 'terminated the war.'"

"I must admit that you are extraordinary in your ability to analyze yourself," I said when he stopped for breath. "Have you no illusions?"

"I suppose that I have seen through myself," he said with dignity. "The years that I studied at Columbia University showed me how completely different your civilization is from mine . . . in what you admire and think is good . . . and what we think is good. It is easy enough for us to pick up Western ways . . . but they will always be artificial for us. But for you people, your ways are the outcome of your creed. Your actions are foreordained, just as ours are, but by completely different principles. I made friends with many Americans at Columbia, but these friendships were never as intimate or as emotional as my friendships with other Japanese. They couldn't be because they were made at a different level."

He was married, he said, to a modern young woman, Ineko, whom he had met when he was at Columbia University and she was finishing two years at Sarah Lawrence. They had been married at a civil ceremony in New York . . . an unthinkable thing for a Japanese young couple. But there had been reasons. They knew the match would be strongly opposed by their two families, both for its unorthodox manner and because Ineko's family had been in the process of arranging a marriage for her to take place as soon as she should go home.

When she had first won a scholarship to go abroad to study, her family had felt that they could not refuse her permission to go. But as time went on they began to feel more and more that all this Western education would make her less than marriageable to the "suitable" and affluent young man they had chosen for her. Ineko knew all this, but was herself determined to marry a modern husband and, being somewhat attracted to Jiro when they had met at a party, she had leaped at the idea of getting married before returning to Japan. Jiro himself had the same motive for haste, as he knew that the first thing his family would do upon his return home would be to marry him off "suitably" . . . by their standards.

I judged that Jiro and Ineko must be scholastically quite brilliant young people, but they were now finding that keen minds were about all they had in common. Ineko was good at many sports, Jiro told us, but she especially loved skin-diving, a sport which he could not enjoy at all as he had sinus trouble. He really only liked golf and that because of its social side . . . which Ineko openly scorned. She was dynamic and filled with frustrated ambitions for both of them, but Jiro knew he was secure in his father's financial standing and he had no intention of hurrying into any eight-to-five job in his father's import-export house.

In fact they were both discovering that her liberal Western education and the American theory of sex equality were too unsettling to make for a comfortable Japanese marriage, even with Jiro, whose liberal ideas were shrinking when put into practice. They now had a three-year-old son whose unplanned advent had temporarily solidified their home life. But now that the first fires of maternal pride had burned down, Ineko was chafing fiercely at the wifely isolation from her husband's world of men and events, and at her own enforced dedication to the all-encompassing role of Japanese motherhood.

Jiro had once advised her to enjoy her companionship with their child. She had answered that an adult woman just couldn't be companionable with an infant.

"Look at yourself!" she told him. "You spend five minutes with the baby once a week — and that's all you can take of his companionship!"

Jiro had been horrified, but later realized that what she said was true.

Now, in talking with him, he seemed to me to be a rather disillusioned but much more mature person than the young man he had described to us of the hasty marriage a few years before.

8

Y ESTERDAY was a wasted day, thanks either to too many
oysters or too many martinis.

Today we read in the newspaper that oysters have been taken
off the market owing to traces of cadmium being found in
them. Maybe that is what happened to me. Better to blame it on
cadmium than on martinis.

Quite accidentally we met Polly Ireton, an old friend, in the
lobby yesterday. She was waiting to meet a friend, she said,
when she heard my American voice and looked up to see me
looking like all the other Americans. This was a blow to me as
I thought I looked rather more respectable than some. Polly
herself looked wonderful, as she always does . . . slender and
svelte in the very best type of American good taste . . . spotless,
fresh, form-fitted, underdressed and with unostentatious but
real jewels. She and Don are on their way to Hong Kong for
two months where they are engaged in some scheme to winkle
out a share in Asia's prosperity.

We had dinner with them at the Copa Cabana Club, of
which Don is an old patron. It seems that Don, who came into

Yokohama with the U.S. Navy at the end of the Second World War, was able at that time to assist a Japanese "Mamma-san," who had a "stable" of girls but no stable in which to put them, to lease the premises of the present Copa Cabana Club. Mamma-san and her girls have been here ever since. If one judges by the knock on the door, the secret password, the low bows, the whispers, and the prices on the menu, this is a select place.

The food looked and smelled wonderful but I was afraid to eat much after yesterday's oyster-martini fiasco. Roast beef was served in a huge, thick slice that was enough for one whole hungry family. What happens to what we don't eat? Harry ordered a bottle of Nuites St. George 1966. Wonderful! As Don and Polly were drinking whiskey and I was being cautious, Harry drank most of it and became very amiable.

The next day we went to the Mitsukoshi Department Store, not to buy but to look, for one learns much about people from seeing what they purchase, and the Mitsukoshi is an education. The abundance and luxuriance of the goods on sale is overwhelming. Anything and everything in the luxury line is available here now. Mitsukoshi today is the greatest possible contrast to what we saw here in 1955 when even one austere, shoddy plastic handbag or a single pair of cheap shoes would be the complete display in a large shop window, and customers lined up for hours for the privilege of buying badly made necessities, and there were no luxuries.

Today, the impression of Mitsukoshi extravagance begins with two king-size lions, three yards long, made of bronze, crouching on both sides of the front entrance to the emporium. These are exact duplicates of the triumphant Trafalgar Square lions in London. All that is needed is Lord Nelson in order to tell when a virgin is passing. The lions symbolize the fact that Mitsukoshi is king of department stores.

The next inducement to shopping is visible from all entrances to the store by raising one's eyes above the heads of the customers and looking toward the center of the emporium where the statue of Magokoro, the Goddess of Sincerity, is to be seen suspended in midair. Magokoro is twice life-size and appears to float midway between the first and second floors in the huge, brightly lighted airwell of the store where she rules benevolently over counters of sweets, nuts and cosmetics. She is carved out of Japanese cypress, *hinoki,* liberally painted with gold and platinum, and she glitters proudly as, wrapped in many tinted rainbows, she descends toward the fruitful earth to the accompaniment of organ music. It wasn't until a kind taxi driver proudly explained the over-size Magokoro to me, calling her The Fairy, personally conducting me inside to the best viewing point and telling me that children came from all over Japan to see The Fairy, that I appreciated what she meant. She might well be a Japanese child's version of a fairy if only because of her Buddha-like proportions. Large Western children like fairies tiny; probably small Japanese children like them large.

Inside the store most of the famous cosmeticians are represented, each with his special line of beautifiers and his own cosmetically made-up saleslady. Some years ago one could only buy white powders in Japan: today the girls are using suntan shades, probably because they are golfing and swimming. I found that French cosmetics were generally cheaper here than in western Canada, but U.S. brands were about the same. A box of French face powder was priced at $5, and the same make had been $8 in Canada when I ceased buying it. A Rubinstein lipstick was $6 both here and in Canada. North American toilet goods, toothpastes, deodorants, hair sprays and most drugs, were priced at about double in Japan.

There was also a large display of confections, some of these imported from England in large, fancy boxes with pictures of English country life and only a few sweets inside, and costing at least $6. There was a wide offering of every type and shape of salty tidbits, locally made, tasty and cheap for use with drinks. Many were flavored with soy or made with soybean flour.

Another popular and extensive section was devoted to the sale of spirits and wines, with an extravagant assortment of all these, and an English-speaking clerk exclusively for American and English customers. A bottle of good Scotch, say Johnny Walker Red Label, was $16.30 an Imperial quart, and not cut. Not surprising, as a drink of Scotch on ice at a bar was $3. All these prices were to double a few months later with inflation. This day at Mitsukoshi, Japanese Suntory whiskey (quite good) was about half the price of imported Scotch. Shortly after, as the dollar dropped further, Suntory best quality cost the same as imported Scotch. There was a wide range of wines, from the local Japanese types to French, Spanish, Portuguese and British imports, costing from $2 a bottle to $30 and even higher. Local Japanese wines were infinitely preferable to the strange concoctions made in British Columbia and called "wine."

A bottle of whiskey or wine when properly wrapped made a very popular present to give to your host after he had entertained you, the leaving of a present being almost obligatory for a visitor. The wrapping of a gift has an intricate etiquette of its own, but fortunately the Japanese are liberal in their attitude toward the ignorance of a foreigner, and if a gift is neatly wrapped in white paper, and tied with a cord of red, white, silver, or gold, the contents will be considered quite drinkable.

The jewelry section exhibited odd collections of costume jewelry which were very extravagantly priced, but the real thing, with literally yards and yards of cultured pearl necklaces, brooches and bracelets, was less exorbitantly priced than the ersatz articles. I have never cared much for pearls, and I do so less each time I visit Japan. Oddly enough, pearls do not sell well to Japanese women, as necklaces don't fit into the kimono neckline and pearls are considered inappropriate and too dressy to use with pants suits and mini-skirts. However, most foreign visitors to Japan feel that they must buy pearls here even if they can't tell real from artificial except by the price. And as real pearls aren't cheap, and tourists usually want both real pearls *and* a bargain, there is always an over-the-counter struggle.

I am glad that I no longer feel any urge to buy souvenirs when I travel. The only things I want to buy in Japan are Japanese books in English translations, and these are expensive. Even in paperbacks the current novels we bought were priced at $2.50 each, and hardbacks were $7 to $10. General travel books were from $50 to $100, and illustrated art books were priced from $34 to $75. We found that many Japanese writers in English translation are published in Tokyo, but fail to reach the North American market because publishers there think there may not be a wide enough sale to make them profitable. The pace of Japanese literature, in most cases, is too slow for Occidental taste.

On the fourth floor we went through the kimono and *obi* displays. We were filled with admiration and more convinced than ever that the kimono as used by Japanese conventions is an elegant, luxurious and sophisticated costume. The design of the material must be appropriate to the age of the wearer, to her status of married or single, to the season of the year, and to the specific occasion of its wearing, such as a wedding, a funeral, or a party. Although to the casual Occidental eye most kimonos are beautiful, to the informed Japanese eye the costume will lose its beauty and authenticity if worn inappropriately. The color combinations and the flower and foliage design on the materials are painted masterpieces beyond verbal description, and not all are brilliant or gaudy. Some of the loveliest are designed especially for older women, with muted shadings from opalescent pearl through silver, steel, dark charcoal and jet. These are to be worn with a somber but opulent *obi,* the proper tying of which is an art in itself. Incidentally, the sleeves of an unmarried girl's kimono should be almost to the floor, but they must be shortened after marriage.

The selection of the correct *obi* to be used with each kimono is again a sophisticated choice and an expensive one. I saw some elegant *obi*s priced at $800 and up. Kimonos ranged from $300 to $600 to $1,000. Mind you, we were at a high-class establishment, probably the finest in Tokyo, and certainly not every girl or woman pays these prices for her kimono, but they explain one reason why Japanese girls have fallen for mini-skirts and pants.

The department for Western women's dress was well stocked with very mediocre garments and goods, but nothing with elegance comparable to the kimonos. Really smart Western styles are only found in small boutiques such as abound in Rippongi and Shinjuku where very chic models are stocked, but, to the disgust of Western women living in Tokyo, only in very small sizes suitable to Japanese women.

Many young women here make their own Western-style dresses and suits by following American fashion book patterns which are widely used. Nice materials are available, and the most popular piece of modern mechanism in use in almost every Japanese home, even in small villages, is still a sewing machine.

Japanese men's tailors are considered to be excellent in fitting Japanese figures, and there are several first class tailors in Tokyo turning out suits of the best cut and materials. I understand that a top executive pays as much for his suit as an American executive does in the States, probably from $150 to $300. Less expensive ready-made suits and clothes for men and youths are readily available, but fully as expensive as those in North America.

To our surprise we found in the household goods section that radios, television sets, electric kettles and most other electric appliances were no cheaper than in the Western world.

It required two separate visits to Mitsukoshi for us to achieve the top floor, "The Roof," as the store is so overheated and crowded that we could remain inside only for a limited time. We avoided the crowded elevators and used the escalators, for the sake of being helped by dainty female attendants who urged us to "Hold tight!" and at the top, to "Step off." As this was their total vocabulary, it was a problem to locate the next escalator upward which never seemed to be nearby. I think they were arranged to encourage shoppers to sightsee the various floors.

On our second day we made it to the seventh floor and discovered the art gallery and exhibit halls where, according to Japanese merchandising custom, exhibits by current local artists are hung. In 1955 we had bought, from one of these exhibits, at Maruzen's fine book shop, an original portrait of a bright-eyed, two-year-old Japanese boy painted by his father, Sadao Tsubaki, and not for sale. When we asked to buy it, the artist seemed to think we must be mad, and asked to know why we wanted his son's portrait. We told him that it reminded us of the many smiling-eyed Oriental babies whom we had loved, who had once played in our Borneo home. This portrait now hangs in our Victoria living room to entrance all those who see its innocent, infant beauty. And from the tremendous increase we found in the prices of original art canvases today, our little Japanese boy is much more than a sentimental investment.

Most of the oils we see here today are obviously in the European tradition, and what interested us more was a special exhibit of Japanese calligraphy by both modern and ancient calligraphers. In Japan, calligraphy is an art even more than a means of communication, and the characters are symbols of ideas rather than pictures of material things, and their beauty is their greatest value. The works we saw today had a delicate black-and-white purity and perfect flow of line which was more sophisticated and satisfying than most of the modern oils.

In other galleries there were extensive displays of fine arts goods, both European and Oriental pieces. These figurines, sculptures, ceramics, and so on, were all to be purchased . . . at high prices. But worth it, I imagine, as I have never before seen comparable art treasures outside of a museum.

Ultimately we made a swift trip to the roof to see the much advertised Fuji Waterfalls, a scene which is cleverly land-scaped with real rock cliffs and growing trees. It is decidedly impressive when you consider the fact that it is eight floors above the city, and 3.15 tons of water tumble over the cliffs every minute from a height of 34 feet. But is it worth the effort it took to make it, one wonders? From the Japanese point of view, yes . . . as beauty, especially when it includes the magic of running water, is its own reward. But from the Western point of view, one asks . . . Does it sell things?

Although neither the Goddess Magokoro nor the Fuji Wa-terfalls, or even the silent bronze lions appeal to me estheti-cally, they endear themselves to my affections because they are so typically Japanese. With their implacable wayside charm, their piped waterfalls defying gravity to splash on the roof, and their undaunted fairy always descending and never arriv-ing on the Tokyo shopping mart, yet determined to make everybody happy, technology here meets its match with dreams and nature.

For those interested in further prices at the time we were in Tokyo, I mention that taxi fares were cheap at $1.75 for 2½ miles. Dining for two could cost from a minimum of $20 at a moderate restaurant to $80 and up and up at more pretentious places. I read in a popular journalist's column that lunch for two at forty dollars was considered reasonable. But then he was on an expense account. On the other hand, we were told that there were humble, untouted Japanese restaurants where you could get a good meal for $3.50 each.

Qualified English tutors to teach English were advertised for at $10 an hour, with the same price and up for Japanese lessons given by Japanese. "Hostesses," all "charming and young, under thirty years," were wanted for a variety of "fabulous" and unspecified jobs at wages from $30 to $50 a day.

And a haircut and shampoo cost Harry $10.

Our three small coffee cups were down to the dregs and even the pot was empty. Teatime here doesn't mean tea, but coffee, and we are seldom alone for it. Plain tea is served free automatically at all hours at business houses, but coffee is a treat for special guests, and the Brazilian mix served in the Okura is the best I have ever drunk.

I squeezed the pot to give Jiro a few last drops. He had dropped in today ostensibly to show us pictures of his wife Ineko and his little son Taro, but I think he is really lonely. An odd young man . . . he can't quite give up Western ways and settle for what he has here. His father owns an import-export business which Jiro is supposed to take over in time. The elder Endo would like to retire now, but doesn't quite trust Jiro's indifference to the business which the old man built up and dotes on.

Although we find that our new young friend is filled with fine theories and idealistic intentions, he is not prepared to surrender his own selfish desire to practice law, something for which he feels his education has fitted him. He admits that for a Japanese whose education has not been tainted by the West there would be no choice other than to take over when his father wished; there would be no moral struggle between obligation and desire, the way would be plain. But poor Jiro can never completely subdue his Western ambition to be an individual, although he isn't ruthless enough to succeed in this. His roots have been gnawed at by parasites and he may never fully bloom . . . and he knows it.

From her pictures, Ineko looks to be a charming, handsome young woman, dressed as I would expect her to be in Western dress. The little boy, Taro, is ridiculously like his father. When I commented on this Jiro said, "Well, naturally. And he is very intelligent, too."

"I think little boys of his age . . . three . . . are at their most interesting and lovable period," I suggested. "They are just becoming distinctively masculine, yet they still are sweet and gentle and loving."

"Oh, he's a boy, all right!" said Jiro proudly.

"Later on would you like him to go to a university outside Japan?"

"No. Why unfit him for what he will have to live with here?"

"But don't you think that in fifteen years' time . . . when Taro is ready for a university . . . the breach between your ways and our ways will be closing?"

"No, I don't. Not here, if you really understood the absolute grip of *on* and *giri*, of obligation, of family tradition and responsibility . . . the grip that these have on us here, you would know that we can never escape them. But I doubt if an American can ever appreciate this," he said gloomily.

"Did you ever think of settling in the States?"

"No! I am Japanese."

"Do you wish that you had never gone to the States?"

"I don't know. But I sometimes wish that I hadn't married a Western-educated woman. Not that I blame Ineko . . . I really admire her in many ways, but I now feel my family was right when they said that Western education didn't make a suitable Japanese wife."

"You love her, don't you?" Harry asked.

"That's not the point. Love doesn't matter much in a Japanese marriage. Any healthy man can enjoy going to bed with any healthy young woman. But that doesn't make her a suitable wife."

"No," Harry said, "but it makes it pleasanter."

Jiro smiled faintly then said, "Of course, you realize I couldn't talk like this if you people lived here. It's only because I know you are going away soon that I can say these things. I suppose we'll never meet again . . . and you'll just remember me as that funny guy who never found out what he wanted."

"You're not alone in that, Jiro," Harry said. "We all have times when we doubt ourselves."

"You know that we are leaving Tokyo the day after tomorrow, Jiro," I said. "Please don't fail to look us up when we get back here in late March. We'll be at this hotel again . . . and we do really hope you'll bring your wife to meet us then. Will you?"

"Perhaps . . ." he said.

9

~~~~~~

ALTHOUGH WE WERE EXPECTING to be out of Tokyo in two days' time, we had to give up our room in the Okura today. They have been fully booked two months ahead for some conference, they tell us. Getting into a Tokyo hotel without reservations is next to impossible, and we tried place after place without finding a vacancy. Then I remembered the Fairmont, which Leonard Pickles had once suggested, and they had a vacant room. I had been prejudiced against the hotel by its name. Who wouldn't prefer to go to the Akasaka Prince or the Kokusai Kanko or the Keio Plaza when in Japan? But now it seemed to be the Fairmont Hotel or the subway station, so we went to the Fairmont, which at least has a pleasant edge-of-town location.

They showed us into a small room on the fourth floor with a three-quarter bed and a blank-wall view. We asked for something larger and the porter guided us around a couple of corners and into a comfortable room with twin beds and a magnificent view overlooking the outer palace moat. The water was rippling like azure silk under a lovely breeze, and far below us the shimmering moat was dotted with small boats rowed by small people whom one could imagine laughing happily. We fell for this entrancing outlook immediately.

The service, however, proved nonexistent, and the atmosphere was that of a middle class English boardinghouse or family hotel such as you can find all over the world. You get one chain pull per night out of the w.c., and the water spends the rest of the time gurgling wearily up and down through too-small pipes to the upper floors, with no hot water or heat after ten. It was a contrast to the Okura, but at least we felt we would be saving money.

Two days later when we came to settle our bill we found the room cost almost twice what we had paid at the Okura. When we inquired about the reason for the high price we learned that we were paying double for viewing the palace moat.

Romanticists call Japan the land of festivals, but it is also the land of conferences, and hotel rooms are all sold out at the same time. Almost every hotel here is expanding, building on or up or over with a goal of twice the number of rooms next year. I wonder if they can enlarge and still continue their smiling, efficient service?

The next day Mr. Honma telephoned to say that our train and hotel reservations were now complete for our tour and we would leave the following day at 9:00 A.M. Our interpreter would meet us for the first time at the hotel tonight.

Meanwhile we packed two large suitcases and took them to the Hotel Okura to be held there for our return. We are taking with us just one small bag each. These will undoubtedly grow heavier and heavier as we have to carry them ourselves on the trains. Of course I also carry my ladies' large, heavily loaded, over-the-shoulder handbag which every traveling female understands is as heavy as her suitcase, partly because it holds all the family treasures which her husband hands over to her just as they leave the house.

We stopped at the Canadian embassy to pick up mail and reassure ourselves that all was well at home before we left Tokyo. Two letters from Lina who says that Pucci, our fifteen-year-old Maltese terrier, misses us and barks constantly. Having seen Harry and me disappear, he now reckons that Lina may do so and won't let her out of his sight. I wish Pucci could understand the time element and know that we *will* be home soon. But to a dog, gone is gone until he sees you again. Well, I suppose it would seem foolish to give up a trip to Japan because your dog didn't want you to go.

After collecting our mail we drove to the end of the Ginza in the Nihombashi District to search for a plaque which marks the former site of the house of Will Adams, the famous first Englishman ever to land in Japan, in the year 1600. Adams, who was a skilled navigator, introduced to Japan both the art of navigation and that of shipbuilding. He was largely responsible for England's opening up trade in Japan through the East India Company. In time Will Adams became a great friend of the current Shogun, Ieyasu, who gave him a large country estate at Hemi, also the rank of *Samurai*, with eighty to ninety retainers to care for him. Adams was never allowed to leave Japan, although he had a wife in England.

He was ultimately reconciled to a permanent separation from England and in a genuine love match he took a Japanese wife, the daughter of Magome Kageyu, a postal official. Adams fathered two children by her, a son Joseph and a daughter Susanna. Some time later, in spite of his love for his wife, he sired a third child by a Japanese woman who lived in Hirado. It would be interesting to know more about what became of these offspring and their descendants, but there is

86

little historical data available about them. We do know that Adams taught his son Joseph how to navigate, and Joseph became a pilot and spent much of his life at sea. It was probably Joseph who built the shrine at Hemi to commemorate the death of his parents. At this shrine, on her tombstone, Joseph's mother is rather touchingly referred to as "Miss Magome."

Although we had visited the tomb of Adams and his wife at Yokosuka many years ago we had been unable to locate the exact site of the house he occupied in Tokyo, or Edo as it was known in 1600, though we had searched several times in what we believed was the vicinity. But today, with the help of a wide-awake driver who didn't mind inquiring in all the little shops, we finally found a simple, unworked stone boulder with a plaque, almost hidden in a four-foot niche between the walls of two new buildings in a small shopping district. A plain memorial stone about three feet by two feet, it is engraved in Japanese characters which our driver interpreted. It tells of Will Adams, born in 1564, the first Englishman to come to Japan, and it gives warm tribute to him as a great navigator who taught the art of navigation to the Japanese. The date of his death is given as 1620.

While Harry was photographing the plaque we were surrounded by friendly neighboring shopkeepers, all anxious to add something to the story of the memorial, and evidently familiar with its historical significance and pleased with its close propinquity to themselves. They confirmed that the street itself is called Anjin Cho, or Pilot Street, in memory of Adams.

The sudden downpour of rain which now came reminded me of the day in 1955 when we had visited the Adams tomb in Yokosuka on the Pilot Mound in the former Hemi Estate which belonged to Adams. It was pouring that day and we went by taxi to Yokosuka on the Miura Peninsula beyond Kamakura, a long hour's drive which cost us a fortune in yen.

Leaving the taxi on the road, we had to climb between private homes and gardens, up a hill, over rocks and through bushes and up a long flight of steps to the top of the hill, where we found the handsome and impressive, though neglected, double tomb of Will Adams and his Japanese wife, Miss Magome. The monument was beautifully executed in Japanese style with a memorial plaque, an incense and food altar, and Japanese stone lanterns which are worth a fortune today.

The combination of steady rain and the rough scramble to get there had dampened my enthusiasm but not Harry's, and he photographed all angles of the tomb and me. Then, crouching under a tree protected from all except drips, we had ruminated on the crass stupidity of waging wars . . . as compared to the virtues of peaceful penetration by men like Will Adams. He had been well ahead of his time, and so was the Shogun, Ieyasu.

On our way back to the Fairmont we were delayed by a large labor demonstration of five hundred or so workers, all with sweatbands or hats and marching in orderly fashion. They were led by some open trucks filled with organizers shouting instructions through bullhorns, and the trucks were led by police cars signaling to the traffic to let the demonstrators through. The walkers were carrying red flags and signs, which our driver interpreted for us as saying that they were demonstrating against some of the large companies and the rising prices and high cost of living. The marchers themselves appeared indifferent and docile and only waved their flags and shouted when ordered to do so. It all seemed very innocuous and innocent compared to the demonstrations we have at home. Although even this mild disruption appears to contradict the popularly held Japanese ethic that workers are always loyal to their companies, I understand that the organizers go only as far as the companies permit them to and that everybody is back on the job the next day at the proper hour.

We were to see many of these demonstrations before we left Japan, most of them regimented, nonviolent, placid, even amiable. Apparently violence was left to the student demonstrators and not usually indulged in by adults who had jobs to keep. Later, when the train unions went on strike, we noticed that it wasn't the strikers who first became violent, but the inconvenienced passengers who threw stones at the strikers, tore up the stations and ripped up the cars until trains ran again.

Tonight our interpreter came to the hotel to meet us. Harry always said Sachiko looked like a Heian girl of the Japanese tenth century, with her long, flowing soot-black hair, a peach-bloom skin and flat Mongolian features. She was tall for a Japanese girl, with a very feminine figure which adequately filled her tight, indigo pants. Over a lavender blouse she wore a sleeveless, chrome yellow pullover and on top of all was a wonderful, flower-embroidered Afghan sheepskin coat. Of soft suede finish and cut like a mandarin coat, it was long and profusely embroidered in bright silks with vari-colored flowers, and it became her perfectly.

Before the Foreign Affairs Ministry had assigned her to us as an interpreter I had suggested that they send us a man, thinking that a male might help to carry the luggage. But Harry had requested a "pretty girl" . . . and we certainly got one.

It was obvious immediately that Sachiko was ornamental and we were soon to find that she was indispensable. In the end she never let us miss a train, except for delays forced on us by the go-slow train strikes . . . and catching trains in Japan is as much of an achievement as interpreting the language. Her slender hands were always filled with sheafs of vari-colored tickets designating our destination, cost, class, car number — and all these she waved under the noses of gatekeepers as we dashed by in close formation, pushed on by the crowds behind us. With her example we soon learned to use elbows and bags to batter our way through crosscurrents of human beings, our one object being never to lose sight of Sachiko's flowing black mane. We admired her from the first and, in the end, I think we loved her.

10

WE LEFT TOKYO at 9:00 A.M. in the Hikari Super Express, New Tokaido Line, headed for Nagoya. The dingy gray suburbs of the city, with factories, smokestacks, rail lines, tenement houses and dilapidated lodgings, extend for miles in every direction. Our train was traveling west, and as the crowded city slums thinned out behind us we began the search for Mount Fuji on our right. When at last a shimmering pearly white shape emerged through the smog it was greeted with admiring comments from the watching travelers, except for Harry who hissed in my ear that Fuji looked shopworn in the smoky grayness, and added, "If they are so efficient, why don't they do something about the smog?"

"Why don't we do something about our own smog?" I hissed back. "Anyway, I read in the paper that the Japanese government is going to take extreme anti-pollution measures soon."

"Soon?" Harry wondered. Sachiko giggled.

Meanwhile the train came closer to the sacred mountain and we saw clearly her bold, elemental shape, and her gleaming cone emerging from the murky air. Fuji has a supernatural, living beauty of her own which to me is different from all other mountains, and I pressed my face against the window, waiting . . .

Some Japanese say that Fuji looks down in disgust on the smoke and pollution about her, just waiting to vomit up her revulsion and nausea. Others whom she irritates will shout, Down with Fuji! And there are modern youngsters who are bored with her as they are bored with cherry blossoms and geisha. It is their mountain, and they may say what they wish. But for me it is always magic, and as the train roars away I press forward in my seat for one final glimpse of its incandescent cone. Those around me are buried again in their newspapers, but only when the mountain is completely lost to sight can I sink back in my seat, content that once again Fujiyama has not let me down.

Less spectacular than Fuji's beauty, but still comforting and colorful, was the view we had later of the hills looking south, the slopes of which were spotted with brilliant mandarin oranges, a profitable Japanese export.

Meanwhile Sachiko and I were talking about the sudden growth of the Tokyo Ginza, and the greatly increased value of the land there, which has driven homeowners out. Today, a piece the size of a postal card is the nucleus of a fortune. Sachiko said that some years ago there used to be a large community bathhouse at the end of the Ginza, well patronized by all who lived near because none of the old houses had running water or baths of their own. No one objected to this deficiency, as a visit to the community bathhouse was a social pleasure as well as a hygienic duty. But with the increased land values the bathhouse was sold in order to put the land to more profitable uses. As the remaining houses then had no access to a bath, and the inhabitants had to travel for at least half an hour to get to one, they soon sold their old homes. Thus ended the Ginza as a dwelling place, and today it is one of Tokyo's main streets with department stores, restaurants and nightclubs with flashing neon signs to scar the night.

We arrived at Nagoya at eleven. In a short taxi ride from the station we passed the fabulous Nagoya Castle and found to my delight that our hotel was located just across the moat from the main building. The whole castle layout is like a spellbound fairy tale, and I expected momentarily to see Rapunzel letting down her golden hair from an upper castle window. The water in the moat is as green and opaque as jade, and it wrinkles thickly in the breeze. In places the moat is filled with water weeds and sandbars where wild deer run, but where the water is deep enough one sees carp and wild duck. The scalloped, copper-tiled castle roofs are oxidized green, and those of the main building, the small castle, and the outlying turrets all match the color of the moat, the green, moss-grown walls and the trees tying them all into a jade vision. At the peaks of the main castle the sculptured shapes of two giant dolphin glitter like gold — and they *are* gold, the story is. The incredible thing about this antique castle miracle is that it isn't antique. Although the original was built in 1610, it was completely destroyed in World War II, and was faithfully restored in the 1950s. The view of it is so lovely from our hotel that I hoped we had no program for the afternoon.

But of course we did. As soon as we could snatch a quick lunch we headed for the Aichi Prefectural Offices of the Forest and Agriculture Department, where an appointment had been made for us from Tokyo. Nagoya is the third largest Japanese city and the capital city of Aichi Prefecture. It is the center of the second greatest industrial area, the first being Osaka.

At the prefectural office we met Toshide Oyabu of the department, and half a dozen of his associates. We loaded into two Toyotas and headed out of town for Inazawa City, admiring as we drove the reconstructed city of Nagoya, which although badly damaged in the war, has since been rebuilt with wide streets and open breathing spaces between new buildings.

Arrived at Inazawa City we met Tomio Sawada, head of a government advisory group which assists the local farmers. Inazawa has about two thousand families engaged in nursery growing, many of these families having been on the same plots of land for many generations. Unlike the Western world where one associates nurseries with the propagation of flowering plants, in Inazawa the nurseries are chiefly concerned with growing trees — pine, juniper, cypress, spruce, fir, beech and others, including orchard trees. Many of the artificially shaped "banzai-ed" trees were very expensive. A single juniper of good size and artificially shaped might cost as much as a million yen, or about U.S. $3,333, as such trees are greatly valued for ornamental use.

Each separate nursery occupied a very small area of land, some only an acre and a quarter. Five acres was the extent of any single holding, in which case only three and three quarters acres would be used for rice growing, as Japan now grows a surplus, and the remaining acre and a quarter would be used as a nursery.

In previous years the total land area had been needed for rice. Today, thanks to modern farming methods which produce a higher rice yield per acre, plus the fact that the Japanese diet has broadened to include more meat and dairy products and cereals other than rice, the demand for rice is less, and land is spared for other uses. Aichi Prefecture is considered a very prosperous area. The average income to an owner per two and a half acres of land is now about Yen 2,500,000, or close to U.S. $10,000 per year.

We left Inazawa City offices with our party tightly squeezed into three small cars. Harry was enjoying himself immensely, surrounded by horticultural and forestry experts who were also delighted with him for being so knowledgeable, and who assumed the trip was arranged for his benefit. It was a great advantage to have Harry to ask questions and elicit the appropriate information, while I was left free to observe what appealed to me most — people rather than trees.

Our cars soon entered a narrow lane, at the end of which we found ourselves on a stretch of green lawn in front of a small, meticulously neat Japanese house. It was raining as we disentangled ourselves from the vehicles and entered the little house at the invitation of its owner, Mr. Kiyoshi Inui, one of our party. He told us that he had lived here all his life and his family had owned this land for five generations. In the past they had grown rice and mulberry trees for silk worms only, but now they grew a variety of crops. The house was seventy-six years old and had recently been renovated.

We squeezed into a small entrance room, leaving our shoes at the door and slipping our damp feet into warm fuzzy crimson slippers placed there for us. As there were twelve of us and twenty-four slippers, the effect was of a splendid red centipede. The room was almost filled with a low table around which were placed enough seats for us all if we crowded. I noticed a bowl with a spray of handsome mauve orchids on the table and I recalled then that every office we had visited so far had had a spray of orchids.

As soon as we were seated an attractive little Japanese lady dressed in Western style entered with a tray loaded with teacups and small bowls which she arranged carefully on the table before us. She was accompanied by a very pretty young woman in Western dress who carried plates of cookies and soybean cakes. I knew we would be offered tea, but I hadn't expected it would be the formal tea-ceremony tea, *matcha,* a strong, thick, powdered green tea which looked just like the water in the castle moat. I knew that serving *matcha* was a compliment to us as guests, but I had to swallow hard to get mine down. After we had all drunk this with the proper laudatory comments we were served ordinary tea in teacups. Fortunately the tea ceremony had been tactfully adapted to the limited time of our visit and our foreign tastes. Especially so as we had just finished drinking tea half an hour before in the Inazawa office, and half an hour before that in Nagoya, and half an hour before that in the hotel . . .

Looking about the polished, spotless room I saw that it had been modernized by installing in the old fireplace an electric grate which gave out a scorching heat. In the alcove stood a glass cabinet which held an exhibit of beautifully dressed Japanese dolls arranged in five tiers on top of a crimson spread. These dolls were not for children to play with or to handle, but to commemorate the Dolls' Festival on March 3, a very special day for all little girls.

The dolls are collected through all the years of a girl child's life, and brought out only for special celebrations. I was interested to see that in this unpretentious farm family the Dolls' Festival was beautifully and gaily celebrated. I was told that Mr. Inui, whose daughter had helped to serve us tea, had a year-old granddaughter in whose honor the exhibit was arranged. I was amused to see a huge, furry, pink and white imported U.S. panda bear seated amicably alongside the dainty Japanese dolls.

Harry asked Mr. Inui if he had any sons to inherit his land and, if not, what would happen to the estate after his death. Mr. Inui said that his eldest son had not wished to farm but had studied law and was now a lawyer, thus leaving the responsibility of the farm to the second son. This boy had been impatient at the idea of carrying on the farm tradition and so, with his father's consent, he had left home after finishing high school and gone to Tokyo University. There he had studied engineering for several years and then decided that he did not like city life. Having discovered for himself that both city and farm life had disadvantages, he had returned more willingly to the land and was now working with his father with the prospect of carrying on the farm tradition when his father was gone.

This decision had made Mr. Inui very happy, he said — although he looked so strong and healthy that I thought it would be some time before his son ever needed to take over. The son and his wife now lived in the house with the father and mother, as did the daughter with her husband and baby. Some of the other Inazawa landowners worked at independent jobs in Nagoya, commuting there every day while their wives and children worked on the land. Others farmed out their land to laborers while retaining ownership themselves, but living in Nagoya.

Mr. Inui opened the sliding doors behind us to show us one of the original, unimproved rooms of the old farmhouse. This large, bright chamber was completely walled with *shoji*, or rice paper sliding panels, and the floor gleamed with the natural polish which comes from decades of *tabi*-clad feet shuttling back and forth. This was the old silk room which every farmhouse once had, where the silkworms were housed, where the grubs hatched and the caterpillars spun their cocoons. It was a room for which there was little practical need today, Mr. Inui said, as silk culture was largely outdated by the competition of synthetic materials. Only the mulberry trees in the garden survived unchanged. This room was true old Japan, he told us with a mixture of pride and amusement. Nevertheless, I took note of a huge television set with a very large, pink plastic American doll seated on top.

Harry asked our host what he thought was the most important change in farming in the last twenty-five years. Mr. Inui answered without hesitation that it was the use of chemical weed killers and mechanized cultivation. Next in importance was the introduction of greenhouses for plant propagation. Everybody present agreed with these statements and added to them the thought that having slightly larger farms now was a great benefit. One of the men, Mr. Kuhara, a well-built, sturdy-looking fellow who was not a farmer but a machinery agent, said that his job was to do any sort of mechanical plowing or harvesting for anyone who wished it, at a price.

When we went outside to leave, Mr. Inui introduced us to his wife, who had served us tea, and was now proudly holding up her granddaughter, a beautiful, red-cheeked Japanese infant of one year. Beside them stood the very pretty daughter, mother of the baby. The little house behind them gleamed in the rain, the garden was meticulously neat, the various conifers all throve, and each one of the family added to the comfortable picture of health, happiness and security. Prosperity seemed here to have followed intelligence, industry and family co-operation.

Before we left Nagoya we paid a hasty duty call on Nagoya Castle, but like most of the castles, its beauty was confined to its exterior. Inside it was thick-walled and dusty, dark and damp, and obviously designed to repel invaders rather than welcome friends. We happily hurried away, content with our hotel room.

Nagoya is the home of one of the oldest, most beautiful and best loved places of Shinto worship in Japan, the Atsuta Jingu. Sachiko, who feels responsible for our doing what we ought to do even if we don't want to, suggested that we should visit the shrine this morning before catching our midday train for Takayama. She herself is not religious, she claims, nor are most of the young people today, but they all like to visit the famous shrines and temples of Japan, going there as sightseers anxious to see places of national Japanese interest. Sachiko admitted, however, that every Japanese is included automatically from birth in whatever Buddhist "parish" or area in which he lives, a fact which seems to me to involve him involuntarily in Buddhism. Anyway, we set off for the Atsuta Shrine at nine o'clock this morning with religiously open minds. Harry and I vaguely remembered having visited the shrine on our honeymoon, but Sachiko had never been there. It was partially destroyed in the war and was later restored.

I have always thought that Shinto must be a rather comfortable faith to follow. For instance, it is difficult not to believe one important facet of Shintoism, that this world is the ultimate reality. And I am personally, as a believer in God, convinced with Shinto that there is no place in which God, or a god, does not reside. Shintoism involves a deep reverence for youth, birth and life, for sun, moon and stars, for fertility and sex, for every aspect of nature and for all the forces of life. It invokes a love of purity, sincerity and simplicity, and its mainstay is the rite of purification. Shinto teaches that man is fundamentally good, and that life has virtue and beauty — two very consoling precepts for anyone to live by. Perhaps they are the reasons that the Japanese today seem so passionately committed to living their lives and enjoying to the very utmost both working and playing. Where suicide fits in I have not determined.

My immediate visual impression of the Atsuta Shrine, which is really a collection of six different shrines for six deities located in the main shrine and forty-four minor shrines, is of its extreme simplicity of line and material. Moderate, inverted, V-shaped roofs are held up by crossbeams and rafters which are supported on unpainted wooden pillars. Large cross-logs are laid on top the thatched roofs to anchor them down. There are none of the geegaws and ornate lines and gilt and crimson decorations which typify the temples dedicated to Buddha.

The original Atsuta shrines were built about two thousand years ago, I learned from a small handbook which we purchased from a gentle, shriveled little man selling souvenirs. More than half these shrines were destroyed by bombing in the Second World War. The modern reconstructions were completed in 1955, the designs of the shrines being the same as those of the original ones. In the restoration, however, a number of auxiliary structures were added for use as cultural facilities as well as for worship, and the Atsuta shrine area is now a center of youth movements such as the Boy Scouts and Girl Guides, as well as scholarly and social activities of many other sorts.

We wandered undisturbed for some time through the grounds, as we were the only people there except for our souvenir salesman and half a dozen young girl acolytes. Dressed gaily in white tops and crimson trousers, and carrying brooms and rakes, they came hurrying out from behind one of the shrines. They were giggling and laughing and sweeping vigorously as they tidied up the ornamental stretches of small, clean pebbles which were laid out in patterns much as we plant grass in plots.

The feeling of peace and sanctuary which enveloped the large, parklike premises was intensified by the presence of magnificent giant camphor trees, some over a thousand years old. Shrines are always built either in a grove of trees or on a mountainside, and in the Atsuta Shrine there were not only forested areas but a body of still water with a resting place beside it for tired pilgrims, and streams of running water flowing under arched bridges, lovely to see and perilous to climb over, but without which no park would be Japanese. There were also some large, priceless stone lanterns. I thought that a little Shinto realism was being employed in a myth Sachiko told us, that anyone who prayed to the well in the Mii Shrine would become immune to worms!

There were large and less large *torii* standing all about us in the park. Throughout Japan *torii* appear as symbols of Shinto civilization, for they are the gateways to shrines, and to pass under them gives purification. The material from which they are made may be wood, stone, bronze, cement, almost anything. However, cypress wood, *hinoki,* is most favored. They appear everyplace in cities, along highways and roadways, on hilly trails, and in small villages where *torii* are built simply of rough tree trunks and unpolished cross-beams, the all important factor of a *torii* being the design. This is fundamentally a combination of four straight lines — i.e., two vertical ones symbolizing two gateposts, and two (or more) horizontal ones at the top to unite the gateposts.

The keynote of the whole Atsuta Park area this day was a rather depressing quietude. I would like to see it on a festive day when tens of thousands of gaily dressed visitors pay homage to its deities with fireworks, dancing and singing, while Shinto joy-worship runs riot. But today the wind is so piercing, the trees so damp and dripping, the pebbled walks so chilled and our feet so wet that we are glad to start back to our hotel. Japan in March is cold.

11

THE TRAINS WERE excellent. It wasn't the trains that made travel difficult, but trying to get onto them. It was carrying our bags up a hundred steps and down a hundred steps and then up again and down again while changing train platforms. Porters were said to be "available" but they were also invisible, and one cannot stand still in a surging sea of people and shout for help. Not if one is married to a Keith, piloted by a Sachiko. And anyplace where trains went directly we never went. Finally, with the correct platform safely attained, and either freezing in a cold wind, or alternatively smothering in a small glass birdcage waiting room, we always had a feeling of achievement. It only remained then to await the right train and get inside it.

As the train approached we pressed closer to the track, pushed forward by those behind us, and sympathizing with the impulse which made incipient suicides hurl themselves in front of trains. When the speeding coach ultimately whooshed to a stop near us and the door slid open, all the passengers inside tried to rush out, only to be met by a human wall of outside passengers trying to rush in.

After a moment of complete impasse during which each man was his brother's enemy, somebody outside would very grudgingly draw back just enough to allow the emerging passengers one by one to squirm through. Their exit was a triumph for our entry and, with Sachiko as a flying wedge before us, and the sheer weight of tens of thousands behind pushing us, we got on board. It was a moment of victory for each one who made it.

Once inside and in our own cars and seats, we all became polite, well-behaved people again, bowing to our seat companions, saying excuse me and thank you, folding up coats, removing shoes, adjusting window shades and ultimately sinking back against the red plush cushions with a feeling of accomplishment. This never lasted long as every few hours we had to change trains. A couple of hours in any one direction and we were in combat again . . . down a hundred steps and up again . . .

On average the trains were better than many in the United States. The best express trains were comparable to the scenic Canadian Pacific in its heyday which travels east–west across Canada via Banff and the Canadian Rockies. In Japan the seats in the Green Ticket first class reserved section, which also require the purchase of ordinary fare tickets, were very comfortable and fully adjustable, with leg space enough even for us. But there was none of this luxury for those who held only ordinary tickets. As the Foundation, thank God, assumed us to be first-class travelers, we did not try these, but the cars rolled past us packed solid with nothing but faces — as there couldn't have been enough space to accommodate bodies as well!

As in North America, some trains were clean, others were

littered with the refuse of thoughtless human beings — whether Japanese or American. As box lunches, or *bento*, were being peddled constantly and tea, beer and soft drinks sold, the arrival at each station found an accumulation of candy wrappers, paper plates, fruit peelings, and empty bottles in the aisles and between the seats. The refuse increased with the mileage from Tokyo, as the rush of travel makes it pretty well impossible for the attendants to tidy up until the end of the line. Meanwhile a lilting girl's voice comes over the loudspeaker in Japanese and English to alert us to scenery and to stations.

A dining car is carried on the few runs that are long enough to require it, but most are too limited to make leisurely dining car service practical. However, as well as *bento* box lunches, a buffet car service is available in the Green Ticket section. This offers such exotic items as hamburger steak, fried prawns, pork cutlets, ham and eggs, and potato salad, to be eaten standing up at the counter, and at prices about what we would pay in the States. That is the way it was in February and March 1973 — but three months later in the grip of inflation Japanese prices had doubled.

The New Tokaido Line from Tokyo to Osaka, the leading industrial cities, boasts of attaining a speed of 130 miles an hour. We traveled on the super Super Express *Hikari* to Nagoya, but Mount Fuji as glimpsed from the racing train window won over my interest from the speed of the train and its mechanical graces. One boast of the express trains is that they are always on time, but the go-slow strikes ruined this record.

Toilets and lavatories have a universal appeal for storytellers. As most of my train rides were about three hours in length, I arranged my internal plumbing so as not to use the train toilets. However, Sachiko said they were "not too bad." Harry never used any public toilets; he said he didn't eat enough to need to. I did a little research in public rest rooms when on foot, and found they hadn't changed much basically since 1934, my first introduction to the Japanese coeducational toilet system, except that now there was toilet paper — sometimes. In most rest rooms one finds open squat toilets where the ladies face forward and the gents face the wall, almost hand-in-hand. Excruciating toilet experiences are a favorite subject for visiting Americans, but as for me, I say as Gertrude Stein might have said — a toilet is a toilet is a toilet — when you need one, who cares which way you face!

In the stations and running for trains was the only place in Japan where I saw many old people. Old ladies trotting incredibly fast were invariably festooned with heavy, bulky luggage — everything from straw mattresses to charcoal stoves. They were usually accompanied by a young woman with a baby on her back and one inside, while the presumed husband was probably well ahead and trying to disown them. As there was a flu epidemic at the time some people were wearing gauze masks over nose and mouth, whether to avoid getting germs or giving them, I never knew. Fortunately, pregnancy wasn't catching. Everybody was overburdened and uncomplaining, and so efficient at plowing through crowds that when Sachiko would turn around and call to me, "Are you all right?" I was ashamed to say "No."

From the very first day sitting beside me on the train headed for Nagoya I could see that Sachiko, a perfect Mongolian beauty herself, was estimating us, but she didn't like to ask personal questions. At last she permitted herself just one. I have a silvery streak in front of my long, black hair, which I wear pinned up on top of my head in a bun. The only question she ever asked me about myself was when she looked carefully at my hair and said, "Can you do up your hair yourself?" When I told her I could, she commented thoughtfully, "The way you wear it, it would look well with a kimono."

When I asked Sachiko where she bought her exotic coat she answered, "I saw a coat like it on a girl in Australia and I asked her where she bought it. She said in Afghanistan so I decided to go there and buy one. But I didn't like the country or the Afghans — they're always angry! They open the border only once a week, so after I bought the coat I had to wait there a week for the border to open again . . . I was glad to leave. I hated the place. The man was very angry with me when I bargained with him for this coat. He said, 'Don't argue! That's my price! Don't argue!' Well, in the end it cost me only about thirty of your dollars. Can you believe it? It's all embroidered by hand."

I decided there was something worth noting about a girl who went to Afghanistan to buy a coat. Determination was the keystone of Sachiko's character, but she also had a quick, inquiring mind and never hesitated to ask for information. Although I knew that she came from the upper strata of society I was amused to discover that she talked freely and happily with every taxi driver with whom we drove and consequently we acquired considerable free guidance and good advice.

The year before, Sachiko had gone to Australia on a student visa and remained there for a year. She had studied art and ceramics and had tutored students in the Japanese language. Living in a youth hostel at first, and later in an apartment, she ended as a desk hostess managing a hotel whose owner had urged her to remain indefinitely in her job in Australia. But as her student visa had expired she had to leave. She was now almost twenty-eight years old.

"But didn't your family object to your leaving Japan, especially to go as far away as Australia?" I asked, knowing that in traditional Japanese family life the disposal of daughters was either to an arranged marriage or to home duties.

Sachiko's answer was simple. "I had earned the money for the trip. They couldn't do anything about it. Anyway, they knew I wanted to go and they know I am determined."

As she sat beside me in the train with her shadowy, soot-black hair falling softly over her face, her almond eyes looking slantwise over at me, her lower lip pushed obstinately out, the twentieth century seemed to be speaking to me through her tenth-century mask. This young woman made up her own mind. No matter how many men might tell me that Japanese females had changed only superficially and that underneath their modern ways they were still bound by old traditions — I wouldn't completely believe it. I had found at least one exception.

12

≈≈≈≈≈≈≈≈≈≈≈≈≈≈≈≈≈≈≈≈≈≈≈

AT 1:00 P.M. we fought our way onto the express train "Norikura," headed for Takayama in Gifu Prefecture in the Japanese Alps. This is old Japan, Sachiko tells us. This train is not as classy as the "Super Express Hikari," but it is better for our purpose of seeing people and places. It stops at many small villages, and where it does not stop it slides through so slowly that we can actually see into the houses which cluster close to the rails. Many houses have scalloped, delft-blue tile roofs which mark them as being quite new, and the buildings themselves seem to have permanent wooden sides and sliding doors. Many have solar water heaters on the roof and also an extra room built there, perhaps an afterthought as the family grows. On the hillsides there are masses of mulberry trees for silkworms to munch on, and it looks as if silk culture has not been abandoned here.

Bento, or box lunches, are soon being sold on the train by very neat little Japanese girls who file down the aisles, laughing and giggling with each other and the customers as they pull or push carts loaded with small cardboard boxes filled with cold rice, fish, and pickles. Almost everyone around us buys one; we do not. Sachiko looks at them rather hungrily but won't take one because Harry doesn't.

The train is climbing all the time and the scenery soon becomes spectacular. The railbed is tunneled through solid rock in many places and we are constantly roaring into the blackness of a tunnel and blasting out again into blinding light to find we have left an entire steep mountain behind us. Other places the rails cling to the very edge of a sheer rock face which almost overhangs the train. These cliffs are festooned with huge, firmly pinioned nets to hold them in place and to prevent slides and loose rocks from falling on the railbed below. To me, this is a new and ingenious idea. Meanwhile we crossed and recrossed the Mashita-gawa, a river which rises in the alps and on which several large power plants are built. The Gero health spa, long famous for the medicinal value of its waters and for the beauty of its autumn foliage, is situated on this river.

Although no snow was falling when we left Nagoya, as we traveled north we saw increasing white patches everywhere and soon the eroded brown cliffs and valleys were almost covered. I have never before been conscious of brownness in the Japanese landscape, but there is an almost total absence of green this year owing to the very light snowfall. Only with the melting of a good snow will the verdure return; otherwise the landscape must await the summer deluges of June. But up here in the alps there is plenty of snow, and I realize now that the crisscross fences running horizontally above the cliffs and across the slopes are snow barricades to prevent snowslides from swamping the trains below.

As we rush upward, the river rushes downward. We see it first on one side of the track and then the other, now white and narrow in rapids, now wide and smooth and lazy, now clear and deep and green over its rocky bed, now frosty arctic blue over shining pebbles, and always a source of beauty as well as power. At Hida Osaka, not far beyond Gero, a large power plant has been built on the river. Shortly before arriving at Takayama the train leaves the river to veer slightly west, and in the distance we are surrounded by high, snow-covered mountains, while thickly wooded areas close in nearby. Much of Takayama revenue depends on wood industries, and Sachiko tells us that the place is famous for its wood craftsmen and wood carvings.

Light snow covers the ground outside and is falling gently as we leave the train. At this moment I much regret having left my boots and my heavy tweed coat in Tokyo, deceived by the spell of spring warmth which suddenly took over in the unpredictable city. February and March on Honshu Island are impossible to outguess, but up to now we found Tokyo much warmer than Victoria was when we left. But it is typical of traveling that one always takes the wrong things and I am inured to this fact and remind myself that everything passes, including cold feet.

After a couple of minutes in a taxi while we zip through a ramshackle little town filled with real old-style Japanese houses and nondescript shops with conglomerate wares, a lovely river, and a couple of dilapidated bridges, we draw up before the Japanese inn Seiryu. Staying at Japanese inns, or *ryokan*, is usually regarded by Westerners as the colorful, sophisticated thing to do ("You *must* stay at one of those *charming* inns!"), and a polite tribute to the Japanese. The Japanese public regards foreigners staying in their inns with tolerance and courtesy but the inns themselves regard foreigners as Buddha's gift to big business. The best inns recommended by the Travel Bureau are as little Japanese as the innkeepers can make them and still attract Japanese, and as high-priced or higher than the best hotels. These inns have modern plumbing, many have private baths, also central heating, and both Japanese and Western food may be ordered. The inns charge 15 percent extra for service, and 10 percent tax on top of that, whereas hotels charge slightly less. The inns are beautifully clean and so are the hotels, and service is excellent in both. Inns always furnish the traveler with kimono for sleeping, slippers, toothbrush, toothpaste and soap. Many hotels do this also, though you may have to request the kimono. Our Tokyo hotel even lent me a typewriter, without charge.

As our taxi swept up to the Inn Seiryu and I read the electric signs outside, in English — Diners Club, Japan-American Friendship Club, Sanitary Food Association, Chamber of Commerce Rally, American Express cards welcome, Lions Club, etc., I had a premonition as to its Japanese character.

Our room on the third floor proved to be a nice, eight-mat-size chamber with a tiny bathroom built for Lilliputians and a bathtub for dwarfs. A charming little glass-enclosed balcony looked out on a narrow alley where a thin, moth-eaten cat crouched shivering, possibly contemplating its ultimate end as part of a *samisen*. Beyond him was another charming balcony like our own where two fat cats were playing. Our balcony contained a small table, two smaller chairs and a small refrigerator stocked with soft drinks, cheese, ice water and ice cubes — to suit American tastes, I supposed. I wondered if a full-size American male could ever get into that balcony.

Naturally the bedroom had no bed, and the only piece of furniture was a diminutive chest, twelve inches high, with two drawers and a little makeup mirror before which I knelt to squint at myself and see if I looked as cold as I felt. Apparently I did, as the maid who showed us up took a quick look at me and then rushed to the heat control thermostat and pushed it to "high." With a happy clanking sound the heat came on.

But we were not to enjoy the warmth for long. The inn proprietor told Sachiko that we should visit a settlement of *gassho-zukuri* (historic farmhouses) which had been relocated in the mountains outside Takayama as part of a government project to protect such historic monuments. Several *gassho-zukuri* were native to the location, and others had been moved from the nearby village of Hida to join them and form a tourist attraction. The proprietor said the drive there was beautiful, and we would just have time to go there and return before dark. So we put on our wet shoes again and got into a taxi.

We were outside Takayama city in two minutes, and the mountains all about were rough and angular and fiercely beautiful under the clean white snow. We drove along a narrow road and up several slopes before we arrived at the end of a long mountain upgrade at the foot of Mt. Matsukura and found a picturesque (the adjective is unavoidable) group of thatched-roofed, *shoji*-paneled old houses standing together on the edge of a small, pale, half-frozen lake. The snow had ceased to fall and was suspended in air like an opalescent mist and the whole settlement was bound together in a bewitched silence. No one actually lived here in winter, the taxi driver told us, but the rest of the year the houses were occupied, and the residents grew rice, vegetables and fruit, and kept poultry and pigs.

The thatched roofs looked bulky and heavy, as they would have to be to resist the wind, and they were anchored by crossbeams and large boulders on top, and steeply angled to shed the snow. The houses were large and substantial, some having second floors, as one could tell by the placement of the *shoji*-panel windows. The dwellings' adequate size would accommodate the several generations of a farm family. There was an old wooden water wheel on the lake, whose waters could be diverted for wet paddy cultivation. There was a hand-powered well on higher land.

For wind protection the houses backed right up against some higher, heavily wooded mountain slopes. When I stood on the edge of the little plateau with my back to the dark heights and looked down to the shining valley below, I had that wonderful sense of freedom that comes from being above the world rather than in it. Here was an ideal location for people prepared to revive the simple life of that pioneer period before the GNP became god. I should like to come here when the houses are occupied, the water wheel turns, the paddy is planted, the well ropes creak, the pigs root, the poultry peck, the hens lay eggs and the little Japanese children dash about.

Meanwhile the light was going rapidly and there was scarcely enough for Harry to take photographs. Although we hated to leave this enchanted scene we were all frozen, and the thought of the warm inn with its clanking hot pipes made us tell the taxi driver to go straight to the Seiryu and avoid the additional side trips, which like any good driver he kept offering us.

Arrived at the inn, we hurried up to our room, as Harry and I had just one thought in mind. We had brought with us only a large zipper bag and a small overnight case, as there is never any place to hang or stow Western garments in a Japanese room. Quickly I located the Scotch in my small case. Then we sat on the balcony and had a drink, and watched the snow-flakes sifting gently onto the tiled roofs outside and felt better with every passing moment and every drink. This was Japan as we remembered it and loved it.

Dinner was to be served in our room, as is always done at an inn, and Sachiko came to eat with us. The maid knocked to say dinner was ready, then entered the room to prepare a place for the food. She took a very low table out of a cupboard, set it in the center of the room, and arranged three backrests at the table for us to lean against. Then she laid out three separate dinners on three red lacquer trays, each meal with its own individual dishes for every item of food. As I watched her doing this with meticulous care and artistry I contrasted the appearance of this meal with that of the all-purpose family casserole in our Western homes. I also contrasted the amount of labor involved in washing and drying these many fragile, dainty dishes we were to use tonight.

To properly appreciate a Japanese gourmet meal one should paint it in colors as well as eat it. Each individual tray contains attractive, vari-shaped dishes which are pictorially arranged as to the color, shape and texture of the foods they contain. Fresh leaves are used to accent the natural color of the viands, and a slice of raw fish becomes ornamental when served on a fresh green leaf. A diner's impression is favorable before food touches his lips. My recollection of the meal at Takayama is more vividly of its beauty than of its flavors, which seem to have been mostly fishy — although as to the eating of raw fish in Japan, I find one soon becomes so accustomed to it that one drops the adjective "raw." The fish served us this night was really a luxury, as Takayama is in the high mountains and for food it relies largely on its own locally grown market vegetables in summer and in winter on salted ones.

The covered rice bowl was on my left and the covered soup bowl on my right and the chopsticks were placed horizontally in front. We started the meal in correct fashion by first taking a little rice with our chopsticks, then sipping a little chicken soup with chicken balls, then a little rice again, and more soup, before we tried out what proved to be several varieties of raw fish delicately flavored and cut in small pieces, one being tunny served with grated horseradish. Then came salted vegetables, then mushrooms and chestnuts, and to finish off, some highly spiced pickles, and then tea. A small hand towel rinsed in hot water and wrung almost dry was beside each place for us to cleanse our hands and mouths. Although very small amounts of each item except rice were served, the food was rich and there was more than we could finish.

If we had been Japanese we would have had our baths before eating and then donned kimonos for our meal. But, being us, we found it much too chilly to sit around in kimonos to eat, and we preferred to delay our baths until just before going to bed.

Not that we were going to have a bed — we had something even nicer and cozier. We had no sooner finished eating than the two maids returned to clear away the dishes, and Sachiko said goodnight and left. With the dinner remnants removed the maids rushed the table back into its cupboard again, and snatched out in its place some lovely fleecy quilts called *futons*, unfolded these and spread them out in the middle of the room where they covered most of the floor. These were to lie on. Then some other warm, fleecy quilts were unfolded and tucked over them and an inviting space for us was opened up inside.

It looked so comfortable that we wasted no time. What with the snow falling gently outside, the windows frosted white, and the central heat clanging pleasantly, it proved to be the most luxurious and comfortable sleeping we had in Japan, as even the best hotels go in for unyielding and indestructible cold cotton bed sheets. True, the little Japanese pillows were brickbats, but we rolled up my coat for a pillow; travel requires versatile clothing.

We awoke early and saw white roofs across the alley and the same thin cat crouched outside the door shivering in the snow. Japanese inns do not serve breakfast in bed and we dressed quickly and hurried down to the dining room. Here we found

the tables half filled with Japanese still in their sleeping kimonos, all eating Japanese breakfasts of bean curd soup, fish,
pickles, rice and tea. They stopped eating long enough to look
us over in a friendly way and to bow and say good morning, a
greeting we returned. One handsome young man with pleasant
eyes and a smiling mouth, sitting at the next table, asked us in
English, "How are you?" We assured him we were well. The
dining room maid gave us one glance and knew we didn't want
a Japanese breakfast and hurried back to us with an electric
toaster, a plate of sliced bread, marmalade, a jar of instant
coffee and a jug of boiling water. By now Sachiko had arrived.
She asked for a Japanese breakfast — but ate very little of it.

13

As the air was clear and cold, and the snow had stopped falling, we decided to walk to the old town to visit the Kusakabes' Folkcraft House. This was said to be typical of the Edo period and Sachiko thought it would be well worth looking at. After asking the inn proprietor for directions we collected our still-wet shoes once more at the inn door and shuffled out onto the snow-blotched, icy streets. For a couple of minutes we wandered through a tawdry small-shop section, then crossed a modern, unbeautiful bridge and strolled along the bank of the Miyagawa. Here a narrow lane was lined on one side with the open stalls of the morning market, whose business hours were almost over. Perhaps because we were too late there was little variety in the vegetables and fruits left on display, but plenty of choice in Japanese biscuits and crackers, which are very tasty.

When we turned away from the river we found ourselves in the old section of the city, in streets lined with houses of once-rich tradesmen, dwellings which are now being carefully preserved both for their historic value and as tourist attractions.

They are all built in identical style, simple and Japanese, their blind-looking rectangular exteriors almost touching on the narrow streets, their time-polished woods and pearly *shoji* giving dignity and elegance to their austerity. It is said that the tradesmen who lived in these houses during the Edo era held financial sway over the whole city of Takayama. One of these buildings proved to be Kusakabes' folkcraft museum, and we paid small fees and entered, leaving our shoes at the door and stepping into toe slippers placed there for entrants. It is difficult for the Western visitor to adjust to the constant putting on and removing of his broken-backed shoes. Most Japanese seem immune to wet feet and cold rooms, but it takes a lifetime to acquire immunization. When they wear Western dress, the Japanese wear Western shoes, and these probably remain soggy all winter. But they are only worn outside the house, and dry, fuzzy slippers are used inside. When wearing kimonos they wear wooden clogs, or *geta,* which are raised above the ground by two wooden crosspieces, and kept on the feet by a V-shaped thong between the big toe and the next toe. These are good for wet weather as they lift the wearer above minor puddles and mud, and dry quickly when left at the door. A *zori,* or sandal, may also be worn with kimono. Both *geta* and *zori* require practice for skillful maneuvering. A *tabi,* or split-toed sock of white or colors is worn with these.

Inside the museum my impression was of space and airiness — cold-airiness, as the only possibility of warmth came from a small oil stove around which a group of young Japanese student tourists already huddled with their little hands, transparent with cold, extended hopefully to the stove. Males and females were dressed identically in blue jeans with bright colored zippered jackets on top. The boys had longish hair and the girls had very long, swinging black tresses which they tossed back and forth on their tireless necks like young colts.

All carried cameras, and the collection of empty, broken-backed sneakers standing at the door was obviously theirs. This was their spring holiday, Sachiko said.

There was, of course, no furniture and the floors inside were on several different levels. The beauty of the interior lay simply in the huge polished beams which supported the structure of the house and then crossed each other high overhead to support the roof. The center of attraction in the living quarters was an old iron teakettle suspended on a metal chain over a glowing fire in a central hearth — but the glow proved to be nothing but electric lights shining under some artificial logs. Most of the girl tourists managed with much hilarity to pose for their pictures, bending over the kettle and pretending to poke up the nonexistent fire.

The building was designed in two sections, one for living in and the other a place for carrying on the owner's trade, such as woodcarving or lacquer work, or pottery. Toward the back of the house we found a well from which to draw water, and several smaller workrooms. Suddenly the *shoji* slid open from one room and a little kimono-clad girl came out and beckoned us to enter the room and have tea — for free, she assured Sachiko. We didn't accept, but saw several young couples inside enjoying the offer.

Returning to the front of the house we went cautiously up the stairs leading to the sleeping quarters, a sort of half-floor or open mezzanine between the main floor and the roof. The stairs were highly polished, slippery and narrow, with a shallow, three-inch tread for my size nine foot, and my slippers, which were always too short and too wide, fell off with each step. Up in the loft were several cupboards designed to hold sleeping *futons*, and I could imagine the room as being quite cozy when occupied — except for lack of heat.

As well as the old, well-polished and perfectly fitted beams, the shining floors and gleaming *tatami* and the handsome latticed *shoji* panels all gave elegance. The winters are severe and protracted in Takayama and, while the exterior of the house was no doubt constructed during good weather, the carpenter probably spent his long winter days on finishing and polishing the interior.

On our walk back to the inn we passed some little stalls which were cooking on *hibachis* and selling hot, savory tidbits. Sachiko dashed over to one and purchased a number of little rolled pieces of dough made from bean curd, a very special delicacy, she said, for which Takayama is famous. We ate these later at the inn with cups of coffee, and they were good. They strengthened us enough to stand up to the shock of our bill from the inn, which turned out to be twice what we had paid per day at the Okura in Tokyo. For us, this exploded the theory of travel by inns being cheap.

For the last time, with the inn retinue all bowing gracefully to us, we collected our wet shoes at the door and forced them on our frozen feet. The only way to do this while standing up is to break down the backs of your shoes and leave them permanently flattened as most Japanese do. Sachiko won out by being young and using platform-soled, backless sandals regardless of weather.

After the usual battle at the station we got inside the Express train "Norikura" headed for Toyama. Once inside a train I was always happy because (a) it was a triumph to get there, and (b) people, including myself, were so improved after they got inside. Add to this the fact that *bento*, or box lunches, were soon being sold by cute little Japanese maidens, calling in sweet, thin voices, "Bento! Bento!" and the atmosphere about us became really jovial. The train, which had originated in Tokyo, already had on board the customary merry party of

Japanese commercials celebrating business deals, or freedom from wives, or just celebrating, and they had their sake bottles with them — now almost empty. These partying men never seemed to become objectionable or violent, just very red, muddled, noisy and hilarious. Those in a party who were least drunk always herded the wobbly ones on and off the trains with much sympathetic laughter and no signs of embarrassment. Obviously, to be drunk carried no disapprobation. There is a Japanese saying that one is free from shame when on a trip. Oddly enough the compulsive drinker is not a social problem in Japan; a Japanese merely "chooses" to get drunk on certain occasions.

Seeing these quite nice little men so drunk and happy made me feel old and chillingly respectable. I wished that I could be young and drunk and stand wobbling vacuously in the aisle of a speeding train. In fact it suddenly reminded me of a night on the way back to college in Berkeley after a big game in the Pasadena Rose Bowl, traveling up with other undergrads from Los Angeles. That night in the tribal joy of a football victory (it seems ridiculous to me today!) with good friends around me, and filled with youth and sensual strength, I saw an opalescent, shimmering world ahead of me to conquer . . . and I knew I could conquer it . . . even without all that red wine! But I guess the wine added conviction.

The scenery was now magnificent. We crossed and recrossed the crystal torrent of the Miyagawa, which rises in the frozen heights of the alps and pours northward to reach the Sea of Japan on the northern shore of Honshu Island. The train track was narrow, running along the foot of sheer cliffs whose horizontal sides were protected from slides by snow barricades and snow fences. Timber was obviously being retained in order to slow land erosion; although trees had been felled in limited areas there were numerous signs of reforestation. I was almost sorry at the end of two hours when we neared Toyama and prepared to change trains for Kanazawa.

By now all the happy gentlemen had simmered down a bit, put on their shiny black shoes, their black coats and bright ties, their scarves and smart overcoats, discarded their empty bottles and picked up their newspapers and shopping bags, and they were standing rather unsteadily in the aisle as the train slowed down. All were mobile. I wondered if any of these were the manufacturers of medicinal pills for which Toyama is famous.

Safely seated again in the Green Ticket car of the limited express train "Raicho" going to Kanazawa, I saw our well-dressed partying friends were still with us. By now I had a friendly feeling for them but Sachiko looked at them out of the corner of one slanting eye and said balefully, "They never take their wives!"

"I suppose the wives have to take care of the children," I suggested.

"No. These are rich men. Their wives have maids. No, Mrs. Keith, Japanese men don't *want* their wives — when they have fun!"

I wondered whom Sachiko would find to marry in this Japan.

An hour later the train slid into Kanazawa. The Japanese gentlemen were ready to go. They were sucking mints and looking eminently respectable, proper executive types; their hilarity had lifted, their audacity had solidified into caution, and dignity had triumphed. They peered anxiously out of the window, searching the platform for a glimpse of waiting wives and children. The bulging shopping bags had gifts for all, no doubt. I wanted to see the women who greeted them, but once out of the train they ceased to be a group and wafted away like smoke.

14

⸱⸱

KANAZAWA IS a famous castle town and, although the original castle burned down almost a hundred years ago, the feudal atmosphere of old Japan remains like the lingering scent of incense. With the population of a third of a million people it is even today described as the center of cultural legacies. The richest *daimyo* of the Tokugawa period, Lord Maeda, established his headquarters here many years ago, and a festival still commemorates this event. That Kanazawa is a city of taste and refinement one feels immediately, even in driving through its historic streets.

Above all our desire in coming to Japan was to meet and talk with people who could illustrate the changes in life-styles since we were last here eighteen years ago. But people are less easy to meet than places — palaces, museums, shrines, monuments. In a museum, civilization has petrified; in people, civilization is alive. Japanese civilization of 1973 and 1974 *is* the people of Japan today. It is Sachiko, educated and searching for freedom; it is merry gentlemen executives enjoying a party; railway strikers going on strike; commuters throwing stones at workers on strike; Mr. Nishiberi with a mind outdistancing his traditions; Japanese inns with Western plumbing and ice cubes and high prices. It is the old and young and rich and poor who ride the speeding trains; the rioters at Waseda University; the fanatic Red Army called *Rengo Sekigun*; the white collar men who commute; wealthy tycoons who arrive at Tokyo hotels in long black cars; and young women who seek to be something more than just wives. Civilization is people everywhere.

It was only by luck that we found people, not places, in Kanazawa, the luck being that it was snowing there. This made the visit to famous Kenrokuen Park, which our ministry advisors had scheduled for us, impractical, as we could not feature ourselves as the itinerary described, "strolling happily through the woods, gently circling the shores of the ponds, and admiring the beautiful natural environment" in a snowstorm.

The name of Mrs. Sachiko Kitamura had been casually given to us by one of our mentors in the Japan Foundation who said it would be interesting for us to call on her as she was director of the Social Education Center for Ishikawa Prefecture in Kanazawa. He gave us her address and phone number in the prefectural offices. This sounded like a comfortable assignment for a snowy afternoon, and Sachiko telephoned Mrs. Kitamura and made an appointment for us. At two o'clock we went to her office.

She proved to be a gentle, unassuming little lady who spoke careful, correct English. She tactfully introduced us to her male office chief, and while tea was being served for all she asked us why we had sought her out. I said I was anxious to know what changes for women had taken place in the last twenty years and I had been told that she could probably help me.

She answered that she had very limited teaching contact now with people, that she was only in charge of a very small library of English books which were housed here in the prefectural office. She showed us several shelves full of worn-looking volumes, including *Ivanhoe* by Sir Walter Scott and *Pickwick Papers* by Charles Dickens, and others of this era, but nothing really modern. When I asked her again if she could comment on any changes in the status of women she hesitated so long that I guessed that she didn't wish to commit herself before her male chief. However, after an hour of pleasant nothings she unexpectedly volunteered the fact that she was teaching English to some young housewives in Kanazawa, and asked if I would like to meet them. Although I thought she might be just getting rid of us politely, and I secretly doubted whether she either could or would arrange it — I said, "Yes, please!" She said she would telephone to her students this evening and call us later at the hotel if she was able to arrange a meeting for tomorrow. We said goodbye without much hope.

On the street again waiting for a taxi I asked Sachiko if she thought Mrs. Kitamura would be able to produce anybody to meet us. First Sachiko said No — and then, Maybe!

Before we went down to dinner Mrs. Kitamura had telephoned to say that four of her pupils would meet us at the hotel mezzanine lounge at ten o'clock the next morning. This was four more than we had expected.

By nine-thirty next morning Sachiko was waiting in the lounge, having arranged with the coffee shop to give us a quiet corner to sit in and to serve coffee and cakes. I was to wait in my room until the girls arrived, as Sachiko said it would not be proper for me to be waiting for them.

At ten she called me to come down and I found three young women dressed in smart Western sports costumes, their ages probably between thirty and thirty-five years. They were all attractive, exceedingly well-groomed and very self-possessed. They explained that the fourth girl who was coming was a trained acupuncturist who shared office hours with her mother who was also an acupuncturist, and consequently the young lady would be slightly delayed.

I explained to my guests that I was in Japan at the invitation of the Japan Foundation and my object was to collect material for a book which I hoped might increase understanding between our two countries. With this in mind I wished to ask some questions about their daily lives. However, I said, there was no obligation on their part to answer if they didn't wish to. I myself would be happy to answer any questions they wished to ask me. As I had a daughter and a son of about their own ages I thought we might find interesting comparisons between the lives and ideas of my children and of themselves.

At first they spoke hesitantly in faltering English and kept retreating into Japanese which Sachiko interpreted for me. But despite this they stayed with a point until they felt sure that I had the meaning, as they had a real desire to be understood, something that is typical of the Japanese today. The girls also apparently welcomed an opportunity to speak English, and they were pleased to talk with a Western woman about the Western world.

The first girl to introduce herself was the mother of two boys, Toshiko Matsuoka, whose husband was employed by a large manufacturing company. She said that she enjoyed studying English because there wasn't enough for her to do at home to fill her time. In the years past it had taken her mother all day just to prepare the meals in her old-style kitchen with wood and charcoal fires; today, it took Toshiko only a short time in her modern electric kitchen, especially so as she used some of the semi-prepared foods the shops now carried. She made her own Western costumes from Western magazine patterns. She preferred to be busy, she said, and enjoyed having something to take her out of the house as her English lessons did.

The second young woman looked rather less girlish than the others. This was Nobu Katagiri, married to a professor of biochemistry who was teaching in Kanazawa University. She also had two sons. She had spent a year in Berkeley, California, she told us, when her husband was teaching there as an exchange professor, and at the time she had regretted being unable to speak much English. She expected to go to the United States again this coming year when her husband would be attending a meeting of biochemists. She was studying English now in order to be more fluent on this coming visit.

Kuniko Komori was an extremely chic young woman with a dainty figure and well-styled short hair. She was wearing a white cashmere turtleneck sweater and a tweed mini-skirt. She had definite plans for her future. She and her husband were planning to go around the world together in ten years' time, and she was learning English as she thought it was the best language for travel. From the confident manner in which she spoke I felt sure she would succeed in her plan. Her husband is an eldest son and the head of his family's business organization. They have a son and a daughter themselves. She asked me what I thought about the women's liberation movement and if I thought women should be addressed as Ms. rather than Miss or Mrs.

I said that if a woman preferred to be called Ms. rather than Miss or Mrs., why not call her Ms.? I thought American women didn't have a great deal from which to be liberated but that they should undoubtedly receive equal pay with men in equal job employment. I asked her how she kept so well-informed and she said that she read Western magazines. She thought the advertisements told as much about Western life as did the articles, and I agreed rather gloomily with her. Her father had been in the Japanese Diplomatic Service, and this she thought had something to do with her interest in life outside Japan. She had been born in Sakhalin in the Japanese section just before the Soviet occupation of 1945.

By now coffee was served, and sweet, sticky cakes were placed in front of us, but we were all too interested in each other to stop talking and eat. I was both astonished and pleased at the apparent freedom with which the young women replied to my questions, and also spoke out on their own initiative. Getting a straight answer to a direct question in old Japan used to be like prying gold teeth out of a corpse. Today, these girls not only answered me but asked their own questions.

It was after eleven o'clock when Masako Kurodo, the acupuncturist, arrived on the scene, dashing breezily up to our table to be affectionately saluted by her friends and introduced to Sachiko and me. I immediately thought Masako one of the most charming and vital persons I had met in Japan and I could not take my eyes off her. With straight black hair cut with a coal-black fringe across her forehead, and a mobile, shining face, she looked like a Japanese doll — except for her wide, wide smile which illuminated her and embraced us all. Tall for a Japanese and very slender, with slim legs which showed up well with her plaid mini-skirt and short jacket, she now looked completely nonprofessional, girlish and charming. I envied her patients their attractive view while needles were being twirled in them.

Meanwhile she consumed her cake with an appetite and drank her coffee with pleasure, volunteering that she had three children ages seven, five and three . . . and that this was enough! She is married to a doctor, a kidney specialist, whom she hopes to accompany to the States on a medical conference later this year. When I asked her how she came to be in her own profession she said that her mother had been a trained acupuncturist before her marriage to her father. But her mother, who was obviously modern in her outlook, had failed to give birth to a son to follow her profession and had instead two daughters. The eldest daughter had married very young and moved away, and this left it to Masako to train for and carry on acupuncture work with her mother. She said she did not mind this as she and her husband and three children all lived together in the mother's large old house in the city. Here she and her mother also have their office and treat their patients.

The night before I had made out a list of questions to ask and one was — Could they name some important differences between their mothers' lives and their own? To this they quickly agreed that the important basic difference was that they had fewer children, and this by choice. They and friends of their own age usually wished to have two children or at the very most three, whereas their mothers, who knew nothing about birth control methods, had given birth periodically and involuntarily.

I asked if they thought their own lives were happier or better than the lives of their mothers. They said that their mothers had probably been happy within their own spheres because they knew no other. However, the daughters could not now be happy living their mothers' lives, or vice versa. They did not seem prepared to say that one way of life was either better or worse, but merely different.

They all considered that their husbands were much more conservative than they were. One said that men had to be more conservative because the weight of maintaining family tradition and honor fell on them. They thought their own husbands did not really like new ways of doing for their wives but they sometimes consented just to keep their wives content. This idea alone, that a wife should be kept content, was a new concept for Japanese husbands, I suggested. They laughingly agreed. They said that their husbands did not object to their going out to study classes such as their English class, but that they would all object to their wives taking jobs. Masako was an exception because she worked with her mother in her own home.

I asked if divorce was frequent among their friends and they assured me it was not. Only one of them ever had a friend who had even considered asking for a divorce. When she found that her husband would not give her a divorce, and that even if he consented he was entitled to keep the children, she gave up the idea of trying for a divorce.

I asked if they had any trouble with their teenagers such as we had in the Western world. They looked confounded and then said that the only trouble they had with teenagers was getting them through their exams — which is the mother's responsibility. This problem they referred to as the "examination hell." Apparently the problem of teenage delinquency did not enter their minds.

They all did their own housework as maids were very difficult to find and no one, except Masako, had any help. Masako said this was only because her maid had been in her family before she herself was born and now the maid told Masako what to do! They all did their own shopping daily and lived on a combined Japanese and Western diet, all of them using some processed foods. Each woman handled the family household expenses but only after her husband had retained about a third of his salary for his own personal spending money and, if possible, another third for savings. Household expenses, according to the wifely budget, included not only food but all expenses for the children and the wife herself. As mothers they had almost entire responsibility for the children both as to activities and studies.

Masako and Kuniko lived in houses and the other two lived in apartments. Any kind of housing was very difficult to find and very expensive. Except for Masako, the parents lived apart from their daughters, a fact which the daughters regretted, they said, but the reason was the shortage of houses of sufficient size to accommodate both parents and married children living together. Their homes all had running water and flush toilets. They had refrigerators and television sets, but TV programs were very poor, they agreed. Only one of them had a vacuum cleaner and none had a washing machine, a dishwasher, or the use of a car, although Masako's doctor husband owned his own. None of them wore a kimono except for a special festival or party. Western dress was cheaper and more comfortable and convenient for modern life, they said. However, they all felt that kimonos were more beautiful.

I asked them what changes they would like to see brought about for their children. There was no quick response and they seemed to be fairly content with life as it was for their children. Finally Nobu Katagiri said that what she wanted most for her boys was for them to pass their university exams, as passing these successfully usually meant joining a good firm after graduation and remaining with it for life. The others nodded assent to her answer. I had expected somebody to say that she hoped her children would never have to go through a war, or would never be hungry, or that they would have better living conditions, or a fine career — or something of this sort. But no one did. It was as if the prosperity of today had blotted out all the past for them, as indeed it has also in the lives of young North Americans. We are habituated to great material security, and prisoners of prosperity.

We were still talking at midday, when our guests said they must go home. I asked them if I might use their names in anything I wrote and they said they were quite willing. I think it was with real regret that we parted.

Masako, however, insisted that she was going to take us home with her to see how she lived, as her house was near the hotel. This was a rare opportunity for me and not to be turned down, for the Japanese home is regarded as a haven from the outside world and one that is seldom opened to strangers. As most Japanese homes are humble and unpretentious the host also feels that his home is not "good enough" to offer a foreigner.

But Masako was urgent in her invitation, and, guided by her, we hurried along through a mist of wet snow and drizzle and after a short walk stopped before a closed entrance door in a long city block. Masako unlocked the outside door and we found ourselves in a small entrance hall which held the usual display of house slippers awaiting the arrival of entrants. I abandoned my soggy oxfords and mounted several steps to an inside door which was a *fusuma*, or sliding paper screen door, with the floor below it grooved to accommodate the sliding movement. The wooden floor beams and steps were so highly polished that we could see ourselves reflected in them.

We followed our hostess down the hall which ended in more paneled doors which she slid open. After dropping our slippers in the hall we entered a room with an electric *hibachi* sunk in the center of the floor. The *hibachi* was covered by a raised wire frame over which were spread some red woolen comforters, an arrangement which filled most of the floor space. This scheme warmed the bedding for nighttime as well as supplying a cozy spot for daytime relaxing if you sat on a cushion on the floor with your feet under the comforter next to the *hibachi*. This was a sitting room, our hostess said, and she slid open the panels on the far wall so we looked out into a miniature enclosed garden which included some tiny, dwarf cherry trees and a sliver of water dripping down the rocks. The scene was lovely and would be especially welcome in a hot, steamy Japanese summer — but today I shivered, and Masako closed the panel quickly.

We returned to the hall and mounted a narrow, shining stairway to the second floor where there were three sleeping rooms. There were no beds, of course, and the *futons* were folded away in cupboards. Beyond one of these rooms was a small one filled with miniature tables and chairs built to a child's size, with a sturdy rocking horse and large plastic toys and shelves filled with children's books, obviously, the children's playroom. Meanwhile a little girl of three, who had been silently following us about with her thumb in her mouth, hurried into the room and sat possessively down on *her* chair, and then smiled at us for the first time.

Descending to the ground floor, we entered another room which looked out through sliding doors into the enclosed garden with its dwarf trees, gleaming white pebble paths, and dripping crystal stream which tinkled faintly. This was the family dining place with a large, low table and at the side of the room a smaller one for the children. From here we entered a narrow kitchen where the elderly maid was busy over a shining electric stove which stood beside a large white enamel sink with taps for hot and cold running water. Masako told us proudly that the kitchen had been completely modernized this year. It was the only comfortably warm place in the house. An orchid stood in a water glass near the stove.

As it was now well past the lunch hour we retreated to the entrance hall to put on our shoes and say goodbye. Before we could do so a sliding panel opened and a tiny, quite beautiful little lady with gray hair severely dressed in old Japanese style, and wearing a pearly gray kimono topped by a spotless white surgical coat, stepped out and was introduced to us by Masako as her mother. She smiled at us warmly, bowed with gracious dignity and thanked us for coming to visit their "humble home." It struck me that here were two women of the same blood but of different generations, dressed differently but doing the same job, both following the different folkways of their different eras, yet somehow miraculously alike in their femininity and their ability and desire to serve.

The mother asked us to stop and take tea with them, an offer we declined with thanks, saying my husband was awaiting us. Our shoes on at last, we bowed our way out into the wet, frosty streets and hurried toward the hotel.

"But they can't be typical!" I said to Sachiko. "I'm afraid they are all very unusual young women. I liked Kuniko's questions about women's lib."

"Her husband wouldn't!" said Sachiko.

15

~~~~~~

Train rides and station waits are never dull. You see people unglamourized, each one intent on his own crisis and prepared to trample down his fellowman till the blood flows, if the need occurs. Yet in moments of ease between trains you look at each other with not unfriendly eyes.

Today as we waited on the Kanazawa platform for the *Raicho* Express for Osaka I became the center of concentrated attention from a group of country folk, or so I judged them to be from their rugged rural attire, most of them being in *mompei*, trouserlike garments which tie around the waist on top of the kimono. Among them were a number of small, very lively children warmly wound about with mufflers, coats and mittens. One little boy was obviously either fascinated or shocked by my appearance and he left his group to come close and stare at me from a few feet away. I stared back and then smiled and waved. He rushed back to his group of youngsters, who all stared at me now, then grinned and waved. Suddenly he hurried back with his hand extended and gave me a warm tight handshake which he evidently felt was more appropriate to me than a bow. Then the rest of the children one by one came over and shook my hand and then retreated, while the adults watched and laughed.

How far we might have progressed with our friendship I'll never know, for just then the train roared in and they fought their way on board. The last I saw of them was small, grinning faces pressed against the car windows and small hands waving as the train drew out. Neither Harry nor Sachiko were included in this get-together and at such times they pretend not to know me.

Before arriving at Osaka our *Raicho* Express ran for almost two hours through outlying slum areas, forests of factory smokestacks, rows of huge, hideous buildings with tiny, dingy apartments into which I could see from the train, so close were they to the tracks, and all this area wrapped in a smelly gray world of smoke. It does not make for a favorable first impression of the city which is second in size to Tokyo and the undisputed commercial capital of Japan.

Yet Osaka has a magnificent natural location on Osaka Bay at the mouth of the Yodo River, which is interspersed with multiple canals. During the 1970 Exposition of which it was the billion-yen site, Osaka piled up a huge surplus of cash from its Expo visitors, and was left with a magnificent new road and an impressive and much-needed new bridge across the Yodo.

Arrived at Osaka station, we dragged ourselves and luggage out and joined the line that was waiting for taxis. My struggle with Japanese taxis never ends. The back seats are always diminutive and the leg space nonexistent, a fact which does not discommode the average Japanese passenger but it does Harry and me. If you pick up a taxi at the station the driver does not expect to open his rear luggage compartment for your bags because (a) he says he can't stop that long, or (b) his engine is in the rear. As far as your bags go, you can get them in yourself or leave them behind. The best thing about the taxis is their moderate rates.

Sachiko always climbed in with the driver in order to give directions, leaving the back seat to us. I have tried several approaches for entering with my arms full of luggage. If I put my bags on the seat and push them ahead there is no place for me to sit. If I put them on the floor before entering there is no place for my feet, not to mention those of Harry who is waiting impatiently behind me. In desperation I crawl after my bags and crouch beside them while Harry loads his suitcase on top of me and stands on my feet and then asks tenderly, "Are you all right dear?" I usually maintain a crouching position until we arrive at our destination. By then my feet are as high as my head, my legs are paralyzed, and Harry has to pry me out in a semi-crippled state.

In this condition we arrived at the Hotel Plaza, which is rather elegant, as one would expect considering the fact that Osaka is famous for good food and high living. But the restaurant prices that night took my appetite. Harry did in fact go to bed without dinner as he had the flu and felt miserable. Sachiko and I ate together in the roof cafe with a lovely view, candlelight, fresh flowers on the tables, string music, excellent service — and a chicken salad. Poor Sachiko. I fear she must be hungry all the time but she refuses to order more than we do, although Harry assures her that a "growing girl" needs more.

Harry coughed all night and I suggested that he stay in bed today but he wouldn't. Fortunately the day is fine, one of the few bright days since we arrived in Japan. After all, it is still winter.

As Osaka is the industrial capital we had asked Foreign Affairs to arrange for us to visit some factories and workers' homes. Consequently they made an appointment for us to be shown through the Asahi Beer factory which Sachiko says is not typical as it is the showplace of all factories.

Taking a taxi the next morning we crossed the Yodo River and drove out in the suburbs to Suita, the home of Asahi beer, which proved to be an extremely impressive plant. We were admitted by guards through two sets of entrance gates and ultimately were met at the office by an extremely attractive young girl dressed in a smart blue tailored suit with a crisp white blouse and a mini-skirt, and ankle socks and sneakers on her very pretty feet. Her face was classically Japanese but she had used eye makeup to lessen the slant of her oval eyes, and suntan powder to give the outdoors look which is popular now with young Japanese women. She might have been chosen for her looks alone, but she proved to be a very efficient guide who spoke excellent English and apparently enjoyed her job.

The plant covered a large area and our guide strode freely along as she never could have done in a kimono. Under her guidance we watched the creation of the best beer in Japan, beginning with the treatment of returned bottles and the sterilization of containers, continuing up through the fermentation of the mash and the working of the huge vats, and ending with the filling and capping of bottles. When we came to the plant for bottle capping the sound was so deafening that our guide told us that the women work here for only fifteen minutes at a time because of the effect on their ears, and then rotate with girls at other jobs. Everything we saw was spotless, including the workers who were dressed in white jumpers, many with masks.

There are six Asahi factories in Japan and the Osaka plant alone employs six hundred people and maintains a large dining room where meals are served for employees for the cost in yen of about 20 cents. There are dormitories nearby for single workers and apartments for married couples, all available at minimum cost. They also have a favorable retirement scheme which is extremely important in Japanese economic life. We asked our guide if there was much labor unrest in Asahi or were the workers content? She smiled and said perhaps 80 percent were satisfied and 20 percent were not. There was, she added, a very strong union in the factory.

After we had toured the plant she ushered us into what she called the "foreign visitors" hall, a large sunny room with a number of tables and chairs. Here she turned us over to a young man who came forward to meet us, a public relations officer. He seated us at a table and provided us with bottles of Asahi beer and dishes of salted nuts and bicuits. Although I thought I couldn't drink beer at ten-thirty on a cold winter morning, I found I could, and enjoyed it.

Our P.R. man was obviously a beer devotee. Among other instructions on how to drink beer and enjoy it the most, he told us there were four tests for a good beer. (1) It must be free of any odd taste or smell. (2) It must have five basic flavors — astringent, sour, bitter, sweet and pungent, and these must be perfectly blended in every mouthful. (3) It must bring a feeling of vitality and stimulus. (4) It must give you a feeling of "fullness," of "good body."

When I said that I had enjoyed my beer this morning even without knowing why, he wanted us to try a second bottle with the tests in mind to prove the perfection of Asahi, but we said No. I asked him if the factory workers got free beer. He said, No — they didn't drink! Couldn't afford to, was my guess.

Drinks in hotels are so expensive that we always carry a whiskey flask with us for a drink in our room before dinner. At Osaka the flask went dry. Sachiko, who drinks only fruit juice, looked at me in shocked surprise when I told her I wanted to buy a bottle of whiskey.

"You drink whiskey?" she said.

"Certainly. We have a drink every night."

"You!" she repeated, shocked.

"Yes. Why are you so surprised? You Japanese drink a lot of sake. I have consumed more sake at a Japanese dinner than I ever drink whiskey."

"Yes, our men drink sake — and whiskey — but not a drink every night. They drink to get *drunk*. You saw them on the train. It is disgusting! They leave their wives at home — and they get drunk. I never saw *you* drunk."

"Of course not. But I like a drink."

She still looked puzzled, and probably will remain so.

At Sachiko's suggestion for a possible place to purchase liquor, we headed for the center of Osaka city where there is a remarkable underground shopping maze extending five floors below the street surface. I had never seen anything like it and the farther down we went the more I felt the weight of the whole city on me. The aisles were bulging with half the population of Osaka doing its Saturday shopping. The counters were piled high with everything, including ladies' briefs, men's long drawers, plastic handbags, Kleenex, Kotex, synthetic blouses and yard goods, costume jewelry, cosmetics, pearls, cameras, pantyhose, platform shoes, men's shirts and vivid ties, tins of imported fruits and every kind of biscuit; but I saw no real silk goods except for kimonos.

One floor was entirely devoted to restaurants, tea bars, coffee shops, snack shops, and cafes all filled to capacity with satisfied customers who obviously didn't worry about the city above them, or experience the claustrophobia that I felt. Naturally there was a large fountain playing on one floor, and live goldfish to be fished out of their tank at a price.

By the time we had descended five floors we had had enough of close air, loud music, and elbows in our stomachs, and we decided to surface without finding whiskey. We went up to the street level by escalator and before we had taken a deep breath of outside air the crowds swept us along into the adjacent Hankyo department store. Here we found the other half of Osaka that couldn't get into the underground. Mothers and babies, crying toddlers, impatient papas, happy young couples, anxious old ones, all forming a solid mass of human beings struggling to move in different directions — and somehow succeeding — and even remaining polite. This was the amazing thing — the friction of people physically rubbing against each other in this kaleidoscope of humanity did not seem to distress them as it did me — and, even more, Harry, who got his For-God's-Sake-Do-Something! look. I feel you have to be born in an overcrowded country to take crowds placidly.

Again we decided to give up the whiskey and head for an exit but the crowd was heading inward and we had to go with it. We found ourselves drifting from counter to counter of fresh and pickled fish, pork slabs, pale paralyzed chickens, and hunks of blue meat of unknown origin until quite by accident we ended up at a display of pleasantly familiar bottles.

Sachiko cornered a salesgirl, but when I pointed to a bottle of Johnny Walker she shook her head and said she could not sell it because it was the only one she had. Accepting this rather unusual no-sale argument, I settled for another brand of Scotch. Imported whiskey is usually about twice the price of Japanese Suntory but this day $14 would buy a moderate import, or a top quality Suntory. The dollar devaluation had done it.

Leaving Harry at the hotel the next afternoon, Sachiko and I took a taxi and drove over the new bridge and out to the dismantled Expo '70 grounds. On the way we went through Senrei New Town, a large, middle-class, apartment house section which was built before the Exposition, primarily to provide housing for the influx of visitors, and has been growing and expanding ever since. The buildings are spaced with free areas between them and they look much pleasanter than the downtown apartment blocks and offer more sizable individual units. But there is not a tree in sight anywhere. I suppose they were all sacrificed to build the housing and the wide, new highway which cuts through this development and connects Osaka City with the Expo grounds.

The grounds themselves are a dismal sight and not kept up as one would expect of such a showplace in Japan. One unavoidable reason for this is the very light snowfall of the past winter, which in melting has failed to supply sufficient moisture to bring back the greenness to grass and shrubs. The large area the Expo covers probably makes it prohibitive to irrigate artificially. But when to the resulting effect of brown turf you add the shabby vacant spaces left by exhibits that have been removed, the specters of other pavilions that are dying on their feet, and the skeletal bare bones of the amusement section which still occasionally functions on fête days, you have a sad vision of the expiring spirit of an exposition. A fine driveway circles the whole area and we drove around the perimeter three times accompanied by the ghosts of what the grounds must have been in 1970. This road has been partially closed in several places by heavy roadblocks placed there by the police in an attempt to prevent young Japanese speed demons from killing themselves and others by racing each other around the perimeter. Today there wasn't another car on the road and we didn't see a single person on Expo grounds.

Our taxi driver gave us a vivid glimpse of the last few closing nights at Expo when people came in such crowds that they couldn't get overnight accommodation near the grounds, nor could they get a place on the overcrowded trains going either to Osaka or Kyoto. They had all huddled together for warmth on the nearest station platforms and prepared to stay there all night. Seeing their plight, the Expo police came to the rescue with numbers of box lunches and soft drinks which they distributed free, and as many blankets as they could secure for the night for the use of the shivering crowd.

Osaka itself has a larger percentage of foreigners than Tokyo, probably because it is such an important port town. Our hotel is just across the street from a modern building which is the home of a Japanese television studio and many of the TV personnel eat in the coffee shop here. Today we watched a girl with dyed, honey-blonde hair and eyes heavily made up to look round rather than narrow and slanting. Although she was by nature a pretty girl, the result of her make-up was to destroy all reality and leave her a plastic doll. Harry asked Sachiko if she was certain the girl really was Japanese. Sachiko said firmly, "Of course. She probably takes Western parts in Japanese cowboy films. That is no funnier than having Occidental film stars play Oriental girls!"

Traveling from Osaka to Takamatsu on Shikoku Island marked the high point in our luggage lugging. During a three-hour trip we changed trains three times and made the last lap on a ferry boat. Part of the way the railway track followed the shore of the Inland Sea, a route which was lovely twenty years ago before the GNP took over. Now factories and slum areas stretch out endlessly, pallidly visible through the polluted haze. Himeji Castle, which I remember as the most beautiful castle in Japan, now hides in a veil of smog.

At Okayama we changed platforms, not forgetting the hundred steps up and down, and battled our way onto the Uno train which was small and already full, Uno being the port

143

from which one embarks for Takamatsu. Arrived at the Uno station terminal which served both for trains and boats, we fought our way through crosscurrents of crowds all shoving in different directions. Shouting indignantly, Sachiko was spun around by a speeding traveler and I was tripped up by a fast-moving old lady, and Harry alone plowed through unharmed. When we finally got on board the boat, the cabin seats were fiilled and people were standing.

Then Sachiko discovered we were not in the Green Ticket (first class) section and again we squirmed between hot bodies to get to the upper deck saloon where we ultimately found seats, although before the boat left port there were passengers standing everywhere. At this point I reminded Harry of the bad reputation of the overloaded Japanese ferries and excursion boats which all too frequently tip over just as they leave the wharf. But he was reading a *Japan Times* in English which a neighboring passenger had passed to him, and he didn't answer. What fascinates me about Japanese travelers is that as soon as they manage to get into a seat they are the nicest people on earth again.

Our scheduled sailing time from Uno to Takamatsu was twenty minutes but it took us an hour. Only then did we realize that we should have been traveling by hydrofoil, but the hydrofoil had collapsed on its last trip.

Meanwhile other passengers were enjoying their box lunches which they purchased on board, packed on neat little plastic plates. I would have liked to try one but I knew it was too much of a feat for me to sit on a rolling boat and juggle a plate from which I ate cold rice and pickles with chopsticks, washed down with tea. I watched a nearby lady consume every grain of rice and every sliver of pickle and a slab of fish, and then she opened a plastic bag containing three oranges and peeled them one by one, divided them into segments, and ate them. She returned the peel to the bag and took it with her.

We would have had a lovely view of the Inland Sea on this crossing if it hadn't been for the heavy sea fog which drifted about us. Still, Takamatsu is a fisherman's port and the smell of fish is preferable to the fumes of city living.

By midafternoon we arrived at the Takamatsu Kokusai Hotel, a rather shoddy-looking place where we had reserved rooms. In the bathroom posted just above the toilet was a notice with illustrations showing the proper method of using the toilet.

We were too late to get any lunch at the hotel but as it adjoins a huge bowling hall, a sport which is tremendously popular here with both men and women, we were directed to the hall in search for food. The alleys were full and in the adjacent restaurant we found food slot machines from which we extracted some sandwiches. In every eating place in Japan sandwiches are the same — vegetable, cheese or ham — and they all taste alike.

We took a taxi and drove to the top of Yashima Plateau from which there is a magnificent view of the Inland Sea and many of its islands. Below us the sea fog had lifted and behind us rain clouds were closing in, but for a moment we looked down from the plateau on a lovely green sweep of land, the ancient battlefield of the rival Genji and Heike clans. It was here in a sea battle off the Yashima Headland that the Genji clan defeated the Heikes. While we were admiring the famous view the rain clouds came in, and by the time we had descended from the plateau it was pouring. We drove to the entrance to Ritsurin Park, one of the three most celebrated gardens in Japan, which was laid out in 1700 to harmonize with the natural forest of pine trees. Harry and I had visited

Ritsurin on our honeymoon trip here years ago and now we decided it was better to remember the park happily from our youth than to struggle through its thirteen hills and around its six ponds in a dismal downpour in our old age. Fate seemed against our garden viewing, as it had snowed at Kenrokuen Park in Kanazawa. Fate — or perhaps just the winter season.

16

~~~~~~~~~~~~~~~~~~~~~~~~~~~~~~~~~~~~~~

OUR NEXT STOP would be Hiroshima. I couldn't sleep at all the night before leaving Takamatsu for thinking about it. One of our strongest motives for wishing to make this trip to Japan lay here in Hiroshima. Not in the nuclear ashes, but in the living presence of a middle-aged Japanese man whose identity was linked with our past.

We left the Takamatsu Hotel that morning and went to the port, again expecting to travel by the hydrofoil which was said to be functioning. We found it was not, and rushed to the ferry which would require an hour longer and cause us to miss the train from Uno Port to Okyama. But we soon discovered there was no object in hurrying, as all trains were observing a go-slow strike, and whatever train we caught would not connect with the one it was scheduled for. Ultimately we got on the Okyama train, which moved promptly out of the city and then came to a halt in the suburbs and waited fifteen minutes in order to ensure that we miss the connection from Okyama to Hiroshima. Everybody took this calmly.

As we had a long wait in Okyama we went down to have

coffee in the station underground restaurant. A mob was lined up outside the door waiting to get in. Once inside, getting a table depended on being the swiftest runner and then sitting down while the seat was still hot from the previous customer and the table covered with his dirty dishes. It was the only dirty eating place I had seen in Japan, and there was as much food under the tables as on them. The little waitresses literally ran all the time between the kitchen at the extreme rear and the hungry patrons who ate with incredible speed, spewing morsels of food all around. I commented to Sachiko that this must be a horrible life for the waitresses. Sachiko answered philosophically that they were probably quite well paid.

In due time we boarded a train for Hiroshima. Very shortly we stopped at a station along the line where a gay and colorful wedding party was seeing off the bride and groom, an attractive little couple dressed in Western attire. The other members of the party were all in kimonos, including the handsome father. He wore a heavy black silk kimono with a number of crests on it, and over the lower part of the kimono and tied around the waist was a thick silk skirtlike garment called a *hakama*. He was the most impressive figure in the party.

The young couple entered our car and sat down in the seats in front of us and busied themselves storing away their shining new white suitcases, removing their coats and shoes, and gossiping happily about the wedding, with their heads close together. Their two heads of hair were shining black, hers wavy and his spiky; their skins were clear pale beige with a slight flush, perhaps from the ceremonial exchanging of sake cups in the wedding ceremony. When the groom turned his head to glance backward over the top of his seat at the mundane passengers behind him his eyes were sparkling and his glance was filled with pride for the lovely girl beside him and the triumph of possession. Her eyes, as he settled down close beside her, were probably filled with a humbler emotion of simple affection and gratitude for finding a suitable husband. In any case, they existed in a world of their own, reserved for honeymooners.

We arrived at Hiroshima at six in the evening after being halted twice again by the go-slow strike. Passengers were less good-natured about it each time, and I imagine if the strike continues for long the "Oriental calm" will break down on both sides.

We were chilled through, exhausted and exasperated before we finally arrived at the hotel, and once in our bedroom we had immediate recourse to the whiskey bottle. Meanwhile I tried to make the pretty, pink, well-camouflaged radiator get hot — and failed. I called the office and they sent up a porter who clucked his tongue at it but couldn't make it work and sent for the janitor, who fixed it immediately by doing exactly what I had done without success. In half an hour the room was stifling and we couldn't turn down the heat. Again I called the office manager who sent the porter, who sent the janitor, who asked us patiently, Please did we wish the heat *on?* . . . or *off?* I said we wished to adjust it ourselves to a comfortable temperature. As he didn't understand what I was saying, he smiled politely, nodded agreeably and turned off the heat. By this time Harry was in bed and sizzling with fever and impatiently advised me to leave the bloody radiator alone. I did.

I went with Sachiko to the dining room for dinner and ordered a tray of food sent up to Harry. When I returned to our room after dinner the food was untouched, Harry's breathing was very labored, he coughed constantly, and the radiator clanked and sizzled with sudden waves of volcanic heat. I gave up and went to bed.

Harry coughed all night in violent paroxysms, and I began to cough, too. Neither of us slept, he from coughing and I from worrying about him. I was frightened. I felt responsible for saying Yes to this expedition and, because Harry knew I wanted to go, he had said Yes, too. But I'm afraid he's not strong enough for this type of travel *plus* the flu. He teases me by saying that I always struggle on through snow and ice bearing a banner with a strange device — Excelsior! He doesn't know how close I am sometimes to giving up the struggle.

While lying awake I tried unsuccessfully to figure out some plan of action to make the trip easier. But even if we give up our Kyoto stop and try to turn back directly to Tokyo, we *can't* go directly. We have to change trains and run up and down those deadly steps several times. In any case we have no reservations in a Tokyo hotel sooner than ten days from now. Although we know a doctor there we have no bed: and without reservations we'd sleep in the streets. Here we have at least a bed in a comfortable room — with heat! And Harry can stay in bed — *if* he will admit he is ill. Men are so obstinate.

Everything seems so modern and Westernized in Japan until you try to get a simple item such as a good cough mixture. Last night the hotel pharmacy offered us sugar lozenges or a packet of white powder. After talking it over this morning with Harry we decided that the only thing we *could* do was to follow our original plan. We have several more days here, and Harry's influenza may be better by the time we travel again.

Meanwhile we are still faced with our most frustrating problem — how to find our un-met friend, Osama Suga. Or the even more subtle question: Does he wish to be found? The sequence of incidents which linked this stranger to us was as follows.

After the publication in 1949 of my book *Three Came Home,* and before it appeared in Japanese translation, I received letters from four Japanese. One was from Giichi Suga, who identified himself as the younger brother of Colonel

Tatsuji Suga, the former commandant of our prison camp in Borneo. Colonel Suga had killed himself after being taken prisoner by the Allied Military Forces who liberated us. He had died believing that his entire family, who were domiciled in Hiroshima, had been killed by the atom bomb. His brother, Giichi Suga, who had read my book in English, wrote to thank me for describing his brother, the colonel, as "a decent human being." He said that the colonel's family had been outside Hiroshima when the atom bomb was dropped and they had survived. He also asked me for a commission to translate *Three Came Home* into Japanese. I told him that an agreement had already been made elsewhere by my publishers.

The second letter I received was from Masao Kawabe, a Japanese soldier who had given me ten dollars to buy food for my three-year-old son when, as prisoners in January 1943, we were traveling on a nightmare voyage from Berhala Island to Sarawak. When the war was over I had sent several food packages from Canada to this young man in Japan, and he had written to thank me.

The third Japanese to write was Toyokichi Matsuda, a reporter on the *Mainichi*, a newspaper in Tokyo. Mr. Matsuda had read *Three Came Home* in English and had given it a very favorable review in his paper. This was especially timely as the book was then being filmed. As the result of his publicity he had received a personal message addressed to me from the widow of Colonel Suga in Hiroshima. She asked him to tell me that quotations from my book which she had seen in the *Mainichi* had helped her to stop feeling "disgraced and humiliated" and had given her and her children "great relief and deep comfort" by assuring them that Colonel Suga "was not a monster, and had probably not committed suicide because of being conscious of maltreatment of P.O.W.s under his charge."

Later I received a fourth letter — this one directly from

Mrs. Suga herself, but translated into English by a translator. This letter repeated her feeling of gratitude on behalf of herself and children for the "just picture" which she believed my book had presented of her husband.

It may seem odd that a book that told truthfully of our often brutal treatment in prison camp could be of comfort to the widow of the camp commandant. I shall leave *Three Came Home* to speak for itself about this. I will only say that in postwar Japan in the poisoned atmosphere of war crimes and the hanging of Japanese war criminals, with the air fetid with rabid recriminations and the angry desire to pin the responsiblty of defeat on somebody, or anybody, there followed a general breast-beating and self-flagellation indulged in by most of the people of the defeated nation. No one knew what to think, whom to blame, or where to stand.

Apparently my own conviction, as stated in my book, that war was the criminal and not the individual, had importance to my readers. Mrs. Suga, who had known her husband as a kind and loving man and a good father, had been able at last to banish the shaming war vision of a monster in uniform and remember him again as the kindly man whom she and her children had loved and respected. Some time after I received her letter, I had learned that she had died as the result of malnutrition and exhaustion from overwork in her efforts to keep her family together through the war years. She was survived by a son and two daughters.

Several years ago, though the assistance of a Eurasian friend, I had located the address of the son of Mrs. Suga and Colonel Tatsuji Suga — by name, Osama Suga. I had been told by the friend who gave me the address that she believed that Osama Suga would welcome a meeting with me. I myself had felt that I must meet him. Just why, or exactly what I expected from a meeting I could not clarify in my own mind

— except that it had to do with my belief that the hope for future peace lies in the goodwill now of each one of us for the other. My generation had all suffered: now that suffering had passed, but it had left scars on us all. It seemed to me that these could be lessened only by positive gestures of goodwill. In our nuclear world the policy of an eye for an eye would only lead to extinction.

For me, the tragedy of Hiroshima was linked with the ill-fated Suga family. One personal tragedy which you yourself experience is just as painful and more possible to comprehend and sympathize with than the wholesale tragedy of an atom bomb slaughter — whose magnitude seems beyond human conception.

Immediately upon our arrival in Japan I had given the name and address of Osama Suga in Hiroshima to our planners in the Japan Foundation and in Foreign Affairs. I asked them to get in touch with him by telephone and to explain to him my association with his dead father, Colonel Tatsuji Suga, and say that we wished to meet Mr. Osama Suga in Hiroshima shortly.

But when the ministry made contact with the address by telephone, they reported that the person who resided there said he had no knowledge of Colonel Suga and furthermore that his own father was alive and well. The ministry advised me that Suga was a very common Japanese name and that, among one hundred and ten million Japanese, there were a very great number of Sugas. They noted in addition that there were many different combinations of characters which could be read as Suga. There had been countless numbers of colonels in military service in the war and probably a number of Colonel Sugas had come from Hiroshima alone. They considered that the search was hopeless as apparently the address I had did not belong to the person whom I was seeking.

Not yet entirely convinced of the futility of my search I had asked three other Japanese sources to make telephone contact with the addressee, something I could not do myself as I didn't speak Japanese. I felt confident, however, that if we met person-to-person we could communicate. But each telephone query had received the same answer, a denial of Suga identity from the person at the other end of the line. This was the position when we left Tokyo.

Now, arrived in Hiroshima, we had to make a decision. We just might be within fingertips of the man we sought. But did he seek us? We could only assume one of two things about him: the man at the address either spoke truthfully when he said that he had no knowledge of the deceased Colonel Suga, *or* he wished to disown any connection with him and found our questions an intrusion. If it was the latter, then we had no right to continue our search, knowing that Japanese etiquette considers a direct approach to a delicate matter crude and uncivilized.

It was tempting now that we were actually in Hiroshima to go directly to the street address and personally question whomever we might find there who had denied the Colonel Suga connection. But we knew this would be inexcusable by Japanese custom, and an intolerable intrusion to go to a man's home without his invitation. So twice again we arranged for phone calls to be made to the house. Each time the person who answered denied the Osama Suga identity. At last I felt forced to recognize that the goodwill I had hoped to convey must forever remain unspoken.

I was both disappointed and relieved by this decision. Any meeting would have held emotional overtones and even stale emotions are exhausting. I had wished to take an infinitesimal step in the right direction toward goodwill between our nations. However, regardless of idealistic philosophies, wars do leave mortal wounds and scars do remain. The events I had sought to palliate had happened almost thirty years before. Now I must accept the verity of what the young generation said: "We have forgotten the war."

By now Harry's illness had for me displaced one worry with another. After a sleepless night and an anxious awakening, with Harry looking like death but insisting in almost voiceless whispers that he could carry on, that he would not hold me back, that he could make it, that he was going to get up, I asked for the address of the best English pharmacy in Hiroshima, and we went there by taxi. All we could find was a bottle of Vicks Extra Strength Cough Mixture. Sachiko, who was coughing also, purchased a bottle of Japanese white powder which the pharmacist said was a sure remedy for influenza. Back in the taxi on the way to the Peace Memorial, Harry swallowed a large dose of Sachiko's powder, smelling and tasting of camphor and garlic, which he washed down with a good swig of the cough mixture. It was nauseating, he said, but he didn't think it would do him any permanent harm.

A bitterly cold wind was blowing at the Peace Memorial Park, a large area in the center of the city which has been landscaped in modern style. The park was cold, austere, dignified, impressive — and completely uninspiring. There were many pieces of modern sculpture, all huge, bulky and solid, and all without the delicacy of the Japanese art tradition. Each one had a specific reference to some aspect of the bomb horror, the Children's Peace Memorial, the Mothers and Infants Memorial, the A-Bomb Cenotaph dedicated to all victims, and the Peace Bridge; all symbolized hope for peace.

The one that touched me emotionally was the slender figure of a mourning female, commemorating the memory of the young students who had lost their lives in World War II. Except for this one the monuments had in my judgment sacrificed human warmth and feeling to monolithic pretentiousness. It was as if the artists felt that a deed of such colossal tragedy could not be expressed in simple human terms. But, as we are all just simple human beings, it seems to me that tragedy must be brought down to our scale, if we are to fully experience it.

The exhibits in the museum are mostly distorted and charred remnants from the actual bombing — ghoulish, horrible and frightening beyond words. I went through the halls and showcases without lingering because they made me physically ill. I smelled flesh burning. Any person who still believes that war is the answer to anything should see these exhibits with the fact in mind that the new war missiles today are incomparably more destructive.

We left the museum so sickened in mind and body that the clean, cold wind blowing outside was welcome.

17

THE NEXT DAY we drove to Miyajima-guchi, a fishing port not far from Hiroshima from which one embarks on a ferryboat for the famous island of Miyajima. The drive is supposed to take an hour, but it took us two hours because of bumper-to-bumper traffic on incredibly narrow roads through small, congested fishing villages. Between the little houses we caught fleeting glimpses of the sea and the islands in the distance, but most of the time we gazed into the tense faces of other struggling motorists or the smiling faces of the cheery villagers, who in spite of traffic on the narrow highroad carried their babies, pulled their toddlers, and dragged their baskets as they skirted their way from doorway to doorway of the shops, which opened directly into the crowded traffic of the road. Most of them were round-faced, pink-cheeked, stalwart, and all were very agile in dodging vehicles. The livelihood of these villagers comes from fishing activities, and the coast is lined with oyster and seaweed beds, and bamboo fences to act as traps and to mark out garden areas in the sea.

Like most people who take their living from the sea, these

are dependent for survival on the whims of tides, waves and weather. These small fishing communities are extremely superstitious — or perhaps superreligious — in their devotion to their gods and their observance of shrine festivals. The most colorful of these is *Kangen-sai*. This event is observed ritually on Miyajima Island and is the festival of the *Itsukushima-jinja*, and all the nearby villages and fishermen of this area identify with it. Annually a portable shrine is placed aboard a fishing-fleet ship and towed about by sailors to the sub-shrines on the island to the sound of music and beating of drums. This festival occurs in July and is the big event of the year. Its proper observance is clearly connected with good fishing fortunes throughout the year ahead.

Arrived at the nearest port to the island, we found that we had just missed the ferry. Standing and looking toward Miyajima we could see plainly the huge scarlet camphorwood *torii*, the gateways to the shrines, built on tidewater island land. With each high tide the scarlet pillars rise up out of the sea and seem almost to float there as they greet visitors to the Itsukushima shrine and the little island. The shrine itself is said to have been built from the wood of a single camphor tree. Near it stands the five-storied pagoda, which is exactly that and has five pagoda roofs reaching upward. It is over five hundred years old and listed as a national treasure.

It was tempting to us to wait for the next ferry and go to the island, but we knew that the heavy mist which was already settling down would by then have obliterated the famous view from the island mountaintop of the Inland Sea, or *Seto Naika*, as the Japanese call it. And as Sachiko remembered that we had arranged to visit the Shudoin Orphanage in the afternoon we decided to return to Hiroshima. To drive through the villages and observe the people was really of more importance to me than the view from Mount Misen, so we inched our slow way back between shops, houses, bicycles and people.

The goodwill of both people and motorists in Japan seems never lacking. Everybody here drives both fast and skillfully and seems to see in all directions at once. They have to in order to survive. The roads are unbelievably narrow, as most were built years ago for men and horses. There are no sidewalks except on large city avenues, and most of the people killed or injured in traffic accidents are pedestrians.

In Japanese traffic their good manners with other motorists may be the result of the fact that their reactions are instantaneous and their judgment of distance is remarkably accurate. Time and again I waited to hear the screech of metal on metal — but always we slid through untouched. If there wasn't that extra fraction of space both drivers seemed to recognize it and one would wave the other one on. Constantly in this swift-moving, aggressive game I saw lightninglike gestures of courtesy which saved both time and crashes. It was very different from the way the game is played in Italy where drivers sit eyeball to eyeball glaring indignantly sooner than give way an inch.

The day in Tokyo when we set out to visit an orphanage we had ended up at the Modern Art Museum. Now in Hiroshima we tried again and actually arrived at the Hiroshima Shudoin Orphanage.

Sachiko had made an afternoon appointment for us by telephone. Leaving Harry at the hotel we went by taxi to a large, rambling, rather shabby house on the outskirts of town. We were warmly welcomed by an attractive white-clad young girl who seated us in a parlor and said that the director would be with us immediately. A moment later a tall, Western-looking woman arrived at the front door and, after giving her name, she was even more warmly welcomed than we by the little nurse — who then glanced at us in confusion. It seemed that she had mistaken us for the honored guest.

The new arrival proved to be the wife of an American doctor who had been working in Japan for several years with the Atomic Bomb Commission. She and her husband had adopted a Japanese orphan girl three years ago, and now, having just returned from leave in the States, the adoptive mother had come to tell the director of the success of the trip and the happy mood of the child. This lady rightly took preference over us and we waited patiently, meanwhile drinking cups of tea served to us by another little white-clad girl.

When the director, Mrs. Sumiko Kono, at last introduced herself to us, I was impressed by her interesting mixture of gentle manners and self-confidence. Obviously she had sacrificed none of her femininity to her role of being an efficient director and a qualified nurse. One felt immediately that she knew every inch of her establishment and probably loved every orphan.

I realized later that she was about forty-five years old but she didn't look it. She had an attractive, strong countenance; her hair was short and waved and dressed close to her oval face. She wore a dark blue tailored suit with a short skirt, calf-length woolen socks for warmth, and soft moccasin slippers which could be kept on inside the building.

She explained to us proudly that her father, Kogi Kitamura, had taken over this establishment on the death of his father, Tozaburo Kitamura, whose private mansion the original building had been. He had turned over his large private home for the care of abandoned children during the famine of 1888.

The original orphanage building had been completely destroyed by the atom bomb in 1945. Total massacre of the children had been avoided only by the foresight of Mr. Kitamura, who, shortly before the bomb fell, had evacuated all the children to the country under the care and protection of his own young daughter, Sumiko — who was later to become the director.

Immediately upon the cessation of the war, Mr. Kitamura had started reconstruction of the orphanage, a work which he accomplished in the face of difficulties, hardships and privations. In rebuilding the establishment, he took the advice of his daughter and added a department exclusively devoted to the care of abandoned infants. As Sumiko Kono was a trained nurse and a graduate of St. Luke's College of Nursing in Tokyo, and had made up her mind to carry on her father's work, he named her as the director of the new Shudoin's Baby Home.

In the years since the war the orphanage had become too small and ill-equipped to meet its growing needs. In 1965 it was once again rebuilt and extended, this work being financed by donations and loans.

In time, Mrs. Kono said, she hopes to have a baby center where *all* mothers and babies may come for assistance in infant rearing. She herself seems very young even now to be so selflessly dedicated. She must have been little more than a girl when the atom bomb fell, and she had the awesome responsibility for the survival of the orphan children whom her father had just evacuated to the country in her care. The Shudoin establishment is now supported by a combination of prefectural and government funds plus private donations, and it is the only institution of its sort on western Honshu Island. In spite of much greater needs, its total capacity is only equal to the care of one hundred and twenty-five children.

In order to live in the home an orphan or an abandoned

child must be sent here by the prefectural government, usually after having been discovered by a prefectural social worker. An infant qualifies for admittance (1) if it is an orphan, or (2) if one parent is alive but cannot care for the child, or (3) if it is the child of a convicted criminal, or (4) if its parents are mentally unfit, or (5) if it has been deserted by its parents. The majority of the inmates now here have been deserted — a fact that is another comment on the change in times from the era when every child was wanted.

We asked Mrs. Kono if it was difficult to adopt a child in Japan. She said it was not and cited the case of the American woman whom we had just met, saying that she and her doctor husband had adopted a five-year-old child with great success. I asked if a prospective parent could choose his own child for adoption and she said, No, it was up to the orphanage to decide what child was suitable. There are no children with American blood here, she told us. The United States now is said to have taken them all back to the States.

She then very graciously, and with assurances to us that she could spare the time, took us on a complete tour of the buildings. As was to be expected, everything was spotlessly clean and polished from floor to ceiling but nothing was on an institutional-size scale. I imagine it was very like the original mansion house. There was a friendly, homey atmosphere and the rooms were small and cozy. The main building is for children under five only, and, as well as several separate sleeping rooms with small beds, we saw three playrooms all equipped with color TV, and children playing, dancing and singing in time to the TV programs. They were being played with and amused by a half dozen young girls whom Mrs. Kono introduced to us as student nurses from the nearby hospital who had volunteered their leisure time. Another room held a beautiful display of dolls for Doll's Day. These had been prepared for a program of entertainment tonight.

There were no uniforms for the little inmates and each child was dressed differently, and most of them looked happy. One little boy with kinky hair and great round black eyes was dancing and miming and proudly showing off for our benefit. Mrs. Kono took him by the hand and did a little dance step with him which delighted him. His father obviously had been black but, according to what she had said, not American.

We went outside to the playground, which was equipped with slides and swings, and here we found some larger boys playing ball. There was a second building for the older children, and from our glimpses inside it looked more institutionalized than the other, with a single long dining hall and several dormitories for sleeping. As we were leaving, a group of five children followed us outside and seemed to wish to attract Mrs. Kono's attention. They clung together looking mournfully at us and she stopped and spoke gently to them, but not one of them smiled. While she was walking with us to the front gate she told us that these five children were brothers and sisters. They had been admitted last week after their father had murdered their mother and another woman. He was now in jail awaiting trial. It seemed probable that these five lonely ones were in the orphanage to stay. They looked indescribably miserable and dispirited. They were the only children we saw who did.

I was glad to leave Hiroshima. Any American coming to this city must involuntarily feel the burden of the atom bomb. Even now, when this once lovely place has been almost totally reconstructed, it emerges with the scarred, traumatic visage of a wounded soldier who must smile to get alms. From now on I shall be haunted by Hiroshima — not only by what we have done to the Japanese by dropping the bomb, but by what we did to ourselves.

Added to this is my own feeling of failure coupled with vague self-rebuke at not finding and talking with Osama Suga. Perhaps I could have pushed harder if I hadn't felt ill with flu. As it stood I didn't know where I had gone wrong, or *if* I had gone wrong. Or if it was just that there is no way of making the past different — of putting a better face on war.

It is all very well for the youngsters to say, "We have forgotten the war." They never knew it. It is not so easy for those of us who wear the war burned fatally into our tissues — regardless of which side we suffered on.

This morning Harry seemed better — or maybe I am just getting used to his coughing all night. Several days under the same hotel roof have certainly done him good but allowed the flu germs to catch up with Sachiko and me. The last two nights Harry and I consumed almost a full bottle of "The Mixture." Perhaps we might have been worse without it? I have always heard that there is no combative drug for influenza itself and that the best treatment is to stay in bed. But bed rest was not our objective in visiting Japan. So with a new bottle of "The Mixture" and another flask of whiskey we got going again — bearing 'mid snow and ice by trains on strike and crowds on the run, the banner with the strange device — Excelsior!

We caught a train headed for Kyoto via Okayama, and along the way we admired the hill terracing which not only makes agriculture possible on steep slopes but supplies practical housing sites. The houses stand together closely like packs of dogs and are of every shape, color and material. They are kitty-cornered, triangular, and rectangular, so designed in order to utilize every inch of leveled space. Each group of houses has its own graveyard, always nicely located on a hillside or overlooking a river, and we glimpsed some fascinating headstones. Mandarin orange groves added brilliant spots of color to the hillsides.

One good thing about the go-slow strike is that it offers some of the advantages of touring the country on foot, as the train moves so slowly that we pry into all aspects of village life along the way. I can remember rolling slowly through the outskirts of American cities by train and being fascinated by private peeps from the moving Pullman car into other people's lives, and seeing things I would never have seen by walking in the streets. There is something completely anonymous and secret about what one observes from a moving train about the lives of nameless persons. It is a drama one sees in a dream without responsibility for its smiles or tears.

As we pass through Shin-Osaka before heading almost due north to Kyoto, a sea of blue-tiled roofs stretches around us broken by reefs of apartment blocks and factories. There are frequent signs of affluence such as numerous bowling alleys and tremendous square-block-size golf cages which enable the rabid Japanese golf addicts to practice the game even in the city. Many office buildings now have roofs devoted to putting greens. Widely distributed on restaurant fronts and hotels we see such names as Rotarians, Lions Club, Diners Club, Bankers Cards, and American Express credit cards welcome, and other bourgeois symbols of Western culture which now adorn prosperous Japanese premises. After an uneventful journey in which we dozed most of the time, we arrived at Kyoto late in the afternoon.

18

~*

K YOTO IS A CITY whose manifest destiny is to assuage the
traumas created by other cities. It anesthetizes the inroads
of the GNP (there is even a shortage of sewers), rejuvenates
tired businessmen, and vindicates feminine beauty as its own
excuse. Most appropriately, Kyoto lies langourous and lovely at
the foot of a semicircle of smiling, wooded hills, basking in a
mild and gentle climate.

For over a thousand years from 794 to 1868 this was the
capital city of Japan and is still its fifth largest city. Its original
name was *Heian-kyo*, meaning Peace and Tranquillity. Today
it still reflects its close contact with China during the sixteenth
and seventeenth centuries, and perhaps for this reason it is
considered the treasure house of ancient Japanese art, which
was itself largely inspired by Chinese art.

Anyone who has read *The Tale of Genji* by Murasaki
Shikibu, and *The Pillow Book* by Sei Shonagon, both women
writers of a thousand years ago, is certain to arrive at Kyoto
with a preconceived idea of the romanticism and sensuality of
its historical life. *The Tale of Genji* is written as fiction while

The Pillow Book is an intimate diary of court days and nights. The subject matter of both writers was the intimate relations between men and women in the Heian Courts.

That Kyoto was not destroyed during the ruthless bombing of the Second World War is credited to one of the few deeds of sheer decency which shines out of that insane war period. The survival of Kyoto is directly due to the influence of an American, Dr. Langdon Warner, the curator of the Oriental Department of the Boston Museum of Fine Arts. Dr. Warner was able to convince the United States High Command that both Kyoto and nearby Nara were without any strategic military value and were in fact the repository of invaluable Asian art treasures which were without duplicate in all the world. One is not surprised when a museum curator of arts speaks like this — but one is surprised when a high command listens as the United States High Command did. As the result of Dr. Warner's plea, Kyoto and Nara were not bombed. Perhaps the survival of these two lovely places will weigh a little in history against the ashes of Hiroshima.

Obviously Kyoto is one spot in Japan that history demands that the tourist visit. Yet despite its countless religious shrines and temples and antique milestones, my own feeling of admiration for it is not for its historic piety but for its quality of extreme femininity. Kyoto is the most feminine city I have ever visited. Not so much that it is obviously beautiful, but that it is subtly and secretly lovely. Its voices tinkle, its winds rustle, its laughter challenges, its footsteps are light and swift and even its traffic is gently subdued.

In years past Harry and I, breathless and shoeless and young, had hurried along the sightseers' route in Kyoto and had done our best with youthful energy to check on its two hundred Shinto shrines and fifteen hundred Buddhist temples. But this time we were determined to avoid all religious monuments if possible and, if not, to visit only the ones without steps. Harry was still feeling weak from the flu and I was now so worried about him that I had given up praying for the success of our trip and prayed only for him to survive it. Sachiko and I also had fever and were aching and coughing.

This manuscript should be entitled "Old Folks Abroad," as we do everything so differently now from when we were young. The hotels are pleasant, the food is good and our own night life is the same in each city — eat, drink and go to bed. Bright-light night tours are out; we save the price. The one comforting thought as we grow older is that we didn't miss much when we were young. "Grow old along with me . . ." but only because there is no other choice! I prefer to, "rage, rage against the dying of the light."

Every night we watch the well-fed, respectable and hopeful foreign tourists lined up outside the hotel door waiting for the Swinging Golden Night Tour bus, or the Bright Blue Moon Night bus, or the Neon Silver Night Tour bus, or the Gilded Goose Guide, or the Queen Bee Cabaret, et cetera. On any one of many such buses, for the sum of only Y7,000 (prepaid) one may dine on real beer-fed beef *sukiyaki* (Japanese *sake* included), or go to a traditional geisha party (beer will be served), or attend a Japanese theater (one refreshment only), or see a puppet play (with café espresso), or watch "torrid" nude dancing (with a choice of beverages), or relax in the care of a "charmingly hospitable" Japanese hostess (hot *sake* served). The travel bureau notes that the Y7,000 must be prepaid, and there will be no rebate, and that the bureau is not responsible for any "'irregularities" which may occur on tours. But as the tours are generally superrespectable; the "irregularities" don't occur no matter how fervently the tourists are longing for them. For the Yoshiwara is gone, *pachinko* is fading, nude dancers work by union hours, and most Japanese cities are in bed before midnight. Wrestling, golf, bowling and base-ball are in. Only the tourists have energy left now for night life.

One of the very happy things about Kyoto is that the coun-tryside wanders irresponsibly in and out of the city, creating quiet, wooded paths and ancient huts and cottages in unex-pected places. Another attraction is the number of kimono-clad girls on the streets who add to the beauty and elegance of the surroundings. Time seems less pressing here than in Tokyo and Osaka and the tempo does not require nor lend itself to pants and mini-skirts.

Kyoto was for some centuries in the past the capital city of these Nihon Islands, and it is only natural that it should remain the headquarters for training that uniquely Japanese profes-sional, the geisha, who is an entertainer, a musician, a witty conversationalist, and by no means necessarily a prostitute. There are geisha schools for training the young *maiko* girls, virgins who are studying to be geisha. All of these females, who are in training here to entertain and to please men, ha-bitually wear kimonos. Although I admire the freedom of modern woman's attire I cannot visualize a geisha following her traditional routine in a pants suit.

There are many popular Japanese novels written around the theme of the geisha who ultimately becomes the mistress or second wife of some wealthy or less than wealthy man who falls for her and sets her up in her own apartment. He may feel as loyal to her as he does to his wife — whom he probably does not feel he is betraying by his relationship with a geisha. After all, his wife's job is to take care of his children, and so long as he pays the home expenses he feels justified in having extramarital fun. But his geisha's relationship with him is far from being that of a prostitute; in fact it may be almost as permanent as that of his wife. In some cases geisha marry into very good families and they are said to make excellent wives. In any case they make excellent wages.

Certainly the women of Kyoto, professional or otherwise, are some of the loveliest of the world. They look soft, warm, dainty, elegant, and they move with sophisticated grace as they drift unhurriedly through the temples, tea shops, boutiques and byways of their city. With white powdered faces and sculptured hair styles they seem to belong to a very special species of delicate female being, though experience has proved that inwardly they are tough and strong-fibered. The pigeon-toed progress of a group of kimono-clad girls fluttering along the boulevard before the wind reminds me of a flock of bright tropical birds, earthbound yet impossible to cage.

And as you watch some spotless little Kyoto miss, well-groomed and with fresh flowers in her hair, dressed in a fragile kimono and drifting gracefully along the Pontocho lanes, you will never guess the truth — that she may have emerged from some tiny hut in the suburbs which has neither running water nor indoor plumbing, where the water is carried up to the house in buckets by the girl and her mother (not by the men) from one of Kyoto's polluted rivers.

There are more tempting articles of fine quality to be purchased in Kyoto by the connoisseur than anyplace else in Japan. Silk weaving is a basic industry, the local brocades are famously beautiful, and the whole city district of Nishijin is dedicated to weaving the finest silks, especially for *obis*. The Tatsumura Silk Mansion offers every type of textile, both old and new. Ceramics and lacquerware are of the highest quality and Japanese objets d'art of all sorts may be purchased — at a price. For this is no place to find bargains or buy tourist oddments; Tokyo and Osaka abound with these, but Kyoto is the place to come for the real thing.

Harry is perpetually searching for a fine *netsuke*, but when he finds one he likes he is never prepared to pay for it. He has a connoisseur's eye and a beggar's purse, and good *netsuke* are very expensive. A *netsuke* is a handsomely carved little pendant of a type that used to be worn as a toggle attached to a cord attached at the other end to a purse or tobacco pouch or medicine box or *inro* — or whatever a man might wish to hang from his sash or girdle when he had no pockets.

Although the purpose of *netsuke*s originally was an entirely practical one, by the seventeenth century they were being used chiefly for decoration and their workmanship was akin in delicacy to that found in fine jewelry. Any suitable carving material such as ivory, coral, jade, horn or wood was being used when this special art reached its zenith in the latter part of the seventeenth century.

We found some fascinating ones in a Kyoto shop. I especially liked the tiny ivory figurine of a Kabuki actor. The face when looked at from one direction wore a smile, but when the head was twisted the smile became a scowl. When I admired it I was told rather condescendingly that it was just a modern *netsuke*. The older ones have as themes some aspect of nature, animal life, fish, bird and plant life, or mythology or folklore. Harry found a fine demon's head of red lacquer which he favored — very old, very authentic, very expensive — but he did not favor the hundred-dollar price.

The search for a *netsuke* reminded me of our perpetual search in Greece for an icon of Saint George slaying the dragon, as Saint George was the patron saint of both Harry (Henry George) and our son George. Finally in an antique shop we found a fine one that I wanted to buy for Harry's birthday. We bargained for it and I almost persuaded Harry to let me buy it, when suddenly he backed out of the shop, pulling me with him and telling the shopkeeper that we would return some other time. All that evening I argued with him that we *must* have the icon, if only for young George to inherit — and I finally had him persuaded to return with me the next day. But next morning as we entered the ancient orthodox quarter of Athens where the antique shops were located we saw they were all closed. It was a Greek holiday and we were leaving Athens early the next morning! I have always regretted losing that icon: Harry has always rejoiced at my keeping the money. But today the money is gone — and if I'd bought the icon we'd have it.

On our second day in Kyoto Harry awakened feeling slightly more alive than dead and we hired a taxi at nine o'clock and told the driver that we didn't wish to see any shrines or temples except for the sake of their scenic backgrounds. This left plenty of leeway as the whole background of Kyoto is scenic, especially now with the hills snow-frosted and the roofs dusted with white. The air itself had such a tonic quality that we agreed to the idea of driving into the hills to the Jakko-in temple just for the ride.

The road was already filled with cars loaded with young Japanese tourists who, in this holiday period just after their exams, are enthusiastically sight-seeing their own country. There was a small parking area at the foot of the hundreds of steps which always seem to lead up to the entrance to temples, and the young people were streaming up and down the steep ascent with enviable agility, laughing and talking and obviously delighted with everything they saw. We did not join their climb. They were all very well-behaved but, as Sachiko reminded us, their interest was not religious but rather that of young people seeing places of interest and enjoying it. The good nature, gaiety, and docility of the young Japanese tourists astounds me when I contrast it with the mood of the city commuter. We then drove to the Sanzen-in Buddhist temple, in the same vicinity and still a functioning monastery. Again we

172

saw it from the bottom of the steps, the ideal manner for temple viewing.

Driving down the very narrow mountain road afterward, we barely escaped an accident. A young man in a small yellow sports car passed us on a curve with no visibility ahead and ran head-on into a car coming up the mountain. The sports car spun completely around and then skidded into a third vehicle, a truck. Bits and pieces went flying everyplace and the yellow car had both sides bashed in, but apparently the driver was not injured. When he crawled out of his smart little car he was as yellow as it was but he tried hard to laugh, being young enough to wish to keep up appearances. Fortunately we were not involved, and as there were three cars to argue the case when the police arrived, we drove on. It was the first accident I had seen in Japan — a fact, I am told, that means nothing!

Meanwhile our taxi driver had learned from Sachiko that Harry was interested in forestry and he drove us to a huge bamboo plantation the like of which I had never before seen. Here a closely packed forest of whispering, whistling, wind-swayed stems, some growing to great height and others just sprouting, were being cultivated for consumption all over Japan. The sprouts, a delicacy for which Kyoto is famous, are harvested in summer while very young and eaten fresh: they are also tinned at that time for winter use and for export.

Previously we had noticed the name *Tahkii* on various signboards and we learned from Sachiko that it was in reference to seeds and the cultivation of trees from seeds. We decided to drive to the *Tahkii* main seed store to see if Harry could find the seeds of maple, black pine, ginkgo and various *Podocarpus* for which he had been searching. Arrived at the shop, we found a knowledgeable and erudite merchant with whom Harry quickly struck up a friendship. The Latin names for trees and plants were known to the merchant, who produced a number of Japanese plant lists with their equivalents. He had seen various forestry publications in English with the name H. G. Keith on them, and when he identified Harry as the author of these he was delighted. His pleasure at this communicated itself to his staff and to the number of interested onlookers who always hang about any warm oil-stove area. We must have spent two hours in the little shop talking, with Sachiko's help, about the many aspects of arboriculture in Japan. Harry says the Japanese are the finest arboriculturists in the world. When at last we parted from our new friends it was with packages of many of the seeds Harry had wanted and with regret at saying goodbye.

We left the magic city of Kyoto at noon the next day for Tokyo. Harry seemed better, but I had chills and fever all night and coughed a lot. Between us we drank another bottle of Vicks Extra Strength Cough Mixture with no noticeable result except slight nausea. Nevertheless we were cheered at the thought of getting back to Tokyo, which now seems like home. Sachiko also has the flu and, regardless of being young and resilient, she looks decidedly droopy.

As for me, I am tired of all the things that go with fast travel. I am tired of drip-drying my nylons on the bathtub, of trying to look fresh and neat from an overnight bag, of sitting in the finest restaurants and ordering the cheapest items, of looking pleasant because I carry my country's banner, of taking an intelligent interest in things, of absorbing atmospheres, of making excuses for myself or others, of being broad-minded . . . in fact tonight I am tired . . . Tomorrow? Tomorrow will be different.

Tomorrow *was* different. We were traveling back to Tokyo by the old Tokaido road made so gloriously famous by the artist Hiroshige in his prints, *Fifty-three Stations on the Tokaido*. Years before I ever visited Japan I had fallen in love with this route through the artist's magnificent, colorful prints. Never had I seen such azure waters, such crashing, spitting, wicked waves as those pictured by Hiroshige, 1797–1858, and his older rival, Hokusai, 1760–1850. I have never ceased to associate those curling, angry spumes of spray with the Japanese coast.

It was impossible to travel as we were now doing over the old Tokaido road without thinking back to the period over a century ago when the capital city of Japan was moved from Kyoto to Edo. The name Edo was then changed to Tokyo by edict of the new Meiji Restoration. Although Edo had in practice ruled Japan for two and a half centuries as regards administration, military power, commerce and wealth, it had not been named as the official capital city until 1868 under the Meiji regime.

For more than five hundred years the Tokaido road to the eastern sea had been in use by *daimyo*s and lords traveling to Edo to bear homage to the Shoguns. After the Meiji proclamation of Tokyo as capital city, this compulsory use by the feudal *daimyo*s and their retainers declined. The road was then left to the common folk, the merchants, peasants, artisans and anyone else who was out to make a quick yen in the newly named capital. It is interesting to note that the road did not follow the shortest route to Tokyo but sought the seacoast from Nagoya on; when traveled today by train over the New Tokaido Line, this route continues to be one of the loveliest in Japan. Although the view is frequently blacked out by roaring tunnels, and majestic Mount Fuji arises from layers of smog, I can still catch glimpses of the miniature, vital countryside which Hiroshige so realistically and lovingly recorded in his exquisite woodblock prints of *Fifty-three Stations on the Tokaido*.

It is not surprising that Hokusai, an older rival to Hiroshige and one whose prints had suddenly lost popularity with the meteoric rise of the younger man, was stung to action by the quick neglect of his own more subtle and intellectual artwork. Setting to work immediately, Hokusai produced a rival set of prints known as *One Hundred Views of Mount Fuji*. These dealt lovingly with the mystic mountain as a perpetual, dominating background to landscapes and seascapes, villagers traveling, fishermen fishing, farmers at work, and to lovely ladies being lovely — but always in subjugation, summer or winter, to the presence of Mount Fuji herself. These prints recorded in picture form the story of the life of the country people. Although they never seriously challenged the overwhelming popularity of the more vigorous prints of Hiroshige, both artists left behind them a living tribute to their own remarkable genius and to the beguiling beauty of the Japanese countryside, a beauty only partially blunted today by the by-products of the GNP.

Perhaps because of the dimming beauty of these islands there is for me no modern artist in Japan today who rivals the fine yet strong line, the noble use of color, the imaginative concepts and, most of all, the sheer Japaneseness of the prints of these two artists. It was this very quality of being so intensely Japanese that endeared these unforgettable prints to me before I ever saw Japan.

And then there is Mount Fuji viewing. Mount Fuji itself is only 12,397 feet high, but every inch is worth a picture postcard. Artists have painted it, poets have sung about it, pilgrims have climbed it, but the myth of the mountain goes deeper than anything recorded on paper. Its viewing is undertaken with religious fervor by the traditionalists, with pictorial enthusiasm by tourists, and with slight cynicism by the postwar young. The name Fuji is of Ainu origin, among which people the fire of an active volcano is called *Fujikamui*, Divine Fire, and worshiped as supernatural. For young or old, scoffers or worshipers, the sublime volcanic mountain, Fuji-no-yama, is the symbol and landmark of Japan.

Most of the time wherever we travel in the Japanese islands we see this gracious masterpiece from different angles until it seems inescapable. But once in times past we made a special trip to Lake Hakone in order to admire an especially famous Fuji view as seen through a gap between two large, dark ominous hills — for this is the kind of thing one does in Japan. The day turned out to be murky, the atmosphere was cloudy, the clouds were low and leaky, and soon it began to pour. But rain, snow or sleet are never allowed to interfere with sightseeing in Japan.

We arrived at Lake Hakone and saw nothing but thick dark nebulae, massive black banks of stormy sky, and the twisted trunks of ancient trees, while a chilling wind howled about us. But the loyal guardians of the indomitable Fuji view were on the job. They eagerly pointed out to us the direction in which we *should* see the sacred mountain *if* she were visible, and cheerfully said, "Very sorry! Cloud today. Maybe tomorrow Fuji-san good. You like to stay here tonight very nice Japanese inn?"

Many people climb Mount Fuji on foot, but usually after having motored halfway up by bus. It is popular for the sake of one's own prestige to achieve the top of the volcano, but it is not the best way to *see* Mount Fuji, whose crest will almost surely be topped with clouds. In any case, the myth of Fuji-no-yama penetrates more deeply into Japanese minds and lives than its pictorial image ever can. It is not just what one sees of Mount Fuji, but what one feels about it that classifies the Fuji devotee.

19

‿⁀‿⁀‿⁀‿⁀‿⁀‿⁀‿⁀‿⁀‿⁀‿⁀‿⁀‿⁀‿⁀‿⁀‿⁀‿⁀‿⁀

WE ARRIVED IN TOKYO all three with the flu and prop-
ping each other up, each with his own set of pills, none
of which worked. We sent Sachiko home immediately as she
was really ill, and we checked in at the Hotel Okura, which
now seemed like home. We spent the afternoon searching for
clean clothes packed in the heavy luggage we had left here, and
feeling grateful for our large, bright, well-heated room and
bath. The manager has promised that we can keep this room
until we are ready to leave Tokyo. After looking around our
commodious room, with a borrowed typewriter already in-
stalled, Harry commented approvingly that Japanese hotels
made North American hotels look like flophouses.

When I tried to catch up with my diary notes I began to
wonder how such an interesting trip could look so drab on
paper. Every scenic spot in Japan has already been overwritten
to the point where one should be thanked for saying nothing
about it — or merely, "Beautiful." But the people themselves
are a never-ending enigma. We had met so many, yet each one
was different from the others both inside and out.

"I hope that young man we talked with at Yasakuni before we left Tokyo looks us up here at the hotel," I said to Harry.

"I think he will. I liked him and he seemed to enjoy talking with us. Don't you have his card someplace?"

"Yes . . . if I can find it." I shook out dozens of neat little printed business cards from the pocket of my notebook. "I think this is it — Jiro Endo. He was a very understanding young man. There's a lot I could learn from him."

That evening Mr. Honma called from the Foreign Affairs office, filled with enthusiastic plans for interviews which he had arranged for me. I thanked God that it was Friday and I would have Saturday and Sunday to recuperate before meeting strangers. It was eight o'clock and Mr. Honma was still working, and happy to be so as it proved the office couldn't function without him. The work ethic again. He said he would come to see us at eight the next night.

We had a large drink of Scotch and ordered Italian minestrone and French bread sent up to the room. It was very good. Fortunately we are light eaters, as restaurant prices are high.

I had a bad night, as I divided it between lying in bed coughing and getting up to drink "The Mixture" fortified with chloroform.

In the afternoon we went to the Mitsukoshi Department Store and renewed our supply of Scotch, our one accomplishment for the day. Mr. Honma did not arrive at eight. This was no surprise. Later he phoned to say he was working late at the office and couldn't be spared. Says he will come Monday evening.

When we awoke the next day Harry was definitely better, and I was still alive. Excelsior!

Today Tomoko is wearing tight plaid pants which fit her neat buttocks like Scotch tape, and she glides along the streets in high heeled wedgy sandals, seeming to skim above its surface. She began to wear Western dress when she was at Vassar, where she graduated with little effort, *cum laude*. Tomoko is the new interpreter-translator who takes the place of Sachiko, who is still at home ill.

I think they must select these girls for their decorative appearance as Tomoko, in a very new-generation, Japanese way, is beautiful. She uses no makeup other than eye liner to accent the upward tilt of her eyes for she knows, as well as does the polite little man who comes with her to introduce her, that it is to her advantage on this job to be Japanese.

Her work with the Foreign Affairs Ministry requires expert facility with several languages and willingness to work long hours. This type of employment is much sought-after and very badly paid, as are most jobs open to educated girls in Japan. Tomoko cheerfully accepts this fact as the lot of her sex, and because she likes her work she appears to feel no resentment at the higher pay her male companion probably commands for doing the same job with less finesse. They both work unpaid overtime without complaint, because this proves they are needed.

At lunch today I asked her if she liked Yukio Mishima's books.

"He is very literary," she answered.

"But do you enjoy reading his books?"

"Well . . . in Japan he is considered a very fine writer."

"Do you think he describes life here as it is?"

"I don't know any people like that . . . but I like to read about them."

"The more I read Mishima," I said, "the less I understand the Japanese people I see on the streets!"

"Yes, I guess we don't see any ex-Samurai running for the buses!" she said cheerfully.

"Did you ever feel that Mishima's women characters were rather ridiculous . . . even repulsive?"

"Well, perhaps. But everybody says he is a wonderful writer. All of his books are on sale in translation in New York. I think he *must* be good."

"He is. A really great talent . . . a slightly insane genius, I suppose. But I dislike his image of women. He makes them all appear mean, weak, foolish or nasty . . . perhaps because of his own homosexual tastes. The peculiar thing is that the first story I ever read of Mishima's had a wonderful heroine. It was a short story called *Patriotism*. I've never forgotten it. It's beautifully written and heartbreaking — a masterpiece. The events take place on the third day of the 1936 February Revolt of the imperial troops against the government. An intensely patriotic young lieutenant is deeply shamed because some of his friends in his own imperial troops have mutinied and he knows he will be called on the next day to attack these young rebels, his friends. He feels that he cannot do this. So after a night of passionate lovemaking with his gentle, lovely young bride he commits ritual *seppuku* or *hara-kiri*. His wife arranges herself beside him while he is doing this and when he is dead she does as a soldier's wife should and takes her own life. The story is filled with all the terrible details of their death and it dramatically links love with death as Mishima himself did in so much of his writing — and ultimately in his own *seppuku*."

"I read somewhere that he was the only Asian writer influenced by Western philosophy," said Tomoko. "If so, then killing himself doesn't make much sense. It was wasteful . . . but of course he was forty-five years old and I suppose he knew he was past his peak," suggested youthful Tomoko. "I read that he always wanted to die a hero's death . . . but his *seppuku* was really more pathetic than heroic. There he was haranguing all those Defense Force soldiers from the balcony of the forces camp just before he killed himself, and most of them couldn't even hear what he said, and others who heard just laughed at him. It was a wasted gesture."

"According to his friends," I said, "Mishima did it as a protest against the MacArthur constitution, which prohibits the Japanese from rearming. They said his suicide was an act of despair because he felt that the old Japanese warrior spirit was dead."

"Well . . . it seemed like a tremendous event to us all at the time," said Tomoko, herself the picture of Westernized sartorial luxury in her skin-fitting suit, "and everybody was terribly shocked . . . but it didn't *change* any of us. We like a little comfort, we like democracy . . . and most of us don't really wish to get involved again in war for *any* reason. Why should we?"

"How do you feel about women's liberation?"

"It's a good idea. But it won't work here . . . the men wouldn't accept it."

"I was wondering, Tomoko . . . are you free to do as you wish here in Japan? As free as you were at Vassar? Or as free as your brothers are?"

She hesitated, then said to my surprise, "The girls are more free than the boys. I am more free than my eldest brother. He has great family responsibilities and obligations. Every eldest son in a Japanese family has these. He must live by *gimu*, that is the repayment of indebtedness. I feel very sorry for our young men sometimes. When I was a child I thought my father was very stern and never laughed. Now I know it was because he was the eldest son, and he had such great responsibilities. From the time his father died, when my father was only a boy, he had very heavy obligations to carry out. About money, family traditions, looking after our ancestral plots, our own behavior, making decisions for the family, and guarding the family honor. Everybody in the family always leaned on him, his mother and his aunts, his grandmother and grandfather, all his younger brothers and sisters . . . and there were ten of them. He had to see that they all had a living somehow. I think he never had any boyhood himself. But of course *now* he is the heir to the family land and all the valuables and treasures."

She stopped and thought for a moment before she continued, "Today he is an elderly man and for the first time in his life he is without heavy responsibilities. He has retired and my eldest brother has taken over the family business. Now my father plays golf, goes boating, bowls, goes fishing. He even made my mother learn to play golf and sometimes she goes with him. He travels where he wishes. He is a different man! When I was a child I didn't understand at all the pressure he was always under. But now I appreciate him. Yes . . . I am really sorry for our young men."

This was a new aspect to me of a young man's life here today. I said, "I didn't realize that in modern Japan such strict rules of obligation were still followed."

"Maybe now there is a little more freedom of choice inside the family than there used to be," she said, "but in good families the eldest son has the authority to command and be obeyed . . . but he also bears the responsibility for all mistakes."

Tomorrow Tomoko is going to Osaka as interpreter for a young American here on a foundation grant to write a doctoral thesis on *Sumo*. A Harvard assistant professor, and a small man himself, he told us today that he had always been fascinated by *Sumo* wrestlers whose weights are from 250 pounds to 400 pounds. He feels that *Sumo* is the one really esoteric sport. He has made five previous trips to Japan to study it, but as a perfectionist he has never been completely satisfied with his results. This trip is to be the ultimate accomplishment, he hopes. Tomoko looks thoughtfully at him, but she has a face which is not easily read.

Harry and the professor had a long chat about *Sumo,* which we watch nightly on television. This classical, pageantlike, body-pushing sport is ideal for TV viewing. The setting is dramatic, the wrestlers are always in focus, and each match reaches a climax quickly, seldom lasting longer than thirty seconds. The determined placidity of the masklike faces of the young giants is in dramatic contrast to the terrific pressures which the mountainous young bodies are exerting against each other.

I have read that most *Sumo* wrestlers are country boys, the sons of poor farmers who cannot afford to play golf or baseball. *Sumo* is the cheapest of all sports, requiring basically only a simple ring and a loincloth.

In championship matches, however, costuming is very different, as an apron is worn on top of the loincloth. This is a magnificently embroidered, brocaded *kesho-mawashi* which usually costs around $800 or more, and is the gift of the wrestler's patron or patroness. The apron is worn for the entering-the-ring ceremony, at which time all the wrestlers who are to contest this night file into the ring. Before the actual physical struggle takes place the finery of the apron is discarded.

Meanwhile the wrestler's hair has been skinned back into a tight queue and then twisted on top of his head in a lacquered black topknot. The spectacle is quite godlike — the young man's placid, masklike face above his naked body, adorned only by the brilliant tapestry apron swinging from his waist in front and the huge hawser or sash which encircles him below his naked belly. Here in the glaring arena lights stands a naked gladiator whom his ring fans adore.

A strict ritual of meeting and greeting precedes the physical struggle between the wrestlers. This ritual is both religious and superstitious, and it follows an unalterably fixed form in three stages. First the hands are clapped to attract the attention of the gods, then the arms are extended with the palms open to show they are free of any weapon, then the feet are stamped to indicate stamping evil into the ground. In due time after repeated sprinklings of salt by both opponents to purify the ring, gestures which must never be omitted, and after some very tense moments of eyeball to eyeball psychological confrontation, the show begins. It is important that the match should never lose its intrinsic qualities of self-control and dignity. At the end of each match the winner passes a dipper filled with water to the next adversary as he steps into the ring for the coming bout.

High mountain districts also produce many *Sumo* wrestlers as the long winters isolate young men from other sports and entertainments. Mountain life promotes physical health and hardiness, and struggling through the deep snow on foot strengthens the hip muscles which are vital to a *Sumo* champion's anatomy. But in the end it is not muscles alone that make a champion but superiority in psychological awareness, which enables him to out-think his opponent and trick him into a moment of relaxation. A match ends when one of the wrestlers is either downed in the ring, or pushed out of it.

According to Mr. Soda, who also joined in the discussion, many young Japanese have again become enthusiastic about this traditional sport, and matches are now jammed with young people, including young women. This comment led to a discussion of the young generation who seem to obsess the minds of everybody today. We agreed that young people everywhere are rebelling against their parents and always have done so, secretly if not publicly. But give them a little time and regardless of everything they may grow up and grow older and become parents . . . and their point of view will change. Not necessarily to become wiser . . . but safer. Rather sad, I thought, but probably inevitable.

20

JIRO ENDO arrived at the hotel last evening, apparently as pleased to see us as we were to see him. I think that to re-meet someone you like gives you the feeling of having known them for quite some time, even if you haven't. Anyway, we were all three unreasonably pleased to be together. He was especially interested when I described my discussion with the four young wives at Kanazawa. He seemed positively proud that they had impressed me so much with their progressive ideas — even while he himself was hesitating to approve of his own wife's commitment to these ideas.

"You know that you ought to meet Makiko Tanaka, our prime minister's daughter," he said. "She is very modern and independent. She likes to tell reporters that her father is a 'male chauvinist'! I think that's going too far, I admit . . . but of course she spent several years as a teenager attending a Philadelphia high school, and she picked up her liberal ideas there."

"She's married, isn't she? I wondered what sort of a wife she is?'

"I've never heard any gossip about her. She is 'Mrs. Tanaka'; her husband was legally adopted by her father so she keeps the Tanaka name. She always acts as hostess for the prime minister. They say that her mother is too shy for all this political entertainment the prime minister has to go in for. But Makiko loves it. She even likes politics and has very liberal — almost left — ideas. I suppose that most Japanese girls who want to do something on their own . . . have careers I mean . . . have spent some time at schools in the West, probably in the States."

"What about this Japanese girl who wrote a book about wife-swapping experiences in the States? The book was called *Lonely Americans*," Harry said. "I think it won some sort of a prize over here. I forget the author's name."

"Oh, perhaps you mean Yoko Kirishima. She's very clever, certainly. But I don't think she stands too well in Japan. She lived with a Scots sea captain and she keeps getting pregnant without being married to him. She's not a girl, though, she's thirty-five or thirty-six. She lived in the States for several years, too. She's not typical of any country, really."

"I see your point."

"The woman that Ineko admires most is this Taeko Matsuda. She's the Director of *Nippon Homes,* and a marvelous businesswoman. Hers is one of the first firms to make prefabricated housing and she built up her own company into a huge industry this year. She says that being a woman does not handicap her. She just says that she knows her own job and knows how to make people work for her. Ineko thinks that Matsuda has the right idea. Ineko is really interested in business. I am not."

Each time we see Jiro I grow more anxious to meet Ineko, who through his words is taking on a definite personality.

This multitudinous, inexhaustible, perplexing Tokyo is at first glance a city of only two classes, the rich and the poor. The poor live in the excrement of the monster GNP. They survive there filling their lungs with smog, their eyes with smoke, and their guts with garbage. Yet in comparison with past years this condition is regarded as prosperity. There are also by contrast some spectacularly lovely places in Tokyo, and these make the squalor seem more detestable.

Many people live in squatters' shacks beside open drains, in stinking huts, in grubby apartments of one room to a family, with a squat toilet over a pit for the fortunate few. Others exist in great grim cement boxes where they awaken in the morning and close their eyes at night without ever seeing the sun, moon or stars. In such shadowy holes babies are conceived and born, grow up, grow old and die, robbed of the birthrights of human beings.

Such things are not unique to Tokyo; we find them in most large cities. But in Tokyo each inhabitant averages just *one* square yard of living space per person, as compared to *ten* square yards per person in London. Even the dead are not left in peace, for graves in Tokyo are constantly being shifted to escape destruction as more neighborhoods become industrialized. All those who can afford it now arrange for a more serene resting place in a temple compound someplace in Kyoto, and only the poor are now buried in Tokyo.

This is how it seems at first glimpse. But take a longer and more penetrating look and you will find a third Tokyo which is neither poor nor rich. This is the newborn white collar city with wide-spreading, comparatively comfortable suburbs. Miles of monolithic apartments, flat buildings and unpretentious but cozy little houses supply living quarters for an extensive, moderately prosperous, salaried class whose sudden emergence is the outstanding event in Japanese modern social history. This also is a by-product of the monster GNP.

These families live quite comfortably as Tokyo suburbanites, although the wage earner himself must usually go to work in one of the three central wards of the city, commuting twice daily by bus or subway in a three hour, time- and energy-consuming exercise. Nevertheless, he and his family live decently, and almost half of Japan's college graduates end up in this group, having been hired for this womb-to-tomb job during their last year in college. A salaried man can't "drop out" of his job, as no other firm will take him. For him the job is his entire life, and his national purpose is good take-home pay. His pastimes, pleasures, friendships, emotional crises are involved in his job. He has everything — in a modest but cozy way; his "office wife," his bar girls, his favorite geisha, his office parties, his business drinks, his subsidized sports and his "fun." Of course he has his family — but that's his wife's job. For he, like the commuter in the United States, leaves home early and arrives back late and his wife bears entire responsibility for raising the children. She is the Japanese Mom.

A step above him and in a different category entirely is the really successful businessman, a *burujoa* as the Japanese choose unrealistically to term him. This man's family lives luxuriously but sees very little of him. His wife is proud of him but lonely, and frequently jealous of his many outside female associations. He has a huge, tax-free expense account which may include household help for his wife, and covers all forms of entertaining. This includes extravagant geisha parties, gourmet meals with unlimited drinks, memberships costing as much as $1,700 to $5,000 in golf clubs, and privileges at bowling establishments, patronage for his favorite bar girls and office girls, and business trips of convenient duration with everything done to create a luxurious impression.

Like the salaried man he commutes daily to the office, but he does so in his chauffered, imported, long black motorcar. He is the commercial brainpower of Japan, its business elite, and he exists almost exclusively in Tokyo. He is the distilled essence of what the salaried man just might become if he hangs on long enough and if enough of his superiors collapse and decay before he does.

So much for the successful Japanese *burujoa* male. Obviously Jiro Endo does not fit into this.

And what of the successful Japanese female, the Mom? It surprises me that in this country, where most women are held in thralldom and have duties rather than rights, the entire responsibility of raising boys as well as girls is left to the mother and any other female relative who lives in the home. Although the schools share somewhat with the mothers, and teachers have some liability for their students, it is the mother who is held to be at fault if the child fails. She alone must see that he does his homework well, must arrange his hours for study, make him eat strengthening meals, give him his rewards or punishments, tell him what friends to make, and arrange for his school exams, which will probably determine the course of his entire future life.

In her relationship with her children the mother is the driving force, often so much so that the sons rely on her energy and initiative for all forward impetus and decision making. In the family, little boys are little gods, but by the time they are sixteen, seventeen and eighteen, the ages when their masculinity most urgently demands that they become self-reliant, they frequently find themselves tragically deficient in self-confidence and independence when separated from their mothers. To this sudden onset during adolescence of insecurity and insufficiency is attributed a share in the blame for the high suicide rate among Japanese young people. And this allocation of over-responsibility to the mothers may be also a contributing factor to the statistics which claim that Japanese women have a higher suicide rate than any other comparable group in the world.

It is interesting to observe that although the American Mom has an almost comparable responsibility in raising her children, and has been blamed for much that is questionable in the behavior of young Americans, there are two qualities which our young people have not lacked — self-confidence and independence.

One vital difference between the Tokyo I first saw in 1934 and the Tokyo of forty years later is the development of these widespread city suburbs which now house a moderately prosperous, salaried middle class. The same type of suburbanization surrounds all large Japanese cities today. This change is precipitated by industrialization, which itself produces the GNP with its accompanying virtues and evils. This has resulted in an even greater time gap existing now in Japan between city life and country life — almost a century's gap, with country life a hundred years behind. In the United States this time gap is very much shorter.

But Tokyo has more to it than squalor, suburbs and bourgeoisie. Despite the destruction by bombings and fires, it has rebuilt its historic monuments to an appearance of genuine antiquity, and has also constructed many new buildings in the image of extreme modernity. Accustomed to destruction by the occurrence throughout their history of earthquakes and fires, the Japanese have formed the habit of tearing down their historic shrines every twenty-two years and rebuilding them in exact replica after the original pattern. This "genuine" relic then provokes the veneration owing to antiquity and provides the endurance of new materials. This habit ensures that Japanese historic monuments survive all disasters, both natural and unnatural. Meanwhile the former shrine material is cut up into charms and sold to pilgrims and tourists.

The heavily wooded grounds of the Meiji Shrine area, dedicated to the old Emperor Meiji, occupy 175 acres close to the center of Tokyo city, where they offer pedestrian visitors escaping from traffic long, quiet, wooded walks. The original shrines were all destroyed in the 1945 air raids in spite of their divine nature which, it had been believed, would make them indestructible. They were rebuilt in 1958. The area includes exquisite iris gardens, not blooming in March, and fantastic water-lily ponds, not blooming now, and a stunning grove of one hundred thousand trees donated by the Japanese people. The shrine and the outer garden area together include fine playing grounds for baseball, soccer and rugby football, a magnificent indoor gymnasium, and both indoor and outdoor swimming pools in the Yoyoji Sports Center, all of which were constructed for the Olympic Games in 1964.

This extravagant garden area close to the middle of the crowded city is a popular showplace and always teeming with sightseers on holidays, come rain or shine. They are there in families, all neatly and gaily dressed, toting umbrellas and picnic baskets, carrying their babies and trundling their toddlers, with husbands inciting them forward and wives trotting behind, but all determined on enjoying themselves. There are shoals of blue-uniformed schoolchildren, some earnest and others laughing, and groups of swaggering boys in blue jeans, and smiling girls in Levi's, each sex seemingly oblivious of the other yet unconsciously titillated by its proximity.

There are many other shrines and temples in Tokyo and all seem to have the same soothing and soporific effect on visitors. I can think of nothing in Western society comparable to this relaxed, innocent, happy pastime of shrine-viewing. Here in the Meiji they forget subway battles, train strikes, racing traffic, youthful suicides, senile old folks, worried mothers and frightened sons – and proudly luxuriate in the unique privilege of being Japanese and viewing their shrines.

The detached Akasaka Palace is just across the boulevard from the Meiji Outer Garden and is by contrast very much not a place for the people. It was built for the present emperor when he was crown prince, and is now occupied by his eldest son, the present crown prince, and his family. The palace, a large, un-homey looking place, can be glimpsed in the distance among handsome formal gardens and groves of magnificent trees which surround it like an enchanted forest. Around the entire secluded area city traffic flows tirelessly and swiftly, and although the royal family is no longer deified they obviously live well.

Almost adjacent to the palace is the Akasaka Prince Hotel, musty and elegant, remodeled from the palace of the former Korean Prince Lee. In search of historical aroma we looked here once for rooms. The lobby, which was really an old fashioned, elegant parlor, felt like an ancient prince's mansion, damp and gloomy, filled with antique treasures, everything reeking with princely charm including chairs that would scarcely bear sitting on and were obviously sized to Oriental behinds. Unfortunately there were only fifty sleeping rooms and all were booked. I was disappointed but decided later that good service elsewhere might be more desirable than musty elegance.

In contrast to the archaic charm of the hotel is the gigantic, rectangular, unimaginative structure of the National Theater nearby. Seen by daylight it always makes me think of a beached whale. But by night, when the dramatically staged and lighted *Kabuki* is playing, or the court music of *Gagaku*, or *Bunraku* the puppet drama, when the cheerful lights inside distract me from the fortresslike exterior, the building becomes the veritable temple of thespian gods.

Japanese theater demands that its audience participate fully in whatever it presents and the audience cooperates because the theater gives them something in which it is worth participating. In *Kabuki* the watchers follow every strangled sigh and flowery gesture, every artificial gesticulation telling of a genuine emotion, and every blushing or blanching of the hero's face, or that of the heroine who is also played by a male. The favorite actor's name is shouted by the audience as he first walks along the *hanamichi,* or platform, through the auditorium to appear on stage, and shouted again and again with each dramatic triumph of his words or his emotions. His fans follow him with adoration and applause even while they nibble their refreshments and sip their tea or beer. He is their escape from the grim outdoors, from democracy, from modernity, from the GNP, from life as it is, and sometimes from their spouses.

Along the same boulevard is the National Diet Building, another uninspiring monolith except for its pyramidlike central tower, and not far away are some equally unimaginative ministerial edifices. Nearby Hibya Park, with both Japanese and Western style gardening, is usually a welcome green oasis in this smoggy city. But this year nothing is green in Tokyo, thanks to the failure of the seasonal winter snowfall, whose melting snows can usually be relied on to coax up a lovely green growth over every inch of unpaved space. I have never before seen parks and gardens so desiccated as they are this spring.

If we saunter in the opposite direction we come to the Yasakuni Shrine where we first met Jiro Endo. Yasakuni is to me the most appealing of all shrines. It is dedicated to the souls of those who have fought and died for Japan, and there is a universal pathos in the death of any young man for his country. Yet I find no sense of depression here among the many visitors who wander about to pray for their dead, or to enjoy the pleasant walk under the magnificent trees and the monumental *torii*. Here one feels enveloped in the quiet acceptance of death which is so truly Japanese.

The Imperial Palace in Tokyo is almost unpretentious compared to some of Japan's old skyscraping, high-turreted castles. In fact, when gazed at through the Nijubashi (Double Bridge) which crosses the moat near the front wing, it looks quite livable and homey amidst its lovely trees and gardens, even for an imperial family. But the palace grounds are the heart and arterial center of this city, and an unfailing source of delight to me. Not only for the dignity and fortitude of the ancient moats built by hand from huge slabs of granite, nor for the lazy swans and sacred carp who swim in its murky green waters, nor for the wind-distorted pine trees with their trunks wrapped around with matting against the winter tempests, nor for the great stretches of open lawn which hopefully will turn green after the first June rain — although these are all matters of satisfaction.

No, the really endearing feature of the Imperial Palace is the fact that any and every day as I pass by I see parties of Japanese sightseers huddled together in group security as they follow the leader of their party who waves his special little pennant overhead to guide them through the maze of that part of the imperial grounds open to the public. All are animated, laughing, talking, smiling, ogling and admiring what they see, with an obvious sense of pride and something very like ownership. For it is said that the Imperial Palace is the spiritual heart of the people.

These sightseers do not belong to the wealthy upper classes, to the Big Five tycoons, the long black motorcar owners. They are from small out-of-town villages, remote farmers on a spree, fishermen from the Japan Sea, curious students, pretty show-girls, white collar families, daily commuters . . . anybody . . . everybody . . . and all of them have sacrificed something to come here to see their emperor's palace. Watching them, I can believe what I am told, that poor or rich, no Japanese wishes to be anything other than Japanese.

No visitor can ever see all of Tokyo. Every time we start out for a new address, new vistas and areas open up on the way. We are constantly saying, "Where are we? We never saw this before!" Tokyo has clear-cut layers of history, but its geo-graphic cross sections are completely confusing. Any natural continuity has been repeatedly broken up by fires, plagues, famines, earthquakes, and bombings. The Japanese themselves have developed a philosophical acceptance of natural disasters, probably from their wide experience of them throughout all their history.

In North America we have had little practice in facing up to country-wide starvation, mass epidemics, or large-scale de-struction of our homes by war or any other means. We expect *not* to have these experiences. The Asian nations expect them. I think one's philosophy develops largely from his experiences. Quite often an American, after reading my story of wartime imprisonment, has said to me, "How could you survive? *I* couldn't stand things like that!" But no Asian has ever said this to me . . . they understand that one survives . . . or else . . .

21

~~~~~~

W HEN WE FIRST ARRIVED in Japan I asked my Foreign
Affairs friends to try to find Mr. Kimpei Shiba, an old
acquaintance whom I remembered vividly from our last trip
here in 1955. At that time he was managing editor of the
Nippon Times, now called the *Japan Times*. He must have
been about fifty years old at that first meeting but so vital and
virile, so clear-minded and forceful that I thought of him as a
young man, except for one un-youthful quality — he was extremely tolerant in his outlook. I had liked him immediately
and felt that I was talking with a friend. I soon found that he
had another unusual quality — he did not mistrust me for being
a foreigner.

We had met apropos of the publication of the Japanese language edition of my book, *Three Came Home*, at which time
he had arranged for an interview with me about the book
During a long talk then, I had learned more from him about
the general aspects of the war than I had known before, although I had been a participant in it. As a prisoner of the
Japanese I had known almost nothing of what was going on

outside our prison camp quarters until the day of release. After repatriation there were other more important things to do than relive the past. But Mr. Shiba, as a newspaperman in Japan, had known a great deal about the overall story, and before we parted that day he gave me a copy of his own book written in English, *I Cover Japan*. He spoke and wrote English fluently, having been born in the Hawaiian Islands and having worked as a journalist in Honolulu and in San Francisco.

I Cover Japan described how its author had been interrogated by the notorious Japanese Secret Police in 1944, when he came under suspicion because of his sympathies with the Japanese peace advocates. As he had been a special correspondent in Japan for the *Chicago Tribune* from 1937 to 1941, no doubt his so-called "foreign" point of view made him suspect. However, by early 1945 almost all Japanese statesmen realized that Japan could not win the war. But they also knew that the all-powerful military machine was determined on the complete extinction of the entire nation sooner than permit a military surrender.

From this point on the author related in detail the true story of the dramatic events leading up to the emperor's decision to surrender to the Allies in order to save his people from being liquidated by the Japanese military order to "Fight till the last man is dead!" As the climax to a series of semi-suicidal events, the emperor finally spoke directly to his people for the first time in history, via the radio. In his message he as their divine ruler accepted full responsibility for the surrender of his country. The emperor's spoken words poured out through government radio all over the ravaged countryside, precipitating scenes of hysteria, tears, whimpers, anger, shame, dazed misunderstanding, disbelief, disillusion and, only at last, relief. Only slowly did their emperor's words bring conviction to a wounded, starving people that they were to live, not to die.

After reading Mr. Shiba's book I formed a completely new outlook on the wartime past. This was at a time in my life when the kindest thing I had been able to do for the Japanese was to not think about them. Harry and I took Shiba's volume home to our library in Victoria and put it on our bookshelves with a feeling of satisfaction and pride. When we decided to return to Japan this winter I brought the book back with me, determined to try to meet its author again and feeling that the book would furnish authentic proof of our past association. Eighteen years is a long time in the crowded happenings of a newspaperman's world, and I realized that many other names might have pushed mine out of his memory.

I had thought it would be simple to trace him through the publishers of his book, but we found the book was out of print and the publishers were out of business, as frequently happens to Japanese publishers, who are constantly seeking more lucrative work. In time, we learned that Mr. Shiba, who had previously spelled his name *Sheba*, had left the *Japan Times* some years before and was now with the *Asahi Evening News*, an English language paper, where he was chairman of the board. Apparently he was considered the dean of English language journalists.

Today we had an appointment to meet him in his office at the *Asahi Evening News*. Although I remembered Kimpei Shiba with very real personal warmth I did not anticipate too much from *him* for our meeting. He had registered with me as a man — an unforgettable one. But I am American and outgoing; he was Oriental and reserved. He might never have thought of me again. And besides, if everybody else in Japan had "forgotten the war," perhaps he had, too?

We arrived promptly at his office in the *Asahi* building where his attractive secretary greeted us with the extreme courtesy which one receives in all Japanese offices, I find. Immediately Mr. Shiba emerged from his inner office to welcome us, saying quickly, "Yes, yes, I remember you well," although I am sure he didn't until he read our cards and I poked his own book under his nose.

I would have known him anywhere; perhaps there is such a thing as an essence of personality. Although I knew he must be over seventy now, his brown eyes were brilliant and still glowed with the same responsive intelligence, his movements were quick and alert, and the impression he gave was of health and vitality. His bony, bisque face was scarcely lined at all and his figure was lean and trim. As to dress, although for most Japanese men I cannot resist the words 'neat and dapper,' Mr. Shiba had the slightly tie-askew look which is typical of most newspapermen.

When we commented on his looking young, he shook his head in denial, and then asked Harry what *his* age was. When Harry admitted to being the same number of years as Mr. Shiba, Mr. Shiba shook his head and said he was "shocked" that we should be traveling so far away from home! He said he himself had now given up traveling outside Japan since he had collapsed in Australia four years ago with a temperature of 104°.

After explaining the reasons for our visit to Japan, I said we would very much value his opinion on several matters. We had observed many important changes in Japan since we were last here in 1955 and would like to know if he believed that these obvious material changes were as deep and permanent as they seemed?

"They are indeed," he answered, "if you mean the mad rush for dollars. Believe me, there is no retreat now from the GNP."

"Do you personally approve of the way things are going?"

"It doesn't matter if I approve or not . . . changes are inevitable. However, a man of my age . . . wouldn't like such changes."

"Take just one difference, Mr. Shiba. Take the sudden emphasis on material well-being of all sorts — goods, money, ambition, the rat race for riches. What's responsible for the Japanese change in attitude and in standards?"

He thought for a moment, then said, "From 1930 to 1945, Japan as a nation did absolutely everything wrong. After 1945, whatever Japan needed according to United States standards was given to her by the United States. It was all free — and Japan didn't appreciate it. No one ever thanked the United States or even thought about it. But now we are stuck with those postwar American standards."

"Are the Japanese people in general really better off today than formerly?"

"People born after the Second World War have no old Japanese standards with which to compare their present circumstances. They all . . . *all* . . . every one of them, have much more than they had before. But each one looks only at the group above him and complains because he does not have the same or better. But believe me, at all levels of society there is more material prosperity today."

Harry commented that in Japan we saw everybody working very hard at every level and not complaining. But in North America people did not expect to work hard.

Mr. Shiba laughed and said, "Japan will soon be like that. Labor is already going after a five day week and higher pay. Well, why not! The capitalist and Communist countries are moving closer together and soon there will be little difference between them. The United States has put into practice many Communist ideas such as payment of welfare, old age pension, an established poverty level and, in some cases, state ownership."

His comments seemed to me to describe Japan as a much more dynamic society than the one suggested by Chie Nakane in her best-selling book *Japanese Society*, which has suddenly become the last word among the Japanese and Western intelligentsia alike. I said, "Chie Nakane sees you Japanese as staying within your own vertically structured society with each man seemingly content to work as hard as he can but always staying within his own frame of progress and not competing horizontally. How do you see this idea?"

"Mrs. Nakane is very clever — in some ways she may be right, but — " He shook his head vehemently. "Everyone — everyone is struggling to get the job of the man above him . . . regardless of his 'frame.' In the future this is going to be a no-holds-barred struggle!"

"Do you know, Mrs. Keith, that in ten years' time China will be where Japan is today? This will bring a leveling off of prosperity in Japan, and then a lowering of standards. That's a good thing! It is inevitable, and it will cause suffering, but people need to suffer. Meanwhile Japan is going soft . . . she has profited too much from both the Korean war and the Vietnam war."

"Have the land reforms brought in under the MacArthur regime endured?" I asked.

"No. They aren't really workable — for us."

"We met families in Aichi Prefecture who told us they had owned and farmed the same land for six and seven generations and were happy and prosperous. They said, like you, that the land reforms were not workable."

"They don't suit the Japanese temperament. We rely on strong family ties and the idea of continuity."

"Can you tell me what MacArthur reforms have endured today in actual practice? At least the changed attitude to women seems to be here to stay."

"Undoubtedly. But you may not realize that Japanese women have *always* ruled the home. Some Japanese say that the man goes in front because he is the horse, and the woman goes behind because she is the driver. Only now the wife trots along by her husband's side in public, and the working girls, like all you Americans, want paying jobs outside their homes."

"So what is going to happen about marriage for your young, educated Japanese woman?" I asked. "She is liberal in her ideas, able to earn money, and comparatively free in her actions. She certainly doesn't think of herself as a second-class citizen. But the girls say that the young men are still conservative in their choice of a wife. If so, who is the modern girl going to marry?"

He roared with laughter and said, "From what I know of modern girls today . . . they'll get married all right!"

"What do you think of this fever for traveling abroad?"

"Mrs. Keith, today all Japanese wish to travel . . . including the lower classes who spend all their money that way. They have a passion to see outside Japan. Taxi drivers take trips to Paris, bus men tour Canada, trash collectors visit Russia, and everybody goes to Hawaii . . . or at least Okinawa. Years ago the travel advertisements were placed only in the English language papers or magazines. Today they are in all Japanese language papers because our Japanese world has expanded. Previously the only Japanese who read foreign language papers were travelers."

"Another thing we noticed, Mr. Shiba. Your young people have much the same customs as our young people . . . the same ways of behavior, ideas and actions. They all dress alike, look alike, act alike . . . alike to our Western youngsters. I'm sure this is more than just a superficial similarity. Our young people are more like yours than either group is like the generation above them. What do you make of this? Today youth is international."

"In some ways they are all alike," he said. "It's true that a culture travels by communications . . . by newspapers, radio, television, by people talking . . . and all these tend to make your young people and ours seem alike. But this is only superficial. Underneath you will find that our young Japanese are still distinctively Japanese. And yours are basically North American."

"Still . . . being young is international."

"Yes, but it doesn't last. Before most youngsters can destroy themselves they grow up." He laughed tolerantly and added, "We Japanese are a people of great extremes, you know. Everything is either wonderful or terrible with us. We are also a people of great contradictions . . . both rigid and adaptable; brutal and gentle; we are aggressive, but also submissive. Our young people are very extreme in their behavior while they are young, but in time they will certainly settle down and adapt themselves to whatever comes. It is in their nature. A few years of youthful rioting will last them a lifetime."

"What do you think about the destruction of much of the natural beauty of Japan in order to create this mammoth GNP?"

"It is inevitable, given the mood of the people. We lost a war. Our belief in our own invincibility collapsed. So now it is necessary for us to redeem our military failure with economic triumphs."

"We are much impressed by the excellence of your English language newspapers here," Harry said.

"And they are all losing money . . . like this one!" he said gloomily.

"But surely that is unjustified! We find that the newspapers here are better informed and print more news about happenings in Europe, Africa and Asia than most papers published in Canada do. Most North American newspapers are bogged down in purely North American happenings."

He smiled and said, "I can't completely agree as to the excellence of Japanese papers . . . depends on the paper. I myself have worked on all kinds. My father published the *Nippon Times* (now *Japan Times*) and half a century ago I went to work for him on that paper. Later I worked for two years in Peking on the *North China Standard*, then for two years in Honolulu for the *Advertiser* and a year in San Francisco on the *Bulletin*. I was also special correspondent in Japan for the *Chicago Tribune* until the war came in 1941. Then I returned to the *Japan Times* as director and managing editor."

"I saw in *Who's Who*," I said, "that in 1927 you accompanied the Japanese delegate, Admiral Makoto Saito, to the Geneva Disarmament."

He smiled rather wearily and nodded his head and said sadly, "Disarmament!" and fell silent.

"So what happens now?" Harry asked. "I see you are still active in journalistic affairs."

"No . . . not very active. You see, I retired once in 1952 but I couldn't stand the quiet! So I founded the *Tokyo Evening News* as its president. Then the *News* merged with the *Asahi Shimbun* and I became director and editor. Now I am chairman of the board . . . and I just sit in my little office!"

I felt as I listened to him that he would prefer to be out of his little office and chasing down a hot news story.

As we got up to leave he pointed his finger at me and said sternly, "You know that Nihon is the Japanese name for Japan and we Japanese are devoted to Nihonism. Nihonism is our creed about ourselves . . . our attitudes and beliefs about ourselves. They are our only real religion.

"Almost everybody writes about Japan . . . except the Japanese," he continued. "Have you read *The Japanese And The Jews* by Isaiah Ben-Dasan? You must read it. Ben-Dasan claims to be a Jew born in Kobe and raised in Japan . . . but I doubt it. He *must* be Japanese. He writes in Japanese essay form and he contrasts the Japanese with the Jews. Anyway, buy that book. You need it."

"We have it."

"When you write you must be critical of the Japanese. Be critical! Tell the truth . . . it's good for us. Remember what I told you . . . people need to suffer. If you send me your manuscript I'll correct it and return it to you. You see . . . we have not *all* forgotten the war!"

Outside his office I said, "He'll never really retire. And Japan will be the loser when he dies."

"I have a feeling," Harry said, "that Kimpei Shiba is the only man we have talked with so far in Japan who has been completely frank with us."

"What about Jiro Endo?" I asked.

"Sometimes, but not always. He's too emotional to see things clearly. His marriage, say . . . He wants an intelligent, independent wife but he wants her to behave like a traditional mother-figure wife."

"And if he had a traditional mother-wife he'd be unhappy because she didn't behave like Ineko?"

"Probably. That young man was doomed to discontent from the time he went West."

"Perhaps his natural intelligence doomed him to discontent," I suggested.

22

∿∿∿∿∿∿∿∿∿∿∿∿∿∿∿∿∿∿∿∿∿∿∿

DON ARRIVED at the Orchid Bar a little late, having gone to the Imperial Hotel first where he had assumed we would be staying. He apologized excessively for his tardiness, saying that he realized this was inexcusable by Japanese standards, as they were a "precision" people, and consequently always on time. This idea was exactly the opposite of my own impressions of Japanese time standards, these being that an appointment in Tokyo for six o'clock tonight might take place at seven, or at five — or the following day — but seldom at six tonight.

Don Oberdorfer, the new representative in Japan of the *Washington Post*, has been in Tokyo for five months, he told us. A welcome change, he said, after three and a half years of covering the White House in Washington, D.C. Out here he has a large geographical area to be responsible for, as he covers Southeast Asia and Korea as well as Japan, but physical distance has little meaning now thanks to telephone and telegraph communications and air travel.

As the big financial news in the United States was the U.S. trade deficit with Japan, which seemed to be creating antag-

onism against Japan, I asked Don for his opinion. He brushed
the matter aside with "Insignificant! Ridiculously insignificant
compared to the whole U.S. GNP! Importance is only being
given to it now in order to protect the U.S. exporters and
companies who have failed to compete with Japanese imports."

"Why can't they compete?"

"Workers are overpaid in the States, and many of our plants
are old-fashioned compared to the Japanese ones, and there is
a lot of plain inefficiency. Almost all Japanese plants today are
modern because they have either been built new since the war,
or rebuilt after the war when bombing destroyed all the old
ones.

"Well, they are not all efficient in the way they function. To
be just . . . what is to blame is the fact that U.S. workers don't
intend to work either as hard, or for as long hours, as Japanese
workers do. Given these disabling factors, most U.S. plants
find it easier to press the government for surcharges on imports
than to control their own plants sufficiently to make U.S. goods
competitive with Japanese goods."

"Listening to you I begin to feel that I know even less about
the United States than I know about Japan," I said, feeling
very unsophisticated.

He laughed, and asked, "What *are* you doing in Japan?"

"I sometimes wonder. By definition I am here to try to write
something that will further understanding between Japan and
the United States. That sounds ambitious but one has to aim at
something . . . and I believe in it. The Japan Foundation is a
Japanese-endowed program with the same objectives as our
longstanding Fulbright-Hays Act — to further international
friendship through cultural exchanges. I think both nations
feel they are misunderstood by the other, and intelligent people
in both countries are trying to find a sympathetic meeting

ground. Ever since the war our relationship with Japan has been that of the conqueror to his conquest. Harry and I have been both the conquered and, ultimately, the conquerors, and neither relationship is pleasant or healthy."

He said, "You're right about the need for understanding. The Japanese don't understand American politics or government at all and we don't understand theirs. In this country politics and government are all conducted with extreme ceremony and according to precise traditions, and their conduct provides an absolute face-saving formula under every circumstance. Every thought and act has been decided upon before it is exposed to public view. An act may be announced initially that seems contrary to the real act decided upon, and then this false act is gradually worked back into being the genuine one."

"Very Oriental," I agreed. "But still I remember some rather undignified photos of Japanese members in the National Diet 'arguing' matters out. I've seen press photos of actual fistfights taking place in the Diet between some of its honorable members."

Don laughed, "Those are the exceptions. Just another example of the Japanese personality which expresses itself in extremes, bowing deeply one day, and fistfighting the next."

"But aren't we all like that — when something really affects us? During the first few days of the train strikes everybody was amiable, including the strikers. Then suddenly everyone, regardless of what side he was on, started throwing stones at everyone else. It wasn't very reasonable — it wasn't very Japanese — but it was human," I said.

"What about women's liberation? When will it hit Japan?" Harry asked.

Don shook his head. "Even today Japanese women don't have the status that American women had *before* liberation. Here they have only just ceased to be a minus quantity. They do have legal rights now, but they have no idea of sex equality. Their men like it like that. When women's lib really strikes Japan it'll be a bomb. Women in the States had a number of years to work their way toward liberation. But here . . . it'll be a bomb!"

"As I remember it," I said, "in 1934 women here had no rights at all. But in 1948 the new constitution, promoted by MacArthur, really a foreign-made instrument, gave them legal rights. I also remember in 1955 we were surprised to see women sometimes walking side by side with their men instead of shuffling several paces behind. This togetherness was specially noticeable among the young people, who even held hands. But what happened after '55?"

"Well, even ten years later, say in 1965," said Don, "the very idea of women asking for factual equality as well as legal equality was ridiculed. Even today there is a huge gap between the theory of sex equality and its practice."

"But don't you think that as the percentage of educated women increases, especially those who work outside the home and are financially independent, this condition will work toward actual equality?" I asked. "I'm sure that when women here have actual equality they'll be quick to use it. Japanese women are intelligent, attractive and excessively feminine."

"A few days ago," said Don, "I interviewed one of the most remarkable women I have ever met, Sawako Arioshi. She is forty-two years old and extremely beautiful. You must have heard of her? She wrote a sensational book, *The Ecstatic One,* a runaway best-seller. The book focuses on the problems of the aged, and the word ecstacy in the title really refers to simple-mindedness . . . well, senility, as found in extreme old age and not to the high joy implicit in our own use of *ecstacy.* My Japanese friends tell me this book is talked about in almost every Japanese home!"

"I read that it had sold over a million copies. Tell me about the author."

"She is quite lovely and very sincere; extremely well-educated, of course. She studied in Japan first, then won a Rockefeller Foundation grant and went to Sarah Lawrence College. She has published books which have been translated and published in Chinese, Russian, Dutch, German and other languages, but never in English. The problem is that her books, like so many Japanese books, are too slow in starting to suit American tastes. Too bad. Especially as some Japanese writers who are less popular and less well-known in Japan are on sale in English editions."

"That seems shortsighted to me, especially now when the problem of the aged is crucial in the Western world also. Has Mrs. Arioshi sent her manuscript in English translation to any U.S. publishers?"

"Yes. Her friend who translated the book into English sent it to several U.S. publishers. I've seen their answers. They all said the story was excellent but too slow in starting to attract the American reader. One editor suggested that she just drop the first fifty pages!"

"If the Japanese can stomach *Jonathan the Seagull* — that's the way they translate it — it seems to me that American readers would surely have the patience to read *The Ecstatic One*," I said. "Meanwhile, we are inundated with every aspect of Yukio Mishima, who really has little connection with our Western world culture. He's far from being universal in appeal and he's neither modern nor young in his philosophy. Then there's Yasunari Kawabata and Jiro Osaraji and Junichero Tanizaki and Soseki Natsume — all old, old men, eighty and ninety years. Yet their books monopolize Western bookshelves without the excuse of being timely. And the classics, *Tale of Genji*, the *Pillow Book*, *Rashomon* — all these have little relation to Japan as it is today. We seem determined to promote our own ignorance."

"What about Kobo Abe?" Don suggested. "He's in his forties. Abe's books are about the struggle of the individual to escape his loneliness. His last books, *Woman in the Dunes* and *The Ruined Map*, are both best-sellers — young people love them — they tell of the isolation of every man whose destiny is to stand alone in society. A bit depressing, but fascinating."

"What started Mrs. Arioshi on the subject of old age?" I asked. "Is she a social worker?"

"No, she's a talented novelist. But a few years ago she started to study gerontology, chiefly because there was such a need for it and she found that nothing was being done to solve the problem of the aged. In Japan there is a crucial old-age problem because of the sudden lengthening of life expectancy. Within the last twenty-five years life expectancy here has risen from fifty years for men to seventy-three years today, and to seventy-five years for women. This is a longer life expectancy than we have in the States. Add to this the fact that the aged have no place to live because of widespread war destruction of old housing and the rebuilding in its place of small, crowded apartments for salaried young city couples. These have no space for the aged parents. It's a changed way of life and it leaves no place for the old folks. It's cruel — but true."

"Mrs. Arioshi must be a strong character as well as talented?"

"She is. Her own life contradicts every generalization made about Japanese women. She completed her Japanese education in English literature at Tokyo Junior College and then decided to enter the business world as manager for the only female performer in the otherwise all male *Kabuki* actors' cast. Her first novel was written with this background about the world of artists. Then she got a Rockefeller Foundation grant to the

States to study. While she was there she visited New York frequently and became fascinated by the city's mixed population and way of life. Out of this experience she wrote a novel called *Non-color* about a Japanese war bride and her black American husband who lived in the New York slums. After she returned to Japan she married a well-known personality in the theatrical world. The marriage didn't work and she was divorced soon after — and left with an infant daughter. That was nine years ago and now she lives in Tokyo with her daughter and her mother. She has written some very successful historical novels, and a number of popular plays. Meanwhile she has become an extreme Japanese nationalist."

"What happened to the royalties on *The Ecstatic One*? They must have been plenty."

"They were huge by Japanese standards, about $330,000. Mrs. Arioshi tried to give it all to nursing homes to benefit the aged, but government tax collectors refused to let her and collected most of the amount in taxes. Then the case was taken up by the Japanese press and ultimately the government permitted her to make a gift of 20 percent to homes for the aged — and then collected most of the rest of the royalties itself."

23

THE LEADING EXPONENT of the youth generation in Japan is no longer young — Shintaro Ishihara, forty years old. Tallish, well dressed, with fine Asian features, inky black hair and an almost naive smile, he greeted us politely in his offices in Shinjuku.

Season of Violence is the volume which won Mr. Ishihara at the age of twenty the much coveted Akutagawa literary prize. I have just finished reading it and find it has few of the attributes of other Japanese books that I have read. The stories open with action, they move quickly, and each one of the characters behaves in a manner to horrify and disgust the Forty-Seven Ronin, or any of the famous heroes or heroines of the traditional Japanese literary world. In *Season of Violence* nobody sacrifices himself for anybody else, or acts out of loyalty or decency, and although some of the young men literally disembowel each other, the act has nothing to do with the accepted motive of hara-kiri. The book doesn't glorify brutality but it accepts it as casually amusing and the very spice of youthful games as played among a group of elite youngsters.

The most frightening quality of the stories is that they do not portray gang war for material profit nor even revolutionary ideals but gang war for fun. The three tales in the title volume are: *Season of Violence, Punishment Room,* and *The Yacht and the Boy,* and all describe a group of teenagers known in Japan as *Taiyozoku,* or the Sun Tribe. These stories have been made into motion pictures and are now superpopular with the postwar generation for whom Ishihara seems to be accepted as spokesman.

I wouldn't have expected the author to look like this modest young man whom I met today, with short, neatly cut hair and a smile crinkling the edge of his eyes. Obviously there has been a change of images between the twenty-year-old writer just out of Hitotsubashi University and this young man who is now a Member of the House of Councillors. It is easy to understand why he won his seat in the Diet with three million votes. His name has been on everybody's lips via cinema and television, a publicity which is reinforced by his genuine personal charm and magnetism. I wonder what he hopes to achieve from his Diet seat beyond the good salary which he doesn't need? Power? Prestige? Opportunity to serve his country? He is considered an avant-garde intellectual and also a fighting conservative, a rare combination. He has been quoted as saying that Japan must have at least one nuclear bomb in order to make itself listened to more respectfully around the world. Young Ishihara is already listened to.

Although Tomoko had come with us to interpret we didn't really need her as Mr. Ishihara spoke excellent English when he wished to, but preferred French. As he had no idea what our motive in coming to see him was I began by saying, "We wished to talk with you because you are the only spokesman of the Japanese youth generation whose writings are being translated into English. May we ask you a few questions?"

He smiled amiably and said, "O.K."

"Do you think your book is typical of young people today?"

"Yes, in a way."

"Are your characters taken from life?"

"Yes, one is my brother."

"It seems obvious that the youth culture is international," I said, "yet it seems to have sprung from different causes here in Japan from the causes in my country. In the United States we explain the qualities of youth — its faults, if you wish, as the result of our participation in the Vietnam war. In Japan you say that similar qualities found in your young people are to be traced back to your having lost the Second World War, as this destroyed traditions and undermined old values. What is your opinion of this statement?"

"I agree that the youth culture is international now — probably because of the mass news media and world communications."

"What do you think is the cause of the excessive violence in Japanese youngsters today as you have portrayed them in your writing?"

He looked thoughtful as he answered, "Perhaps a reaction to pressures from above. Perhaps the result of war destruction. And certainly today there is a lack of any recognized authority."

My first impression as we conversed was that he didn't talk as well as he wrote. However it is difficult to explain shades of meaning in a foreign language.

Harry asked, "These young people about whom you write — the well-to-do upper middle class — what do they have to complain about in this rich, prosperous country today? What is it they want?"

At this question Ishihara turned to Tomoko to interpret, which meant we wouldn't get a direct answer. The two of them went off into a long discussion in Japanese at the end of which Tomoko interpreted the gist of his answer to us as, "Mr. Ishihara says that young people think that society is all rotten. They say they are going to tear it all down."

"What are they going to put in its place?" Harry asked.

"They don't know. They have no constructive plans."

"I notice, Mr. Ishihara, that you refer to young people as 'they' now, not as 'we,'" I said. "Your own position has changed. All your characters, who you say are from life, were very young when you wrote about them, and so were you. Has there been as great a change in the people you wrote about as there is in you? You are now forty years old, middle-aged, conservatively dressed, obviously respectable, and a Member of the Diet. Have your characters changed too?"

He looked a bit self-conscious but laughed as he said, "Yes . . . I think they have changed."

I'm not sure what started us on the next subject but he suddenly began to describe with great enthusiasm his own venture into capitalism.

"Ten years ago," he said, "I traveled in Europe and the United States with a friend. After we got home we decided to build a theatrical center — something like Lincoln Center was in our minds. We finally got the idea financed by a couple of very rich Japanese businessmen and we built the center close to the Imperial Hotel. We called it the *Nisei* Theater."

"Has it been successful?"

"In a way, yes. We put on some plays that we either wrote ourselves — we liked that — or that we chose ourselves. But then the Communist party — they're very strong here, you know — they jumped on us for being capitalists. They said we must stage some Communist plays." Here he laughed and shrugged his shoulders and said, "So we staged some Communist plays . . . and everybody was happy."

"And now?"

"We stage what we like. We employ many out-of-work actors and this is very good. We have some beautiful people acting for us."

"Are you still writing?"

"Yes . . . when I have time. But I am quite busy in my office."

"I hope you continue to write. There are plenty of Diet Members about, but there is nobody but you who writes about today's young Japanese — and is translated into English. *Season of Violence* tells of a world that Americans don't know exists in Japan."

Here he interrupted me to say in a tone of intense disgust, "That book is very badly translated into English. It has turned my story into rubbish. Garbage! Disgusting! The French translation is much better. Do you read French? Please read the French edition."

As we had been with him over an hour we stood up to leave, but by now he seemed to be enjoying himself and said, "Wait! Wait! . . . How much longer will you be in Tokyo? We should meet again."

"We'll be here ten days more."

"But there are people you should meet before you go. Have you met Taizo Kato, the writer?"

"No."

"You must meet him. He's a wonderful fellow! I shall arrange it now. Have you met Shoji Terayama? A funny guy . . . a swell chap. I will arrange that also." Saying which he jumped up and dashed to his secretary in the outer office and told her what he wanted. She started phoning immediately, while he smiled and said, "She fixes it!" Before we left his office we had appointments with "the wonderful fellow" and "the swell chap."

When we finally said goodbye and left, Mr. Ishihara seemed happy with himself and us, and we were happy too. My last view of him was a handsome young Asian dressed in impeccable Western style, bidding us farewell with two-world good manners. He had both hemispheres at his command because he had intelligence and sensitivity from both cultures — and money! I hoped that the young people in *Season Of Violence* had grown up and matured as much as their author had.

However, the next day after I had reread *Season Of Violence* I felt that they couldn't have. I asked myself — Could these be the idealistic, non-material-minded young people of the youth generation of Japan of which we hear? Or were these still the brutal young Japanese guards who had made our lives miserable in prison camp so many years ago?

Mr. Ishihara had said of his book in English translation, "Garbage!" In justice to him I tried to buy the French edition but it was sold out.

I think the line of demarcation for differences among the Japanese is about the age of forty. If a man is under forty years old then he must have been a child or adolescent sometime during the postwar years: then he hates what his parents' generation brought about in his country; he thinks the old people made a mess of life; he wants to throw out the government; he wants freedom. Freedom for what? He doesn't know.

If a man is over forty, then he was a child or an adolescent before or during the war years, and he is pleased to be alive still. He has worked hard for small rewards but he is grateful for his existence; he has little patience with the young generation who, he feels, seldom get off their fannies except to riot about something they don't understand. They have it easy compared to the boys of *his* youth, he will tell you. What more can they want, he asks himself and you, sadly and sourly.

Yet Jiro Endo is in his thirties and he contradicts this diagnosis. He seems to have no revolutionary impulses. Perhaps because he comes from the rich and the elite? No, because some of the revolutionaries are from the rich and the elite. The answer must lie in personality.

24

~~~~~~

TWO PEOPLE OF QUALITY by the name of Hachiya are meeting us today. He has white hair, forceful features and heavy black eyebrows. She is tiny and elegantly feminine and although she is over fifty years old she is still a dancer of high repute. He drives his own motorcar through Tokyo traffic, a feat for any man, but especially for one of seventy-eight years. They are taking us to lunch at the rooftop French restaurant Prunier, the best in town, on top the Kasumigaseki Building, the tallest in Tokyo. The Hachiyas have quality — as witness his driving, their manners, her beauty, his wicked wit.

Mr. Teruo Hachiya was formerly the Japanese Consul in Vancouver, British Columbia. It is through a letter of introduction from some Canadian friends that we are meeting them now. Mr. Hachiya is currently the Director of the American-Japan Society, Inc., one of many cultural exchange societies.

Today he drove with flair and daring and talked to Harry all the time, while Mrs. Hachiya and I exchanged expressions of gratification and congratulation at each near traffic miss. After adroitly parking his car in the Kasumigaseki underground park, he escorted us upward via a series of elevators which ultimately delivered us to the thirty-fifth floor. Here he commenced an amiable argument with the hatcheck girl about checking his very old felt hat which he adored and which his wife, he said, hates. His indifference to fashion endeared him to us and apparently it did to the hatcheck girl who very tenderly placed his old hat in exactly the position he designated on the shelf. Meanwhile tiny Mrs. Hachiya smiled graciously during a discussion she had probably heard many times before.

A shining jet black edifice which looms up out of the grubby Tokyo gray is the Kasumigaseki Building. Inside everything is black, polished and glittering too. From the top floor the Tokyo view takes command over everything else and I was irresistibly drawn toward the huge plate glass windows which framed a misty city below where the occasional beams of the sun were caught and reflected in the windows of other buildings.

Out hosts seated us at a table where I could look out of the window and watch the city skyline against the opalescent sky. The word *Kasumigaseki* means misty barrier and it was a perfect description for the city as we saw it from the thirty-fifth floor.

It was wonderfully easy to feel acquainted with our hosts for two reasons: one, they spoke English beautifully and, two, they were completely natural. They did not assume any attitude for us, they just existed with absolute sincerity. I think this is rare in a relationship between Japanese and Westerners, especially Americans.

Mr. Hachiya was a fine looking old man, well-dressed but in old-fashioned taste because he liked it that way, and very much an individual. He behaved as he wished to do within his own traditional code. He had a keen, not always kindly sense of humor, he was outspoken and blunt but never crude, and had great self-confidence and polish. I think many Japanese of his class and generation are more sure of themselves and more independent in their thinking than are the young generation who all seem joined in one mass impulse — to revolt against everything.

Mrs. Hachiya, twenty years younger than he, had been a gifted dancer, and still danced the *Fujimusume*, or Wistaria Maiden dance, for festivals, and also held classes in dancing. She was very ornamental, tiny and resilient with a look of fragile invincibility. With beautiful hands and feet, all her movements were small and fine and graceful. She conveyed the impression of extreme femininity although she was dressed in a bulky, figure-concealing green tweed suit. Harry and I agreed later that she reminded us in her gracious ways of our Canadian friend, Elizabeth, who gave us this introduction.

Contrary to custom there was no problem in deciding the menu, as Mr. Hachiya promptly chose two prize items for us all, sea food cocktails followed by veal steaks accompanied by a bottle of choice wine.

Suddenly Mrs. Hachiya turned to me and said, "I understand that you are a great student of the Japanese language?"

"Far from it!" I said in surprise. "I only wish that I were. No, I am here to study the people, not the language."

"But you were four years in Japanese custody?"

"Yes, but we were forbidden to speak Japanese or to study it. We used only the Japanese numerals for our muster roll call. I never understood why we were forbidden to study Japanese — unless it was to prevent us from talking with our guards."

I had noticed that a gold maple leaf, the emblem of Canada, was pinned in the lapel of our hostess's coat and now I asked her, "Were you happy in Canada? Or did you find it difficult to adjust?"

Her fine face glowed as she answered warmly, "We were very happy there. It is a wonderful country with fine people. We were especially content in Vancouver."

By now Harry and Mr. Hachiya were involved in international politics. When Mr. Hachiya was excited he talked in exclamations. Now, banging down his fist, he said firmly and loudly for all about to hear, "Russia must never, never be trusted! This I know! I have very strong convictions against Japan dealing with Russia. Remember . . . remember Russia broke her nonaggression treaty with Germany when she invaded Poland!"

"What do you think about President Nixon's trip to China?"

"He should never have had any dealings with China without first talking it over with Japan. But never mind that . . . I am not afraid of China. I feel certain that Japan and China will not fight. Even our religion, Zen Buddhism, came from China. We will never fight. But it is not the same with Russia!"

It wasn't the same, I knew. Asians must stand together . . . and in the future they would.

"We do not like Russia," he continued. "Japan must never, never make a treaty with Russia until she has first settled the question of the northern Islands, Sakhalin and the Kuriles."

"What do you think about Prime Minister Tanaka cozying up to China . . . maybe even Russia, now?"

"He is making a big, big mistake! He should not be friendly with either of them at this time."

"How do you feel about the present relationship between Japan and the United States?"

"It's very wrong! Japan must become a completely independent nation. But the United States doesn't treat Japan as an independent nation. That is all very wrong!"

By the end of lunch we had moved into a less controversial field of discussion, when Mr. Hachiya discovered that Harry was a dedicated gardener like himself. Mr. Hachiya told us that he had been prominent in arranging for the Garden Club of America to visit Japan a year ago. At the end of the club's very successful visit the members donated to a fund to publish a guidebook in English called *Garden Plants in Japan*, in expression of their appreciation of Japanese hospitality extended to them. Mr. Hachiya promised to mail one of these to Harry in exchange for a copy of my *Three Came Home*.

In concluding the Garden Club discussion Mr. Hachiya described the visiting American ladies with their very high heels, short, tight, mini-skirts, hearty laughs, strong voices, good intentions and tireless enthusiasm, leading the way through the gardens of Tokyo with their footsore husbands trailing behind them, limp, sweating and exhausted.

When we left the restaurant Mr. Hachiya was happily reunited with his old felt hat and his equally time-honored overcoat, while the hatcheck girl bowed to him most respectfully as the just due of a real Japanese gentleman.

On reflection, I think the Hachiyas are unlike anyone else whom we have met here. This very dissimilarity is at least one quality all our Japanese friends have in common. We meet no duplicates. Every time my mind is made up about something, I have to unmake it again. And yet I find myself frequently using the same adjectives of description — delightful, charming, energetic, tireless, vital, courteous, hard-working. I would not use all those adjectives for most other nationalities or groups — for Libyans, Muruts, Dyaks, Bajaus, Tuaregs, North Americans. I might for some Filipinos.

25

~o~o~o~o~o~o~o~o~o~o~o~o~o~o~o~o~o~o~o~o~o~o~

G ETTING TO THE OUTSKIRTS of Tokyo was a nightmare of
stalled traffic, inching along with huge oil trucks, with
trailer trucks loaded with new Toyotas, with autos, buses, taxis,
bicycles, baby buggies and Hondas all crawling along together,
the occupants staring into each other's glazed eyes hour after
hour and wondering why they had come.

We wondered, too, until at last we began to creep through
some pleasant small villages where we saw cheery, healthy
faces beside the road, and ultimately in the fourth hour we
were bordering on Kamakura. About thirty-five miles south-
ward along the coast from Tokyo, the trip should have been
only an hour's easy drive but it took us four hours. Our driver
blamed it on the train strikes which have greatly increased
road traffic.

Along the way we asked the driver to locate a toilet stop of
some sort and after considerable sympathetic consideration he
turned in at a train station. Modestly located among the adjacent shrubbery I found three open, dirty, squat-holes. Harry

and the driver chivalrously stood out in front to warn away other customers. In such circumstances one doesn't linger.

The historic city of Kamakura nestles among steep evergreen hills on three sides and on the south side faces the limpid, today placid, waters of Segami Bay. The surroundings all exude a pleasant atmosphere of antiquity, serenity and orientalia as we follow the motor road between the bay waters and the old Japanese-style houses which perch on the edge of the hills defying gravity, termites and earthquakes. There are no factories here, and we felt an air of relaxation and unworldliness.

This was the seat of the Shogunate Government under Minamoto Yoritomo in the twelfth century and it is still the dead center of Buddhism and the home of the most beautiful *Daibutsu*, an Amida Buddha image, in Japan. This is cast in bronze, and stands in the precincts of Kotokuin Temple at Hase, Kamakura. Here, unsheltered, overwhelming and amiable, the gentle Daibutsu lives among a forest of pines and gazes toward the sea. Although this is not the largest Buddha, I think it is the most benevolent and amiable in expression and the most pleasing in art form, which many Buddhas are not. On the bay beyond Kamakura lies Hayama, where the imperial household has a summer palace, as the Segami Bay shoreline is the nearest, most convenient place in which to escape from the humid, hothouse heat of summer Tokyo.

As today, Saturday, was a holiday, the roads were lined with pedestrians and cyclists on the way to temple-viewing, swimming, boating and picnicking. Boys and girls went racing along, babies traveled on their mammas' backs, mammas trotted behind papas, while papas carried large paper shopping bags, the trademark of the country, bulging with picnic victuals, sake, spare diapers and pocket radios, and everyone looked festive and gay. I often marvel at the fact that the

Japanese always appear to look happy even though they may be stepping up to the very brink of a catastrophe, saying, "Excuse, please," as they do so.

Segami Bay waters are always full of sailing vessels. Many are large, obviously expensive yachts, as wealthy Tokyo executives keep their boats here and spend the summers in the shore cottages. Some large companies even maintain dormitories here in which their employees may summer. Less wealthy sailing fans also patronize the bay, and every type of floatable hulk may be seen as well as small, disreputable-looking craft for barefoot boys to putter about in and toy paper ships for wading toddlers.

We turned in for lunch at the Marina, a pretentious looking establishment with very poor food, we found. Our driver had lunch with us and he proved to be an interesting and surprising man. The differences among these people still astound me more than their similarities. Our driver, Fumiko, said that he had a Japanese friend who had traveled all over Canada and whose brother owned a Japanese restaurant in Toronto. Through his well-traveled friend Fumiko had gained a surprising knowledge and interest in Canada — enough so to ask us some informed questions that were better than our answers.

"What are the political differences between French Canada and English Canada?" he asked Harry.

"As far as I can understand it, it is chiefly a matter of language differences," Harry said, "and different standards of living. But heaven knows I'm no expert on politics!"

"Is it true that Canada may separate into two independent countries? Such a thing would seem terrible to a Japanese. Unthinkable!"

"I don't believe Canada will ever separate. I think the height of the separatism movement is passing."

"Do you prefer life in Canada to that in the United States?"

"We live in Canada because we have owned a home there for many years and it was the obvious place for us to settle when I retired. I have become a Canadian citizen and we are happy there."

"What is the cost of living in Canada compared to the States . . . or to Japan?"

"Basic living in Canada, food and housing and taxes, are more expensive than in the United States. But for a traveler, I think the cost of good hotels and meals is about the same in the three countries. But the difference here in Japan is that we get wonderful service included in what we pay. The custom of good service without tipping is a blessing. If for no other reason than this, and there are plenty of others, I'd recommend Japan to travelers."

"Here in Tokyo, what is the approximate cost of living for a working man?" I asked Fumiko. "Yourself, for instance?"

"I am forty-three years old," he said. "I am not married, but I own my own home."

"Isn't that unusual?"

"Yes. I am very fortunate. My home is in the poorest section of Tokyo and it is only one room with community kitchen privileges — but I *own* it. But still it costs me about ¥50,000 [U.S. $200 with yen at 250] a month to live."

"If you were married?"

"If I had a wife and two children I figure it would cost about double — or ¥100,000 [U.S. $400] a month."

"How much do the drivers in your company average a month?"

"We average about ¥100,000 and this includes bonus and extras. It's a good job; the company isn't bad."

"What do you do in your spare time?"

"I don't have much. I read — books, newspapers and sometimes *Time* magazine. And of course I am a devout Buddhist."

We all had the same meal which was listed as seafood salad but arrived minus seafood with a few scattered vegetables and no dressing. However there were, as always at any meal, bowls of good rice. Fumiko ate everything with industrious enjoyment, even the pieces of plastic pie that he and Harry ordered extra. He ate daintily, and I liked him. He was intelligent, dignified and self-respecting. Most Japanese, regardless of their profession or class, impress me as having those qualities. Yet I often see them referred to by Occidental writers as having an inferiority complex and lacking self-confidence. I do not think this is so.

Before we left the Kamakura area we revisited the Tsuru-gaoka Hachiman Shrine where Minamoto Yoritomo is enshrined. We then went one last time to say goodbye to the beautiful Amida Buddha nearby, whose calm and happy personality I so much admire. The shrines and temples in Kamakura, like those of Kyoto and Nara, gain interest and beauty because they blend into their hillside surroundings and lend to the natural landscape a supernatural element. One of their charms is that they are part of the everyday life of the people.

We got back to Tokyo about seven o'clock. The wind outside was very cold, the motorcar was very hot as the heating system was uncontrollable, and we were very tired. But we were sorry to say goodbye to Fumiko — one other person whom we would like to meet again, and probably never will.

Miss Nagano of the Japan Foundation is a tiny young woman dressed in an ultra-respectable brown tweed suit. She has a Dresden skin, an infectious laugh, well-waved hair and huge horn-rimmed spectacles. She arrived at the hotel with tickets to take us to the Unique Ballet Theater to see the "modern" Japanese ballet in which we had expressed interest.

231

A dancer in this company is the brother of a young man in the foundation who had described the new ballet to me as being ultramodern. He said that his brother adored dancing and was very enthusiastic about the new company and less interested in the salary than in the idealistic concept of the productions. He liked the freedom of the group of young artists to dance out their own ideas. Freedom and originality are the opposite of the qualities found in most Japanese dramatic art, which is almost completely traditional and performed within a given framework. I do not include the many Western style musical revues and modern Western dramas one finds here because they are in no way Japanese.

Fortunately, Miss Nagano called for us early as she did not have the specific address of the theater and knew only that it was in the Roppongi area. We started out in a taxi and drove about questioning various amiable pedestrians without finding anything that looked like a theater. Finally the driver delivered us to an unlighted office building and pointed to the rear entrance where some steps led down to a basement with a dimly lit doorway. This was it.

A number of smiling, whispering youngsters all dressed in blue jeans were standing in line at a basement window for tickets. Miss Nagano showed our tickets to a pretty girl usher, also in blue jeans, who led us carefully down a number of steep, narrow steps not designed for Western feet. Below in the dusk of the basement we found our seats and arranged ourselves on very small folding chairs. Harry and I are both narrow and Miss Nagano is almost invisible, but I would not advise any very fat people to travel in Japan.

Once seated we looked around at an incredibly small "Little Theater," with less than a hundred seats by my count. Before the show began every seat was occupied and people were standing at the back. There was no elevated stage and no curtain to rise, but the moment the music commenced there was absolute audience attention. The only other foreigners we saw were a handsome couple near us who, we thought, were South Americans.

The first half of the program, Miss Nagano told us, symbolized the passing of time, and some very pretty girls dressed in leotards, azure at the back and white in front, occupied the stage for ten minutes. The choreography was unremarkable, but the girls had lovely supple young bodies in spite of rather bulgy, muscular legs, and they danced as if they loved it. They were accompanied by uncontrolled bursts of canned music, with spasmodic switching off and on of stage lights.

Suddenly, dashing down the darkened steps behind us, came the prima ballerinas, a tallish boy and girl who were wrapped together in a spangled, glittering cape to look like a two-headed apparition with the boy's head facing forward and the girl's head looking behind. It was weird but effective. After reaching the center of the stage they gradually unwrapped themselves down to body tights, which are certainly the discovery of the century for young bodies. They were very attractive to look at and they staged a sprightly dance whose chief merit was in the dancers themselves. Throughout the program the enthusiasm of the performers and their dedication to dancing and to communicating with the audience was the outstanding feature.

Now came a fifteen-minute intermission during which all the performers turned to and changed the scenery which was pseudo-psychedelic and scanty. It was draped from the rafters and it required considerable effort and dexterity to shift. Ultimately the cast hung up some very large fishing nets to represent the sky.

This second episode was a lament for the Vietnam war. It opened with all the girls dashing onstage and hurling themselves down as if under bombardment. The music and assorted offstage noises were deafening and produced a terrifying effect of bombs bursting and artillery fire thundering and over all there came the unremitting moan of human sobbing, weeping, crying, screaming until the sum of the sounds became almost unbearable. And at that moment a chorus of men in black tights rushed to the weeping women and all danced together under spotlights. In the finale the lighting changed and nothing could be seen but the glowing white skeletons painted on the men's tights in phosphorus paint, making them seem to be fleshless corpses dancing.

The show was received with tremendous enthusiasm. This would have to repay the performers, I imagine, as there couldn't be much box office take in such a tiny house.

Tokyo surges with vitality. Nobody saunters or strolls (except us), nobody looks behind, nobody dares to lag. When I first came to Japan forty years ago I saw an old, old country being strangled by its traditions. In those days we Westerners saluted these picturesque islands in somber and affectionate admiration for their past antiquities, even while we accepted the fact that the golden era of Japan had passed.

How wrong we were! Today this is the most vital, forward-moving country in Asia, perhaps in the world. Out of the scorched black stretches left by the Second World War, out of the hideous wounds of the atom bombs, and the massacre of a generation of young men, out of the very soil of Japan made fertile by its own blood, has arisen the new prosperous state.

Yet this is only half a nation while its women are denied their proper place. There is the capacity here to be a supernation built on a superior race — but this will require both men and women working together with combined strength. This ultimate, all-out effort is something that women are not yet permitted to make.

Although Japanese women today only partially realize their power they already compete in their own way. And *if* they fail to come out on top it is often because they are too smart to do so. They are clever, cautious, gracious — and they know they need the men on their side. When you look into a Japanese woman's face, gently and permissively smiling, do not necessarily expect to hear her say Yes.

Many people tell me, and there is some truth in it, that I am meeting only the exceptional women here, women with education, some of whom have been abroad. They are able to think of themselves in terms we both understand. We do not need to talk about women's liberation. We accept ourselves as equal to the masculine sex, but content to be different.

Such women are an important growing minority in Japan now; they were rare exceptions twenty-five years ago. They are the proof of what the future can be. And when the time comes they will not be like North American women, for we don't really fit into Japan. We are strong where they will be pliant, forthright where they will be soft-spoken, intellectual where they will be intelligent. We will see only the journey's end, while they will be enjoying the journey. We are incurably Occidental; they are incurably Asian. But we are both women.

Our new interpreter, Tomoko, is clever, intelligent, decorative and charming. But we do miss Sachiko. We have been unable to meet her since our return to Tokyo. We have talked on the telephone several times and she speaks of still being ill and unable to go to the office. But this doesn't sound like the girl who went to Afghanistan to buy a coat, the stoic Sachiko we knew, to stay away from work, or to be unable to meet with us somehow, somewhere.

I wonder if we became too friendly while traveling and she was taken off our "case"? I wonder if Foreign Affairs was annoyed with us . . . with her? I wonder if it is policy to disrupt friendship with foreigners? But that is what we came for. Or is Sachiko really ill? We'll probably never know. I feel sure of one thing — while *in* Japan she is not a free agent. No Japanese woman is.

There is a long article in the newspaper today about the need for Japan to develop a nuclear self-defense. Alarm made me open my pocket atlas. It is true! When you look on the map you see that this country is physically indefensible from every point of view.* Nothing can defend her from Russia or China, for she simply has no place to go. And if Japan should choose to attack first as her own best form of self-defense, you need only to look at the map to see the vast territories of Russia and China into which their people can run for refuge, and know what the end must be.

Japan has rebuilt herself magnificently since 1945. Tremendous expenditures of energy and vitality have gone into creating new factories, office buildings and housing. Yet these are not fireproof nor bombproof nor earthquakeproof, and cannot be made completely so. It may all happen over again — as it has in the past. Even the ability of the newest, tallest Tokyo

---

* Location of Japan:
 Approximately 100 miles to South Korea across the Korea Strait to Pusan. 175 miles to Russian mainland from northwest tip of Hokkaido.
 Only 25 miles from north tip of Hokkaido to Sakhalin, Russian-occupied territory. Only a stone's throw from the east coast of Hokkaido to the small, Russian-occupied Kurile Islands, called the Northern Territory.
 500 miles to the China coast (Shanghai) from the southern tip of Kyushu, the southernmost Japanese island.
 Reference: Reischauer, *Japan Past and Present*, p. 275.
 Reference: *Japan Almanac*, 1972, p. 35.

buildings which are especially designed to be earthquake-resisistant still remains to be proved.

Fire is the waking nightmare of every dwelling owner. In every hotel room the first thing you see is the diagram of how to get to the nearest fire exit. The walls are hung with large printed notices telling you not to smoke in bed, and not to fall asleep while smoking. As most Japanese men are chain smokers the request is appropriate.

Everywhere you see constant reminders that after the earthquake in 1923, Yokohama and Tokyo were destroyed by fire. And in 1945 Yokohama, Tokyo, Hiroshima and Nagasaki were flattened to black ash in the fires from Allied bombs. All over the Japanese islands earthquakes and fires are traditional natural enemies. And in this twentieth century these islands continue to be indefensible against the bombs and missiles with which their enemies can precipitate fire.

Meanwhile, Japan is bravely and indefatigably achieving one of the greatest Gross National Products in the world, the speediest economic rate of growth, and the longest individual life span. Yet today she balances in the most precarious world position, awaiting a kiss or a kick. And, as Dr. Minami said about earthquakes, "We can only wait and see."

26

S HOJI TERAYAMA has the reputation of being so far left that
he is an anarchist. He is also the "funny guy" to whom
Shintaro Ishihara, the young author of *Season Of Violence*,
and presently a parliamentarian, referred us.

We were to meet in the cocktail lounge of the Keio Plaza
Hotel in Shinjuku, a gaudy, pretentious place, I thought, to
seek out an anarchist. A huge, new, sparkling palace, it is a
symbol of the present prosperity and a popular meeting place
for the young. Here the synonym for beauty is glitter, and the
lounges sparkled with glinting crystals, shimmering chandeliers
and mirrors flashing back more mirrors. The interior was the
work of a new young woman decorator, said Tomoko, who was
with us just in case we needed an interpreter.

Although the tiny tables in the huge cocktail lounge were all
filled with young people, Tomoko with unerring instinct led us
directly to one by the window which opened out on the elabo-
rately landscaped water gardens. At this table sat a modern,
smartly dressed young man with a huge briefcase and a tiny

Japanese girl. They were deep in conversation, but the girl tactfully got up to leave when the young man greeted us and asked us to sit down. This we did with some difficulty as the spindly little table had neither foot space underneath it nor elbow space on top for four quite large people.

Once wedged in we all eyed each other at close range with mutual curiosity. Mr. Terayama looked to be under thirty, with a round face, very low hairline, short-cut hair and brilliant, brittle, penetrating eyes. He wore a dark business suit, a chrome yellow shirt and a wide black and yellow striped silk tie — all very smart and far from cheap. For an anarchist he did himself pretty well by the Establishment. He showed less poise than Mr. Ishihara and was somewhat on the defensive. He made it obvious that he wasn't in a mood for social chitchat so we commenced immediately with questions we hoped to have answered.

It is almost fifty years since, as a reporter on the *San Francisco Examiner*, I interviewed strangers as I am doing on this trip. I hate doing it. I feel I am prying. Nevertheless there is no gracious way of asking people questions that they don't wish to be asked. If you must have the answers it is best to speak out and be blunt.

"Where are all the old people in this city?" I asked.

"Everybody is young in Shinjuku and Tokyo," he replied with a complacent look around him.

"Why does everybody in Tokyo run, rush and hurry?"

"Because we are young," he said proudly.

"But I read that this country now has an old age life span of seventy-five years for women and seventy-three years for men. Where are these old people?"

"Where they should be . . . home, watching television," he said rather smugly.

This was the second time I had been given this answer.

"What do young people think about the book *The Ecstatic One*?" I asked.

"Young people don't ever think about that book. They never expect to grow old," he said simply.

"By your own standard, when will *you* cease to be young and become old?"

He laughed then and said with a very attractive smile, "I am already considered old by the young ones — but I am young by *my* standards. You know that I write plays and poetry? I have been very popular. But I am already beginning to lose popularity . . . so . . ." he shrugged.

"They say that you are a radical left politician. What is it that you young radicals want to do?"

"We wish to destroy what is wrong with Japanese society. But not necessarily to destroy it *physically*. We dislike the whole rotten social structure. We condemn the government and the political system. We want it *all* done away with!"

"What will you replace it with?"

"Ah! But it is not our business to know the answer. We just destroy what is wrong. We will allow no interference with our own freedom. Young people feel the same in your country. They just want to do their own thing."

"Isn't that anarchy you are describing?"

"Yes, maybe. You old people always ask, If you destroy it, what will you replace it with? Young people always say, That is not our business!"

"Are you a Communist?"

"No."

"What is anarchy in relation to Communism?"

"We must have anarchy first — then we will see . . ."

As I saw no end to the argument, I tried a new subject. "What do you think of trial marriage?"

"Well . . . we have communes out in the country where men and women live and work together."

"I don't mean community living. I mean when individuals, a boy and a girl, live alone together as husband and wife without marrying. Does your society accept this?"

"Some people accept the idea, but not the fact. You know we have a comic strip magazine with stories about trial marriages? These comics are very popular with young people and they have been made into a TV show. This angers the older generation, as trial marriage offends *terribly* against all Japanese tradition. But why worry? Though young people may like the idea of trial marriage . . . not many would dare to try it. But they love that magazine!"

"I've heard of that comic strip and I'd like to buy a few of the magazines. Can you write down the name for me? Please write it in both English and characters."

"The name is *Dozei Jiday* by Kazuo Uemura," and he wrote down the title as I had asked, in English and in characters, and handed me the paper.

"What kind of plays do you write, Mr. Terayama? Please tell us something about them."

"They are all very modern. The audience enters into them and becomes part of the play. The audience must *live* the play — not just observe it. I like my plays . . . they speak for me."

"But you also write books?"

"Yes. But I hate books! I would like to burn all the books. The book I wrote is called *Throw Out the Books!* I'll send you a copy to read."

"Thank you," I said, admiring his ability to play on both sides. "By the way, do you think Communism is the answer for Japan?"

"No."

"Do you come here often . . . to this hotel, I mean?"

"Oh, yes. Young people all meet here."

"Will you destroy this place, too . . . when you destroy society?"

He picked up his bulging briefcase, tucked in his flowing yellow striped tie, adjusted his well-fitting jacket, bowed politely to us and instead of answering said, "I may be traveling in Canada this summer. Shall I come to see you?"

"Please do so. Here is our address in Victoria, and our telephone number. You will be most welcome."

We all shook hands and he departed. I hope if he does come to Victoria that I don't forget which angry young man he is.

In thinking about it afterward I decided that Shoji Terayama had probably missed his moment to destroy. He was now too well entrenched behind his bulging briefcase willingly to set the world in flames either to serve nihilism or any other ideology.

Both Terayama's denial of being a Communist, and his comments on it interested me. Everyone I spoke with about Communism said that it was not the answer for Japan. The strong family structure of the Japanese, their traditional values, and their entire code of behavior all denied the precepts of Marxism. But the fact remains that the parliamentary strength of the Communists is growing rapidly. The Communist party, the JCP, is now the third largest in the Diet lower house, and by far the best organized. The Japanese Socialist party, the second largest in the lower house and backed by the unions, now favors cooperation with the Communist group. A popular front composed of Communists with all left-wing parties, of which there are many only slightly distinguished from Communists, seems almost inevitable.

Almost inevitable. And yet at the same time there are strong

242

rumors, even a conviction, that radical changes in government are going to come from the right.

Komeito, a religious party emerging some time ago from the *Sokka Gakkai Buddhist* revival movement, has become a threat from the right. At first its religious fervor and other extreme features were reminiscent of the European Fascist movement, but these features it is now discarding. As it gains strength and growth *Komeito* has become more moderate and now aims to present a picture of sweet reasonableness. Perhaps it does so, as it is now the fourth strongest party in the lower house.

The Liberal Democrats are the dominant party, and the Socialist party is second, followed by the Communist party. The threat of the JCP is not just in its own membership but in the large number of other extreme left groups which are close to being Communist, and are certainly Marxist. The JCP is almost the only Communist group in the world which is not friendly with Russia *or* China. The JCP now professes to gain ascendency by parliamentary action and not by militant action.

The prewar goal of the JCP had been to abolish the "Emperor System" and stop the then "Japanese wars of aggression."

The party's present goal is, to quote the *Asahi Evening News*, "A new democratic revolution against two enemies — American Imperialism and the control of Japan by monopolistic capital." Although the party is not affiliated with any major Japanese labor unions, it has great influence on the Japanese Teachers Union and therefore on the young generation.

By the end of World War II, the Communist party had a membership of only 1,000. By 1972 it had 300,000. It is now affiliated with five other organizations whose total combined membership is 350,000. In 1973 the JCP has 38 seats in the

Diet lower house, and 10 seats in the upper house. The party has plenty of money, as its income is derived from the sale of the party newspaper, *Akahata* (Red Flag), and three periodicals. *Akahata* is reported to be the largest Communist newspaper publishing business in a capitalist country.

The Japan Communist Party Central School is located on a steep hillside surrounded by mandarin orange orchards near Atami City in Shizuoka Prefecture. Here it trains party leaders in a stiff, concentrated program which includes physical labor as well as academic studies. Its students range in age from the early 30s to gray-haired old age. Women are not refused but are greatly in the minority.

This party school does not appear to be responsible for the bloodthirsty indoctrinations of the excessively violent student and youth groups such as the *Rengo Sekigun* (United Red Army), the *Kakumaruha* (a revolutionary Marxist and Maoist faction), the *Hanteigakuhyo* (anti-Imperialist League), and others whose violent excesses and murderous methods discredit them with almost all Japanese. The Communist party now disowns all such groups and actions.

Although many capable, hard-working people in Japan have shared in the new prosperity, the level of living of many of its aged, its ill, its incompetent, muddled, or impoverished elder generation has scarcely been raised. Welfare programs, pensions, health insurance, and social security payments all depend on fulfilling stipulations, understanding reservations, calculating exemptions and exceptions, many of which it would require a legal expert rather than an aspiring pensioner to interpret. Merely to exist in misery without food or a roof overhead seems to be the least important qualification for obtaining government assistance.

Regardless of who should be doing what, this condition exists, and the Communist organization is trying to do something about it. In Tokyo they are helping to provide free medical clinics which are open day and night. They are fighting high-rise projects which close off sunlight in slum areas, and in the country they are resisting land speculation by large corporations.

People in the United States have fought long and hard to establish their Social Security benefits. I wonder who in Japan will fight to clarify the social security, pension and welfare situation so that the needy cease to starve? Now in 1973 a person of seventy years or over receives about $11 per month in welfare from the government. This, it is predicted, will go up ultimately to $17 monthly. These figures are subject to change — to be increased — it is hoped before too long.* As regards the National Pension Scheme, the majority of old people cannot collect *any* pension because they are required to have made more than twenty years of premium payments. It is easy to believe that poverty is the cause of most suicides among the aged.

A rally of old people was held recently in Hibiya Park, Tokyo. The spokesman for the aged called on the government to increase the pension from $11 to $100. He called, but no one answered.

Social security payments to recipients in Japan are a much smaller percentage of the Japanese GNP than are similar payments to elderly pensioners in Great Britain, which has the highest percentage payments in the world. In West Germany, France, and the United States, the percentage of the GNP paid to dependent persons is also much higher than in Japan.

It was publicly stated recently by the Modern General Research Group in Tokyo that, "the state of welfare in a country

* In 1974 the welfare payments to the aged were dramatically increased. The payments to needy families of four members were also raised to Y65,295, or about $217 monthly for four people.

245

is measured by the pension scheme adopted by the country." These are excellent words. Meanwhile humanists like Sawako Ariyoshi record the sordid facts in *The Ecstatic One.*

Of all the people I talked with in Japan I found no one to disagree that the poor, the aged and the ill were in crucial need of help. The only thing lacking was the help.

Several times we have asked Jiro to bring his wife Ineko to the hotel some evening to have dinner with us, as we are very anxious to meet her. But he always backs away from the suggestion. Obviously she exists in a separate compartment of his life, as we probably do, too.

He dropped in this evening and I asked what he thought of Ishihara's *Season Of Violence* and the *Taiyozoku*, the Sun Tribe described in the book.

"There are brutes like that in every country," he said hotly. "Those kids are not typical of Japan. You have motorcycle gangs in the United States who murder each other in the same beastly way. They are only proof of the worst side of human nature. I don't think that Ishihara should write about them as if they were a normal manifestation here. They are not normal."

"What about the *Rengo Sekigun*, the United Red Army?"

"They're thugs of the very worst type and far from being typically Japanese. They wish only to destroy. There are only about three hundred of them and they are very unpopular. They are hoodlums!" he said indignantly. "They're some of the brutes who massacred those people at the Lod Airport in Tel Aviv. No decent Japanese feels anything but disgust at their behavior. In 1970 they skyjacked that JAL plane and ended in Pyongyong, North Korea. They're still there; they've never been tried. They are fanatics and sadists first . . . and revolutionaries second. They tortured and murdered thirteen of their own gang who were disloyal . . . one was a pregnant girl. The frightening thing is that the *Rengo Sekigun* began among extreme radical university students in Osaka. One of the leaders was a girl. What are these young people coming to!"

"You don't think of yourself as belonging to the young generation any more?"

"Not *that* generation!"

Before he left I told him of my desire to meet Osama Suga, and the reason behind it and of my failure to do so. When I finished I asked him what he thought about it and if I should have gone directly to the house in Hiroshima regardless of the occupant's denial of identity. He listened to me attentively and made no comment for several minutes. I thought he might be going to offer to try to get in touch with Suga for me. Instead he said at last, "The war was a long time ago in Japan. We all wish to forget."

27

~~~~~~

THE FIRST THING to say about Taizo Kato is that he is a very attractive man. About forty years old, he has a warm, outgoing personality and a wonderfully tolerant, alive face which is responsive to every spoken word and to his own thoughts. He has bushy, coal black hair cut short, twinkling eyes, a square, bony face marked by deep, thoughtful lines. Not boyish at all, he impresses me as being mature and very vigorous. He was wearing a bulky, beige turtleneck sweater of Icelandic fleece like the one Harry wears at home, with gray slacks and sandals. He looked to be the well-dressed man of any country at his ease at home.

We had had difficulty in locating the house of this "wonderful fellow" whom Shintaro Ishihara had arranged for us to meet. Our car meandered all over the western section of Tokyo, searching for the address Mr. Ishihara had given us. But street names and numbers have little relation to locations, as Tokyo residents themselves agree, and taxi drivers, like detectives, must wander from clue to clue. But they don't give up easily, and in the depth of an apparent ghetto our driver jumped out and dashed into a small food shop whose amiable proprietor said, "Sodeska!" at hearing the name of Taizo Kato. He then supplied us with directions by waving his arms around, a system which our driver evidently understood, and ultimately we arrived at a modern-looking stucco house partially enclosed by a high white wall.

The door was opened by a pleasant, middle-aged Japanese woman wearing a gray sweater and tweed skirt. She invited us to enter and we abandoned our shoes and slid into the habitual fuzzy red slippers. Encumbered with these we stumbled up two flights of very narrow stairs to the third floor, with my slippers falling off at every step. I can think of no action less graceful than picking up your slippers from the step below you on a narrow stairway.

At the stair top Mr. Kato was waiting for us with a friendly, if quizzical, smile. He led us into his study and, although the rest of the house was freezing cold, the study had achieved a passable degree of warmth with an electric heater. The walls of the small room were lined with bookshelves all closely packed with books, some in Japanese and others in foreign languages.

Generally speaking, the people we go to see have no idea why we come, what we are doing in Japan, or why we wish to speak with them, and almost certainly they have never heard of the Japan Foundation. This makes it difficult for me to find any graceful opening to match the courtesy with which we are unfailingly met. Every time we head for a meeting I think this matter over without finding any solution. Today I merely trusted to the tolerance that Mr. Kato showed in his face to forgive any crudity in my questions.

As I knew that he lectured on Social Changes at the University of Tokyo, I started with a question to which everyone gives a different answer. "Today, young people everywhere are restless," I said, "dissatisfied and rebellious. You deal constantly with young people. Can you tell me what they really want? What are they after?"

He answered promptly and with equal bluntness, "One day I asked my class: What do you young people really want? They answered me: We want freedom! I asked them: Freedom from what? They said: Freedom to do what we want to do. So what do you want to do, I asked. They were silent, they were puzzled and uncertain . . . and finally they just said: We don't know what we want to do. I think their own uncertainty frightens them."

"I have been told that you have lectured in the San Francisco area to university students and talked with many different groups of young people all over the United States. Can you make a comparison between young Americans and young Japanese?"

"I find that American students are more self-reliant and independent than Japanese students. They are no more intelligent, certainly, but I think they study harder throughout their university years. You look surprised but this is true. Japanese youngsters work to a great extreme to pass their entrance examinations . . . their whole future life depends on passing, but after they are *in* the university they fool around, or maybe riot a bit in a last desperate plea for independence, I suppose. But when their last year comes they give up rebellion and fall quietly in line and wait politely for a suitable company to select them, after which they have it made. It is not like this with French students. They graduate from rebellion into an active state of revolution. But there is your American student . . . he graduates into a void, with plenty of book knowledge and little desire or opportunity to use it."

"What about the *Kakumaruha* . . . aren't they violent revolutionaries?"

"The *Kakumaruha* are a student revolutionary Marxist faction who have caused a lot of trouble at Waseda University. They even lynched a student who opposed them. But they are only a small group of young men, and there is also a strong anti-*Kakumaruha* group. Generally speaking, I am correct in saying that most students are quite finished with rioting and violence by the beginning of their last university year."

"Some of your young people that I have talked with," I said, "tell me that their generation hates the word *tradition*. It turns them off, they say. Yet in the holiday week after exams we saw crowds of youngsters sightseeing temples and shrines all over Japan. Doesn't this show a reverence for tradition?"

"No. It is not from respect or reverence that they visit such places. They go to temples and shrines just as they would go to any amusing or exotic foreign form of entertainment. It is someplace to go . . . but not because these places are part of their own religious tradition. Most Japanese today are atheists."

"One of the facts here that strikes us Westerners as most inexplicable is the very high suicide rate among young Japanese. Can you give me any reason for this?"

"They cannot face reality, that's one reason. As you know, the children in Japan — especially boys — are terribly spoiled at home. They are completely protected by their mothers and they have no idea of the realities of life. When they ultimately leave home and are faced with reality, many of them cannot face it."

"I have heard that said before. Can you give me an example?"

"Yes. We have one young man in the university now who comes from a very small village outside Tokyo. Almost immediately after arrival at the university he developed a nervous breakdown. It was my job to question the boy to find out what was behind his trouble. We studied his condition and he told us that he had always slept with his mother until his last year in high school. This is not an unusual condition, you know. We found that it was impossible for this boy to make any friends on his own."

"Not even in his own village?"

"We asked him about this and he said his grandmother had always told him with whom he should be friends. He had never tried to make his own friends. Yet this was a very intelligent boy and physically well able to be on his own away from home. But emotionally he was still a small child."

"Yet your young people always seem — on the surface anyway — gay, happy, laughing," I said. "They look to be the last group that would welcome death. Isn't this a contradictory attitude?"

"To you, it is. But that is based on the difference between yourselves and us. You Westerners refuse to accept death, while we Japanese accept it as part of life. Its acceptance is part of our philosophy. Remember, we are a people of great extremes. Also, we are able to believe two quite contradictory facts at the same time." He smiled at me, quite at ease with an idea that was confusing to me.

I had observed before the Japanese ability to believe in contradictory facts, but to have it put to me as reasonable by this young intellectual . . . well, my Western logic still choked on it. However, I understood what he meant when he spoke of Japanese willingness to submit to death for I had seen this demonstrated many times in other Oriental peoples. As to our Western refusal of death and our tenacious struggle against it, I suppose our Christian faith itself is based hopefully on belief in the life everlasting and the world without end. Life is the goal, not death.

"There's something else I wanted to ask you," I said. "You know that the curse of the American youth generation is the drug culture, the abuse of drugs. But Japanese young people are almost the only youth group that has managed to escape the use of drugs. Why is this?"

He laughed. "Japanese youngsters would use drugs, too, if they could get them. The fact is that they cannot get them in Japan. Our government is very strict about drugs."

"You are the first person I have talked with who thinks it is primarily inability to get drugs that keeps your youngsters outside the drug culture, and not their natural good sense."

He laughed again and said, "I know young Japanese! Why do you think your Western young people use drugs?"

The answer was obvious. "Because they can get them."

He came down to the street door to see us off. I had the feeling as we said goodbye that I had met him many times before in many different lands. I couldn't possibly imagine this civilized man as doing any of the cruel things that our Japanese captors had done during our captivity in the war. Cruel things that some of us may also have done to them.

As soon as we were seated in the Orchid Room the dark, intense little Japanese leader of the three-piece musical combine came to our table with his mandolin and began playing his favorite tune, "Mack the Knife." This is next in popularity here to "Happy Birthday." The members of the Oriental combine dress in vermilion-colored monkey jackets and play Occidental tunes with forced smiles and tired rhythms. They work long hours without overtime pay, so the leader has already whispered in my ear. Heaven knows that they all look underfed in contrast to their overfed audiences. On their five minute mid-evening break they sit grumbling outside in the hall with instruments dropped, shoulders slumped, eyes down in attitudes of despair, plotting how to get even with the parsimonious management and still keep their jobs. Then one by one with dismal steps and desperate smiles they file back to their task of gaiety.

There are few things that make Harry more uncomfortable than being singled out and played at, yet the well-intentioned little leader plays to us regularly, chiefly because we are the most regular Orchid Room customers. As always he hangs over the table and urges us to make "a request" to which Harry always says "Next time," less from penury than dislike of being in the spotlight.

Tonight we have guests and, seeing this, our musical friend is more determined than ever to give us a treat. Fortunately Muriel and Leo respond graciously to "Mack the Knife," and Harry's look of boredom is not too obvious. The fact that we have been staying here for longer than the three days which most foreign travelers remain in a Tokyo hotel makes Harry and me noticeable.

Leo Pickles is chancellor of the British embassy and has lived in Japan for many years. He is an excellent Japanese scholar and a well-informed student of Asian affairs. His wife Muriel is English and very charming, with a lovely voice and laugh and a quick sense of humor. She is, incidentally, a very handsome blonde, but appearance is not the quality one thinks of first with a really charming woman.

We had hoped that Sachiko would be with us for dinner but at the last moment she telephoned to say that she had not yet recovered from the effects of flu and our travels and was still at home from work. We were very disappointed not to see her again. It seems to me that we have started many happy relationships here that we would like to continue with, but probably never will.

In discussing our travels with Leo and Muriel, we told of the many helpful and informative meetings we had while traveling and also here in Tokyo. They were surprised at the number of stimulating and outspoken people we had managed to talk with, thanks to the combined efforts of the Japan Foundation, Foreign Affairs and ourselves. Muriel said we had met more "exciting" Japanese since we had been here than she had in eighteen years in the embassy. I think embassy lives are almost completely hedged in by embassy requirements and contacts are always made within a small circle and at a diplomatic level. Leo, for instance, works extremely hard and most of his time is spent in obligatory prearranged meetings that have to do with embassy affairs. He is another scholastically very well-informed person who *should* write a book . . . and probably never will.

Next day —

To my surprise I had a phone call from Mr. Nishiberi last evening. He was full of apologies for not having seen more of me in the past weeks. He said he was about to make an appointment for me with a famous playwright, and he would take me there himself. He would call me up the next day. I thanked him and said that I would like this. I don't expect to hear from him again.

28

∿∿∿∿∿∿∿∿∿∿∿∿∿∿∿∿∿∿∿∿∿∿∿∿∿∿

THIS AFTERNOON at Sophia University we met the handsome Canadian Jesuit priest, Father Conrad Fortin. I had commented previously to him over the telephone that I found many apparent likenesses between young Japanese and young Canadians. He had dissented instantly and fervently. Now, meeting him in person, I modified my comment by saying that perhaps I could not judge just how deep these resemblances went. Would he give me his opinion?

He would. "You are completely wrong!" he said. "Any apparent resemblance is entirely superficial. Japanese young people don't have either the stamina or the strength that Western youngsters have. Japanese lads work extremely hard to pass their entrance examinations to get into the university, but after that they do as little work as possible. They cut classes, fool around, and generally just wait for the time to come in their last year to be chosen for their 'family' job. That is their predestined niche in the social structure. This appointment in youth assures them of a lifetime job and paternal care from the hierarchy above them. There's nothing comparable to this in

Canada or the U.S., and our North American youngsters know it."

I looked at him in surprise, as somehow I had expected him as their mentor to be a strong advocate of Japanese youth. Especially so as I had listened to many testaments to the diligence of Japanese students.

"You sound a bit fed up," I suggested.

"No, they are delightful people. But I am just telling you the facts about the kids. I've been here eighteen years and I ought to know."

Reverend Conrad Fortin, S.J., M.A., is a French Canadian professor of French literature at the Jesuit-staffed Sophia University in Tokyo and he is Director of the Canadian Information Center in Japan. In asking him for an interview I had thought he would be a good counterbalance to Taizo Kato, and he was. A noticeably handsome man of forty-five years, well-built, well-dressed in civilian clothes today, Father Fortin looks like someone who is used to leading and being followed. Like Taizo Kato he has charming manners and much personal magnetism.

He seated us in an empty schoolroom and then proceeded to interview me.

"What are you doing in Japan?"

"I am here under the Japan Foundation. I am trying to draw comparisons between Japan as it is today and Japan of forty years ago and of twenty years ago. Without hurting any feelings, I hope, as the object of the foundation is to promote understanding between our nations."

He looked skeptical and asked, "How long have you been here?"

"This visit, six weeks."

He looked more skeptical but added kindly, "Well, good luck. So why did you wish to see me?"

"Because I know you are in touch with young people here."

"What do you know about Sophia University?"

"Very little, except that it has been established for some time and is a Jesuit institution with a fine scholastic reputation."

"We are a private Catholic institution," he said, "but operated on Japanese lines. Our total enrollment is ten thousand students — coeducational. It is not easy, as all schools and universities in Japan are overflowing now. This year we received twenty-two thousand applications for new entries. We could accept only two thousand. That tells you something about us. Our standards are high."

"I have a friend in the Japan Foundation who was a student here," I said, thinking of Su Ogino. "He's very bright and attractive and ambitious."

"What do you think of our establishment here?"

"Well . . . the buildings are a bit dreary looking . . . but I expect they're functional," I said, repressing my first impression that the place looked like a red brick prison.

He looked surprised at my lack of enthusiasm and said, "These buildings are excellent for their purpose. Of course today is a holiday and there are no youngsters dashing about. Perhaps the empty halls do seem a bit gloomy."

"And cold," I said. "But when we were looking for you we noticed a very pretty little chapel outside with what seemed to be a wedding party waiting. A good-looking young man in a neat black suit, and a pretty girl dressed in a white wedding gown with a long white train and veil, and some weedy looking lads in cutaways . . . they were all standing just outside the chapel doorway. A wedding?"

"Oh, yes. We have seven or eight weddings a week in that chapel. Not for its religious significance, but because it is such a pretty little building."

258

"You spoke of the Japanese boys as lacking stamina. Why is that?"

"I attribute this condition to their poor diet. Although the diet is better now than it was twenty years ago, it is still very poor compared to that of young North Americans. I've coached many athletic events here both in the university and outside and I've been shocked at the utter lack of physical vitality and resistance of young Japanese athletes. I've also coached their athletes for the Olympic Games and found that even they were terribly lacking in staying qualities compared to competitors from almost any other country. It is definitely the diet. Here they live from meal to meal and the food just cannot support prolonged physical effort at top performance."

"I suppose that as you are in a private Catholic institution you are not troubled by riots?"

"On the contrary . . . we have had very serious student riots . . . extremely violent ones inspired by a small radical Marxist group. These riots continued all through last year and they aren't over with now.* Some of our Jesuit Fathers were seriously injured by the rioters and are still suffering from the effects."

"Can you get redress from the government for injuries?"

He shook his head in frustration and said, "It's almost impossible to get any action on behalf of the injured Fathers because of the complicated structure of university responsibilities. Without doubt these riots are Communist inspired. The Communist party is growing steadily stronger . . . but only a small percentage of the students engage in the riots. However, the great majority of students are completely passive and will take no stand — either for or against. This passivity on their

---

* Some time later a Japanese professor from Sophia University who was studying in France was expelled from France for having some connection with the Red Army, *Rengo Sekigun.*

part is more proof of their immaturity in comparison to Western students. Young Canadians at least line up on one side or the other."

"How do you explain this immaturity in your students? What is the cause?"

"They are almost all overly sensitive. They require constant babying along. They are brought up by doting, overpossessive mothers who prepare them for a world that does not really exist. When they finally leave the family womb to struggle for themselves they just cannot face up to the realities they find."

"Taizo Kato said much the same thing. And he said that one important cause of youthful suicides was this same inability to face reality. There is something else I want to ask you. I see a tremendous change in the pattern of the lives of Japanese women today . . . comparing them to twenty years ago. What do you think about this?"

"I disagree completely. There is no basic change. You have been talking to the wrong women!"

"They can't all be the wrong ones. We've been talking with women of many different types in many parts of Japan . . . not only single, working women, but married women. We found that many of them are interested in matters outside the home and they could be self-supporting if need be. I admit this probably isn't the majority of Japanese women but it is a very important minority."

He shook his head as he said, "You've just met the exceptions, that's all. It's not that the girls aren't smart . . . some of my best students are girls. But that doesn't mean girls are smarter than boys, although some may be, but they just work harder. Of course Japanese women have always had a great deal of concealed power in the home, but it is always exerted indirectly."

"I'll bet you, Father Fortin," said Harry, "that four or five years from now women's lib. will be a factor to be reckoned with here."

"I disagree! I disagree! All that the girls here are interested in is marriage . . . and marriage still has to be arranged by a go-between." Then looking at me and shaking his head with tolerant disapproval, he said, "You can't possibly collect enough information in a short visit here to enable you to make any accurate comments on conditions."

"Perhaps so, but for us this is only one of many visits to Japan over a period of forty years. During all that time we have met the Japanese people repeatedly in changing circumstances. We've known them as their guests and also as their hosts, we have been their prisoners and their conquerors . . . and now, I hope, their friends. I don't want what comes from this final meeting to be either prejudiced *or* sycophantic. I just would like to find the truth. Nothing else is worth writing."

"Well, I've been here eighteen years now. Perhaps when I've been here *longer* I'll think I know enough to write a book."

"In that case you'll probably never write a book. By the time you spend a year writing it and another year getting it published, what you know will be out of date," I suggested.

"I understand that you are very active as Director of the Canadian Information Center," Harry said. "Can you tell us about some of your activities?"

"Every summer I take a group of about thirty students on a two-and-a-half-month tour of Canada. A month of this is usually spent in some Canadian summer school — a great help to the boys with their English."

"How much does this cost?"

"About sixteen hundred dollars per student all in — travel, everything. We arrange that the young people live in Canadian

261

family homes and I find that they almost always continue their friendships by letters with these families long after they return to Japan. A trip of this sort has tremendous value for the boys. They never forget it."

We left the university feeling that Father Fortin was a fine man and an ardent Canadian, and one who was fulfilling his scholastic responsibilities well. He had the self-confidence and authority necessary to lead young people to an orthodox goal. I believe that after he leaves Japan he will discover that his years in Asia have profited him as much as he now sees that contact with the Western world profits his young students.

It is impossible not to compare these two educators, Taizo Kato and Father Fortin. Both are intelligent, well-educated, well-informed and in a position to know and understand young people. But each one of them looks at the same world through different lenses. One seems unconscious of his race, the other wears his race on his shoulder; one is searching for truth, the other is convinced that he has found it. Both hold strong views but have different ways of expressing them. It is in the manner of expression that the difference in their racial cultures shows.

The Canadian Father seems opinionated compared to Taizo Kato and to other Japanese with whom I have discussed controversial subjects. Father Fortin enjoys bluntly refuting any opinion which challenges his own. By contrast, Taizo Kato, and most Japanese, put forward any contrary opinion they have without bluntly negating the opinion that has just been expressed. This avoids an atmosphere of confrontation — something which the Japanese greatly abhor, and Occidentals seem to enjoy. A Japanese will not answer Yes, or No; or Good or Bad. The Japanese approach makes it easier to accept a correction pleasantly and avoids anybody being wrong, but the truth may sometimes get lost.

To our surprise and pleasure our friend Jiro turned up last evening bringing his wife, Ineko, to have dinner with us. Social engagements are seldom made far ahead in Japan and we were not surprised by the short-notice acceptance of our standing invitation. I suspected that Ineko had insisted on her husband bringing her, as at first he was not his usual easy self.

Ineko impressed me as being rather shy, but poised in her manner and not lacking self-confidence. I felt she was totally sincere with herself but not necessarily so with us. She seemed less Westernized than Tomoko or Sachiko, I supposed because of her three years of Japanese wifehood which had intervened since her U.S. college days. But soon I decided that she was just being cautious at a first meeting, as it was obvious in her manner and attitude to her husband that she had lived outside of Japan.

She had the new generation figure, which is marked by greater length from the waist down and more shapely, usable legs. Like many of Tokyo's chic young women, she emphasized the slant of her eyes with eyeliner and made the oval shape of her face an asset. Her clear, almost honey-colored skin had a very slight suntan and was untouched by makeup. She had the natural look which her mother probably never had nor wanted.

As Jiro was maintaining a glum silence I said to Ineko to make conversation, "Tomorrow I'll be shopping for some suitable presents to take home to friends. Can you make any suggestions about where to look and what to buy?"

"Most Americans want to buy cultured pearls and cameras in Japan," she said promptly.

"Much too expensive for us."

"Is the gift for a lady? Perhaps a fine *furoshiki?*"

"Good idea . . . it's traditionally Japanese."

"You know that anything 'traditionally Japanese' is more expensive now," said Jiro, "than something imported from the West. Of course it would be easy if you were bringing a gift from the States to a Japanese girl . . . just bring some Levi's, a Maidenform bra and some pantyhose!"

Ineko laughed and said, "Jiro is right. The girls are crazy for those. Actually the only cheap things in Japan today are Western-style products manufactured in our own factories, such as electric appliances — electric kettles, toasters, TV sets, radios, washing machines — they're all cheaper and better here in Japan."

"But those won't do Mrs. Keith any good as gifts," reminded Jiro. "What about a piece of good coral . . . or a Japanese doll . . . or a lacquer box, or a piece of cloisonné? Or a book about growing *bonsai*? They're crazy about *bonsai* in the States."

"I always go to Mitsukoshi for gift shopping," said Ineko. "They have best-quality goods and they wrap their gifts beautifully. We in Tokyo value a gift from Mitsukoshi. Of course I never go there to buy anything for myself . . . too expensive! I go to Akihabara, a discount center, you know."

Jiro looked his disapproval at this frank statement and said defensively, "Ineko has a very well-equipped modern electric kitchen . . . and that's still quite a luxury in Japan. She even has a portable dishwasher."

"I know, Jiro, and all that saves time," she said quickly. "But what can I do with the time I save? Mrs. Keith, a woman in Japan has nothing to stimulate her in her life at home. It was all right for my mother because she needed all of her day just to prepare meals on her charcoal *hibachi* and her *kamado*, and to care for the children. But it isn't all right for me. I know I can do something more interesting . . . better . . . with my time . . . anyway, I'm bored to death now!"

I had the feeling that Ineko had been saving this up for some time and possibly she wanted to put Jiro on the spot by speaking out before us. I sympathized with her frustration but I was embarrassed for him.

"What would you like to do?" I asked.

"I'm not certain. I studied journalism at college and I always thought I'd like to try that. But here in Japan they wouldn't take a married woman on a magazine staff."

"Anyway, you couldn't possibly take a full-time job," Jiro interrupted indignantly. "Who'd take care of Taro and me? Japan isn't like the States where parents are content to let their babies be raised by babysitters and everybody eats TV dinners. Mothers here are expected to bring up their children themselves . . . and properly, too. You knew that when you married me."

"I know," Ineko agreed, "but I didn't know how dull it would be! Sometimes I almost wish for something bad to happen . . . sooner than just *nothing* happening. It isn't that I don't love Taro. I do . . . but sometimes I get tired of him."

"Do you ever think of having another child?"

"No," they both said together. Ineko added, "Japan is already overpopulated." While Jiro said, "And anyway, we have a son."

"How old is Taro now?" I asked.

"Almost three years."

"Perhaps before long you could put him in a nursery school for the mornings. Then you'd have time to yourself to try some freelance writing," I suggested, but without any real expectation of finding a solution.

"But what is there to write about . . . living as I do?" said Ineko.

"You could write about the problems of a Western-educated Japanese wife."

"Japanese journals wouldn't be interested. All they want is happy housewife items . . . how to market cheaply, holiday recipes, festival descriptions . . . and how to please your husband," she said.

"And you don't know much about those things!" Jiro snapped.

"Ineko, your English is excellent," said Harry. "Why don't you write an article about a Western-educated Japanese wife and try it out on an American journal? Don't discourage her, Jiro. U.S. periodicals pay quite well."

"I suppose she'll do what she wants in the end," said Jiro. Then more gently, "Of course I want her to be happy, but a wife having a career just doesn't work in Japan, at least not yet. Maybe for an unmarried woman, yes . . . there are plenty of Western-educated career women. But for a wife, no!"

"That's because wives here are too lazy about using their minds," said Ineko. "It's easier not to . . . and men don't want us to. They say that the ideal bride knows just enough to talk intelligently with her husband . . . providing he stays home long enough to hear what she has to say . . . but not enough to have ambitions for herself."

"Let's go down to the Orchid Room," said Harry tactfully, "and order dinner. The orchestra leader will be waiting to play 'Mack the Knife.' "

Before we said goodnight that evening Jiro assured us as he had before that, "You do understand that we wouldn't talk like this with Japanese friends? It's just that . . . that . . ."

"That you know you'll never see us again? Yes, we do understand."

We watched them hurry off across the wide hotel lobby holding hands like young lovers, stopping a second to admire the cherry tree in the center, then turning gaily to wave back

266

to us. No matter what their problems, I thought, the world lay before them, for they were young.

"Look at them!" Harry said. "They'll never get over those years in the States. He'd never have brought her tonight except for that."

"And she would never have wanted to come."

29

〜〜〜〜〜〜〜〜〜〜〜〜〜〜〜〜〜〜〜〜〜

O NE OF THE TRAGEDIES of the "forgotten" war is the number of unmarried women now in their late forties who
were of marriageable age during and just after the war. At that
period able-bodied, unattached young men did not exist in
Japan. Instead, there were the hero dead, the white boxes of
ashes, the wounded and maimed and blind, the nuclear victims — but few suitable bridegrooms. Today Japan suffers the
quiet tragedy of a generation of women who have been passed
over as wives.

Chiyo, the elder of the sisters, is a handsome woman with a
perfect oval face, delicately modeled features of traditional
Japanese beauty, and long jet hair dressed in the old style. Last
evening she was wearing a kimono and carrying a *haori*, both
in pale pearly grays. I thought she resembled the idealized
female of the eighteenth-century artist Kitagawa Utamaro, but
I soon found that she was far from eighteenth century in her
life-style.

She teaches art and ceramic design in a Tokyo upper secondary school, the equivalent of our high school, and last evening

she brought me a beautiful pale yellow and green medallion of trees which she had made. She also brought her school yearbook with photographs of her classes and students, who looked to me incredibly like our own American youngsters in their schoolrooms. They had the same temporarily serious and dedicated expressions which one knew would vanish into laughter with the sounding of the bell.

Chiyo had made notes in English in the page margins about hours of study, subjects and other facts she thought would interest us such as the following. School attendance is obligatory after six years of age and until fifteen years, and almost all children attend. By upper secondary school age (fifteen and up), students begin to specialize, and courses fall into many different categories. These categories are technical, commercial, agricultural, fishing, domestic arts, fine arts, and science-mathematics. The percentage of girls in the upper secondary is much smaller than of boys.

These notes were made in English for our benefit, although Chiyo says she doesn't "speak" English. We also learned that she is extremely interested in politics in relation to social conditions, in a form of state Socialism which is not far removed from Communism, but does not consider itself such. She has no desire to visit North America, but is saving her money to go to Russia on a travel tour this summer.

Isoko, the younger, has short waved hair and a round smiling face. She was wearing the same tweed skirt, knitted jersey and red coat that she wore at our previous meeting, and looking like any little American business girl. Unlike Chiyo she wears the kimono only at home. She had just come from the large Tokyo hospital where she works as a dietician. Both women commute to their jobs via the underground transit system, a journey that requires an hour at rush time. They have one day off a week.

Isoko is full of vitality and energy, studies piano and has a piano in her home. She also has a *koto*, a favorite Japanese six-stringed instrument which is played with plectrums attached to the fingers and has a tone similar to a piano. When I asked her what she did for amusement, she answered simply that she played her *koto* and her piano.

Their mother, a widow, owns a small home in the center of Tokyo city. Here she and her two daughters, her son, who is divorced, and his small daughter all live together. They are fortunate, they say, to have a place to live in the city, which is now impossibly overcrowded. In Tokyo there are ten times as many people per square yard as there are in London, and land there, I am told, costs twice what it costs in Manhattan. As the sisters describe their lives to me their faces are cheerful, and there is no whine in their tones as they tell of a routine which would impress most North American women as dull drudgery.

Isoko visited Canada last year with a group of dieticians who came to North America to study Western hospital management, which she found was conducted on an extravagant scale compared to that in Japan. She discovered that the Japanese hospital diet would never have been accepted outside of Japan, but that considering the daily home diet of most patients, it was what they were accustomed to. She spent a week with friends on Vancouver Island. Her first comment to them on seeing their acre and a half of Canadian homeland was, "Does all this space really belong to just you two?" The spaciousness of Canadian living was unbelievable to her after Japan.

Harry and I had previously decided to take the sisters to dinner at a restaurant on the other side of the city, chiefly because we enjoyed the charm of the glittering night drive across Tokyo. The restaurant looked out on a sunken garden, the food and wine were good, and the room was always humming pleasantly with people of all nationalities.

But tonight the garden was there but no diners. We asked the headwaiter what the trouble was, and he said that the establishment was a BOAC overnight stop and the money crisis had cut off the flow of tourists. The gloom thickened as he spoke. The dapper, anxious little man kept hovering over us and urging extra servings and special tidbits. At last a young couple came in, she Japanese and he European, and they were speaking French and having fun. This got the headwaiter off our backs while he went through the elaborate hospitality dance for the arrivals. They were young and brought gaiety and laughter with them, and good appetites, and it lightened the gloom of the restaurant.

Diligently we ate our way through every course — minestrone, fresh shrimps, veal steak, ices and cheese, cheered on by a good wine. But even the wine didn't seem to cheer Harry who ate almost nothing and for some unexplained reason scarcely talked at all, although he is the one who usually keeps things going. I think he was disappointed by the atmosphere of the deserted restaurant — which his own silence didn't help. Perhaps he felt the evening wasn't going well and didn't know what to do about it so he withdrew from it. Anyway, our guests, not knowing Harry well, probably thought that he *never* talked nor ate!

We managed to communicate fairly well considering that the sisters claimed they didn't speak English and I certainly didn't speak Japanese. They were patient in their determination to make me understand choice pieces of information they felt would interest me, such as the school curriculum, the extreme overcrowding of most schools, the eagerness of the children to learn, and the methods of homemaking which were stressed for the girls. They worked diligently to get the facts

271

into my head either by English or with gestures. Soon we were all using pocket dictionaries and diagraming characters on the tablecloth with our fingers. Harry was helpful here as he has studied Chinese and many Chinese characters are used in the Japanese syllabary.

Before we said goodnight our friends had invited us to visit their home on Sunday — our last Sunday in Tokyo. Isoko, knowing the difficulty of finding addresses in Tokyo, offered to come herself by subway to our hotel and escort us back. I was very anxious to accept her offer, as invitations to foreigners to Japanese homes are very rare, but we already had appointments for Sunday with Mr. Honma and Father Fortin, and we had to refuse. The sisters urged us to change our minds and seemed puzzled at our continued refusal. Making social appointments for some days ahead is not a Japanese habit, and probably they had not anticipated that we would be unable to accept. Perhaps they were relieved that we couldn't come, Sunday being their only free day. Anyway, they had done their duty by asking us. But I was truly sorry to miss the opportunity.

We drove them to the underground station where we said goodbye, although they insisted that they would be at the airport to see us off on Tuesday. We sternly forbade this, as nothing is more frustrating than trying to locate people at the Haneda Airport — not to mention the perils of trying to arrive there by public transport at rush hour. But seeing people off and welcoming them home is an ingrained habit in Japan and a gesture of courtesy which is made no matter how inconvenient to everybody. We have watched Japanese gentlemen almost miss their trains by reason of bowing and being bowed to in the act of farewell. So the sisters just may turn up.

After we got back to our hotel we stopped in the bar for a drink. By then Harry was hungry; soon he was able to talk. He asked hopefully, "Was the dinner any good? The place was like a morgue! Do you think they enjoyed themselves? They really are charming women, aren't they?"

I kicked myself mentally then that we hadn't had dinner right here in the old reliable Orchid Room among black-suited executives and partying relatives and beautiful babies having fun, with "Mack the Knife" to cheer us.

After several long telephone talks yesterday we have convinced Isoko and Chiyo not to go to the airport. I also took part in an introduction by telephone to their mother. Our conversation was conducted fluently in two different tongues but the message of goodwill was understood by both. Language can do no more.

I had wanted to meet sometime a doctor, a lawyer, a university leader, a business executive, maybe an actress, someone — anyone — flamboyant and colorful among women professionals. Instead I met a laughing little dietician and a gentle, gracious teacher of ceramic art. They were not spectacular, they were not even "exceptional." They were representatives of a generation who worked for a living because they had to, and whose jobs now contributed to the good quality of life of their community. By their own determination they had escaped being unpaid babysitters and objects of charity in the homes of their married relatives. They were the generation to whom work gave freedom.

We have just had a visit from the young Endos. Apparently they had been arguing rather hotly for just as I opened the door to their knock Jiro was saying, "I tell you there's no place in a Japanese marriage for a career woman! You *know* that, Ineko! You knew it before we got married."

After we had exchanged polite greetings Ineko turned to me and said, "I can't convince Jiro that things are changing here for women. Why, even the P.M.'s daughter has found herself something useful to do . . . and Jiro admires *her*. You admit yourself, Jiro, that Makiko Tanaka is thought well of by everybody and is very happily married in spite of what she does."

"But she doesn't carry on an independent career of her own," said Jiro. "She just acts as her father's official hostess because her mother is too old-fashioned to enjoy all that public entertaining. Makiko does it as a family obligation."

"And loves it! She's a real politician, too. Anyway, what about Chie Nakane and her book about Japanese society? Everybody admires the book . . . and her."

"But I don't think she's married now. So . . . let her write!"

"Well, there's Sawako Ariyoshi and her best-seller, *The Ecstatic One*. I know that she's married."

"She *was* married, you mean. That proves my point . . . she's divorced. Another marriage that couldn't stand up to it," said Jiro triumphantly.

"What about Setouchi Harumi? She writes wonderful novels and she writes beautifully."

"Ineko, you're not proving anything. Setouchi Harumi is a career woman, certainly, but I don't think she has a husband. The two don't go together in Japan."

"Career women who might make very satisfactory wives are geishas," Harry suggested.

But Ineko did not give up easily. "Well, there's that woman who is in television," she persisted. "I mean the one who hosts a show about world-famous people. She even produces the show herself. You know who I mean . . . Nakamaru, I think her name is . . . Kaoru Nakamaru. *She's* married."

"I'd have to ask her husband," Jiro said, "before I knew how good that marriage was."

"Naturally *he* wouldn't like it. She's probably too smart for him," said Ineko. Then turning suddenly to me she demanded, "Mrs. Keith, I'm sure you know of our great Mitsui business combine? One of the *zaibatsu* — the family business. Mitsui is one of the largest economic and political influences in the world. They opened their first shop in 1616 where they brewed sake and made soy sauce for sale. But do you know who was the real driving force for that shop and who managed it? It wasn't Mitsui Sokubei Takatoshi, the aristocrat who wrote poetry . . . all he had was the idea and the Mitsui name! No, it was a *woman* . . . his wife, Shuho, the daughter of a merchant, who made it a success. She married him when she was only thirteen years old and had eight children, too. She not only knew how to make sake and soy, she knew how to sell them — and also how to lend money at interest!"

"Ineko's right about that," conceded Jiro. "The Mitsuis were the first family of the Samurai, warrior class, to change to the Chonin, the merchant class. I guess there were too many unemployed Samurai around under the peace-loving Tokugawa Ieyasu!"

"It was a change from the sword to the abacus," said Ineko, "but it took a woman to make a success of it . . . the first Japanese business enterprise!"

"Ineko, what do your own women friends think about having careers," I asked.

"She doesn't really have any women friends," Jiro interrupted. "She doesn't cultivate them."

"Well, all they talk about is their babies," Ineko said. "They're not interested in anything else. Or if they have sons they talk about the exams coming up. Jiro has no idea how dull *most* women here can be."

It was completely un-Japanese that a wife should argue like this with her husband in public. But Ineko really seemed to be enjoying arousing the very antagonism which ordinarily any Japanese would try to avoid. Her Western indoctrination in female behavior appeared to be durable.

Or so I thought until I asked her a question. "Ineko, did you ever think that you and Jiro might like to settle in the United States?"

She looked at me then with the special brand of shocked horror which the Japanese reserve for anyone who suggests that they might permanently uproot themselves from the soil of their islands. She simply said. "But we are Japanese!"

Someone has written about Japan that her greatest resource is her hundred million people — of which fifty million are females.

It isn't that women have lacked importance in Japanese history. Throughout all recorded time females have served as bargaining aces in the game of politics and government. Daughters, sisters, wives, nieces, cousins and mistresses appear and reappear like brilliant, pulsing veins and arteries carrying lifeblood to connect the careers of important men. Success accompanies the pleasant female faces which are backed by the silent strength of their family fortunes and influence. One Big Name's daughter is the Other Big Name's wife, whose niece is the bride of another Big Name, whose sister will marry his Big Name nephew who is himself . . . etc. And in this fashion great names, enterprises and titles come together and flourish . . . but not necessarily women!

30

SHINJUKU is our favorite area for Sunday walks. Unlike downtown Tokyo the shops there are open, people are always hurrying about, and the huge underground station arcade bursts with activity and echoes with youthful voices and hurrying sandaled feet. Shinjuku is the center for Tokyo's very young people — not addicts or bums, just the very young who always seem to be rehearsing frantically for some great dramatic event which never takes place. Every moment for them is intense and exciting and every action is exaggerated, bold and youthful. I envy them their youth knowing that it can never be replaced nor imitated and even while I am watching it is slipping away.

Some have Mongolian cheekbones, sucked-in cheeks, glittering eyes, tobacco-tinted skins, long, lanky black hair, skeletal hands and feet and concave chests — and I wonder what diseases they may have. But statistics show they haven't. For the appearance of exotic decadence is a life-style here, not an illness. Some of the girls look like discarded Japanese dolls dressed out of a gypsy ragbag. But most of the youngsters of both sexes look healthy, vital and animated, although incredibly sloppy. They are gay but not rowdy. And odd though we must look to them, no one stares at us or seems curious. They don't want to know us . . . they want only each other. Shinjuku makes me feel older than any other place I know.

A few years ago we visited San Francisco's Haight-Asbury district at the height of its hippie occupation. Dazed, runaway youngsters from all over the United States lolled in the gutters, their eyes glazed and their minds blown, too stupefied by drugs to stand on their feet. Their filthy hair and skins and their bizarre costumes meant absolutely nothing, for even if they had been well washed and dressed in the height of fashion it would have been just as pathetic and terrifying to see these young people who live in the richest nation in the world sunk into a self-induced drug coma. Not *all* the young people of that rich nation, of course, but to see any of them like this was too many.

The reign of drugged hippies in Haight-Asbury has now passed. The doubtful distinction of being the Mecca of the drug scene has been bequeathed to Telegraph Avenue in Berkeley, once the humble, innocent little avenue which leads up to the dignified Sather Gate entrance to the prestigious University of California. In my day at the university we collected in the small, friendly Telegraph Avenue shops to drink coffee; today young people collect there to smoke marijuana. And if a flower child gets stoned and can't make it home, he or she can always rest unmolested in the gutter outside, for the Berkeley police are long past the stage of doing anything about marijuana. Gutters possibly — but not pot.

After the U.S. scene I was prepared for anything I might see in Shinjuku ward in Tokyo, which is described as the hangout for hippies, runaway teens, and all youngsters who are alienated from conventional society. The first time we went there I thought the chill weather was keeping them inside. The next time the day was bright and young people were everyplace hurrying for trains, subways, buses, all chattering, buoyant, animated, and none of them doped nor drunk. Since then we have strolled there many times searching for the degradation we had both feared and expected. It may be locked away somewhere inside but at least none of the young people we ever see is sitting in the gutter stupefied. Here in Shinjuku they are younger than in Tokyo which is itself a young man's town, and they are disestablished but not depraved. I am told that the comparatively healthy condition of these wanderers who congregate here is the result of the Japanese government's severe and unswerving policy against drug use or drug sales.

The treatment of a drug addict here is one of no nonsense, no tapering off, just "cold turkey." The cure is permanent whether the addict lives or, as he sometimes does, dies.

Many of the young people are not dropouts. The large proportion of youngsters is legitimately greater here because of the number of universities of varying excellence in this district. This includes famous Waseda University which boasts next to the highest scholastic rating in Japan, being second only to Tokyo University, which leads them all.

The scarcity of hippies now in March is probably thanks to the season, which is too cold for park sleeping. In summer in Gyoen Park just across from the huge railway station, many young wanderers — Japanese and foreign but seldom American — sleep on the grassy lawns which are now frozen and brown. The shortage of American hippies is owing to the high cost of fares between our two countries. In the park there are many walkways, paths, benches and rest rooms and toilet facilities, and in good weather people of all ages stroll, sit or sleep here in hippie costumes or kimonos, for dress conforms to no pattern except one of nonconformity.

Today we came to the Shinjuku station to search for a newsstand selling the comic book *Dozei Jidey* which Shoji Terayama had described to us. Sunday is a popular outdoors day for everybody and hippies passed us in a steady parade, most of them with long lanky black hair, a few with bleached red hair, and all with either cold bare feet and sandals or shiny black high boots. Tight patched blue jeans are universal, topped by Oriental tunics or skinny sweaters without bras, and many chains of dangling beads and huge shabby shoulder bags for both sexes. I saw some mangy tippets of wolfy fur wound about thin young necks, male or female, I couldn't tell which. Some unnamed fuzzy animal had been made into a very short fur coat which was worn over nothing but panty-hose, by a girl — I think? They were all too petite and finely boned to be Americans. They looked to be European, Latin, East Indian, Korean, but predominantly Japanese — and they all walked with a freedom and swing I envied. Somehow I find the untidiness of the hippies here — and God knows they are scruffy enough — less distasteful than that of ours at home, perhaps because the Oriental version seems less *my* responsibility and I don't associate it with any threat to my own grandchildren.

We located the comic book *Dozei Jidey* edited by Kazuo Uemura, at the newsstand. Terayama had said it was popular with young Japanese because it discussed the problems of youth and especially the question of trial marriage. When we opened to the editorial page we found photos of the four young staff members, two men and two women, all attractive looking young people.

The crude pop art style of the drawings inside is similar to that of our own comic books. Many pages were filled with boys and girls struggling with emotional extremes, either very happy or miserable, very loving or furious, laughing or weeping, and usually embracing each other. Other pages were devoted to drab, tear-shedding mammas and papas, to sun-blest Super-men, and to a series of mythological and other-world characters who were always interfering one way or the other in the actions of frantic young lovers. Facially, the characters have disowned their Oriental heritage of narrow slanting eyes, and they appear here as round and goggle-eyed as American comic book characters. There was nothing to suggest obscenity or pornography, and nothing censorable from my point of view. But from the traditional Japanese viewpoint the mere suggestion of trial marriage, or of two decent young people of opposite sexes being intimately associated before marriage, is completely unacceptable.

Another aspect of Shinjuku district is a go-go center with a variety of Western entertainments. These include motion picture theaters, Kentucky fried chicken emporiums, coffee bars, Coca-Cola bars, snack bars, nude photo studios, discotheques and dance halls. There is also a huge stadium for ice follies and symphony, and jazz concerts and rock music; as the youngsters here are all crazy about Western rock. There are massage parlors with near-nude female attendants to "massage" patrons in private rooms, and pinball or *pachinko* parlors, although the latter are fewer than they used to be. This whole area is tawdry by day, but artificially exciting by night with the lights sparkling on narrow alleys like rhinestone jewels on a wrinkled neck. Or perhaps there is a more apt comparison to a handsome woman with dirty underwear.

After purchasing *Dozei* we went to Kanda, the book shop district. Here we visited a number of shops and found them, as always, filled with readers of all ages, but especially young people, all standing two deep and reading from the shelves. Japan has the highest literacy rate in the world and bookshelf reading is universal and not discouraged by the shop proprietors.

The shops generally have pornographic sections located well

to the rear of the establishment and such books are usually in English or French. But today we entered a shop with a large section up front devoted to pornographic, illustrated, English language magazines. In the interest of legal restrictions, tiny scraps of black paper had been pasted loosely over all the sexual parts displayed in the journals. All these scraps had been lifted and peeked under. Most of these publications originated in the Western world. We also found *Playboy, Penthouse,* and *Oui* on the stands, but these were less crude and obvious in their presentations, and better printed and illustrated. These latter journals made an appeal to the eye, while the others seemed to wish merely to arouse sexually the reader.

It is especially interesting to recall that the Japanese were experts in the art of erotic works at least two centuries ago at a time when the predominant spirit in the United States was puritan and the Spirit of '76 was an extrovert drummer boy beating his innocent drum. In Japan in the 1700s and early 1800s under the *daimyo* families the *Ukiyo-e* erotica became famous. In this pictorial art form all popular artists paid tribute to sexual activities with explicit detail in their prints and woodcuts. These illustrations were considered so usefully instructive that they were given to virgins before marriage to prepare them for the activities and pleasures of the wedding night.

In the twentieth century something happened to this ingenuous attitude toward sex as an approved pleasure. The change came in the era preceding the Second World War when Japan's military-minded government determined to focus the nation's effort on making war, not love, and anti-obscentiy laws were passed. After the war, with the Japanese people in a state of shock and questioning what was right and what wrong, and with the country flooded with American G.I.s who didn't care what was right or wrong, a state of public prudery accompanied by private licentiousness was arrived at. This permitted journals carrying explicit sex scenes to be sold only so long as genitalia and pubic parts were covered by scraps of paper or ink daubs. Thus what might begin as a photo of two naked people became a lesson in how to copulate. It is an interesting commentary on public tastes in Japan today that over half the feature-length films produced in the country last year were erotic in content and for adults-only audiences.

When I first came to Japan in 1934 I remember being puzzled by odd-looking objects on sale in drugstore windows. In my ignorance I asked Harry what they were. He told me. In those days you went to the Orient for such things: today we send them to the Orient.

In some Western cities respectability is confined to one clearly defined area, and its opposite is as specifically located someplace else. Not so in Tokyo, where you can step out of any top-flight hotel and make one wrong turn and be in some place more challenging. Not that its Bohemian establishments are necessarily disreputable, but they are nonconformist compared to any tourist hotel lobby. One of the enjoyable aspects of these hideouts is that you may visit them day or night without danger of being mugged. The narrowest alley that leads from the broadest boulevard and ends in the darkest dive is very probably safe for you, for Japan has the lowest crime rate in the world.

The most skilled geisha are said to be found in the restaurant districts of Pontocho in Kyoto, and Shimbashi in Tokyo. Good geisha houses are very expensive and by no means dives. The word geisha is too wide a term to define satisfactorily in a paragraph. Its literal meaning is "accomplished person" and a geisha originally was and still is just this. A highly trained musician and dancer, she is hired to entertain at stag parties, at restaurants, and at tea and geisha houses. Some geisha houses are as exclusive and as difficult to enter as any elite private club in the Occidental world and entrance to them by foreigners is made only via Japanese friends. Such establishments stand far back in lush gardens surrounded by high walls in an atmosphere of patrician elegance and far from the tourist bus route. But other houses are less selective and when the desires of stag party participants vary, so sometimes do the duties of the geisha. Unfortunately the term geisha, entertainer, has come ultimately and wrongly to mean exclusively prostitute.

Quite aside from the expensive pleasures of geisha houses Tokyo offers the most expert prostitution in Asia. Countless establishments here are dedicated to the fullfillment of sexual appetites, both normal and deviant, in gay bars and transvestite cabarets as well as bisexual brothels.

There are also small unorthodox art shops, artists' clubs, potters' workrooms, tiny pharmacists' shops, hamburger stands, eating places and grocery shops. And squeezed in with all of these are crowded dwellings where plain, simple people live, grateful to call anyplace home and happy to celebrate each year with gaudy paper flowers, their own modest version of cherry blossom viewing.

We wandered through the narrow alleys on a goodbye tour the day before we were to leave Japan. The cherry blossom festival with its cherry dances would commence the day after our departure, but the inhabitants of the narrow by-streets were celebrating already, and overhead from every light and power fixture and festooning every pole were strung fantastic arrangements of the brightest, pinkest, gaudiest paper cherry blossoms imaginable. Through the misty rain the narrow passageways glowed with a lovely rosy blush while a spirit of credulous fantasy and devotion to their own tribal mysteries animated the people on the streets. There was a wonderful identity of race, people and nation. Undoubtedly they all envied themselves for being Japanese.

It was so very typical — first that the opening of the real cherry blossoms should be almost arbitrarily determined for a certain date by an apparently higher authority than nature, the festival schedule. Only the Japanese, the finest horticulturalists in the whole world, could achieve this. But annually they do achieve it. Second, it was wonderfully Japanese to proceed happily to decorate with artificial blossoms in the poorer parts of town because real flowers, plants and trees were too expensive. All along the narrow lanes they were celebrating the festival at minimum cost with paper blooms that have blossomed year after year and thus they enable even the meanest city dweller to do his blossom viewing on his way to work. Yet this is not really surprising. These are the people who survived on weeds throughout the war, and lived through the horrors of Hiroshima . . . to look with joy on blossom time again.

Here in the hotel we have been watching for several weeks a large, live cherry tree which has been skillfully transplanted into a commodious and ornamental receptacle standing in the center of the lobby. The burgeoning tree is gradually working its way from pale buds into full, fragile, pink blossoms. Of many things of beauty I have seen in Japan this tree gives me the most moments of pure pleasure. It awaits us morning, noon and night and we watch its blossoms slowly opening in the lobby warmth. We often join with its circle of never-failing admirers, local and tourist, in kimono or in pants, who haunt the magic ring of this transplanted symbol of the renewal of life. With its blossoming we know that winter is over and spring is on the way.

But cherry blossoms are not only symbols of beauty here, but symbols of death, because they are most lovely just before they fall. One thing I know . . . the tree in the hotel will bloom fully but it will be removed from view the night before the blossoms fall . . . like the old people who are not to be seen here now that Japan is in full bloom.

Just before we left Tokyo I dreamed about Victoria, where we live. Much of the time in Tokyo I had been contrasting the two cities because they were so different.

Victoria is chiefly a city of gardens and old folks. Snow melts as it falls, wind brings down the oak leaves, duck manure is fragrant, people are gracious and courteous, and life touches most of us gently as it passes politely by on the other side of the street.

Here we have not forgotten our wars. Armistice Day is a reality and on Remembrance Day we bloom with Flanders poppies. On National days we fly the Red Ensign or the Maple Leaf. Motorists stop for pedestrian crossings, dogs obey traffic lights, buses halt at doorsteps, the fire department keeps an ambulance for heart attack victims, and the banks are crowded on pension days, for Victoria has the only tolerable climate in Canada. Those who hail from the Old Country greet each other with, Beautiful Day! Those up from the States say, Does the rain never stop? Victorians say, It's good for the garden!

Old folks lurch along the streets tapping with white canes, blind to signals, deaf to sirens, dumb to tears, crippled with arthritis and swallowing pills for angina pectoris, but uncomplaining and proud. Each one pursues the same humble goal — to live without charity and to die with dignity. When cherry blossoms fall in Victoria, they fall gently . . .

I awoke suddenly to the hot neon glare of electric light signs flashing in at our hotel window in Tokyo.

31

~~~~~~

THIS MORNING we called at the Japan Foundation to say
goodbye and thank them for their assistance which has
grown steadily and become invaluable. We saw Messrs. Soda,
Noguchi, Horiuchi, Ogino and Miss Nagina, who were all very
cordial and hoped that I had seen what I wished and been
pleased with what I had seen, and enjoyed myself. I said "Yes"
to all of this and thanked them for the unfailing kindness and
courtesy which had been shown to us by everyone. Mr. Noguchi asked me to send copies of any articles which I wrote
apropos of my visit. I told him that I expected to work for at
least a year on a book, as my contract with my publishers called
for a manuscript in that time. Meanwhile, I did not anticipate
writing any articles but I would send them copies of anything
I published.

Before we left the office a Harvard professor who had just
arrived in Tokyo under the auspices of the foundation was
introduced to us. To my surprise he complimented me on my
books and on being "Who I Was." This was very timely and
helpful as I often wonder who I am. Frequently since being

here I have found myself asking, like the man in the cartoon who awakened to find himself stark naked in a large party — "What am I doing here?"

Meanwhile Mr. Honma from Foreign Affairs came rushing in to say that he insists on taking us to the airport tomorrow when we leave the hotel at four o'clock. He will surely arrive late, and Harry will surely be frantic.

Ultimately we said goodbye rather sadly to everyone in the foundation office. They are all exceptionally nice people, as so many people here are after you know them.

Lewis Bush came to the hotel at midday and brought us two books of which he had told us. It was very generous of him as the volumes are privately printed and one is a personal presentation copy to Lewis from the author. I could never have found either of them on bookshop shelves.

Lewis is an extremely knowledgeable, friendly, kind person and an accomplished writer. As I have mentioned before, he has published a number of books about his life in Japan. One which I think most helpful is *Japanalia, A Concise Cyclopaedia*. With its entries arranged in alphabetical order, this deals briefly with numerous pieces of information which the writer has collected through his own wide experiences here and by extensive research.

He and his wife plan to educate their son later in England. Meanwhile I was amused to hear that this young five-year-old scion of two worlds enjoys the best of both diets; he likes rice but also enjoys toast and jam at breakfast time; he likes tea but he also drinks milk; he likes steak but also enjoys raw fish.

I asked Lewis if it was a fact that the American Occupation authorities had banned Shinto as a religion. He said certainly not; that they had banned Shinto only as a *state* religion. He said that recently one of the political parties had been trying to reintroduce Shinto as a state religion — an act which it was feared might lead in a roundabout way to reestablishing the emperor as a deity.

After reading through the two small volumes Lewis gave us I can understand why they could not be published publicly here, as they are extremely outspoken. *Be A True Japanese* is by Sazo Idemitsu, a well known industrialist millionaire. His philosophy is the essence of paternalism, realism, pragmatism and papa-knows-best. My reaction to the statements in the book was to argue with almost every page.

The other book is *Views From Here* by Satsuki Mitaro, and it is written from two shifting viewpoints. On the surface it appears to be satirical and to ridicule the author's own race, but underneath the writer points out the injustice of many labels and libels which are placed on his race. He commences his book by saying, "I have betrayed my ancestors and my beautiful country . . ." and the rest of his book proves that he hasn't. And I wouldn't wish him to.

One of the few pieces of advice that Mr. Shigiei gave me before I left Victoria was to be sure to call on Mr. Hidemi Kon in Tokyo, the president of the Japan Foundation. Mr. Shigiei is the Japanese representative of the foundation in the Japanese embassy in Washington, and he first informed me of my foundation appointment.

Apropos of his advice, Mr. Kon's name was the first one I put on my list of must-meets which I gave to the Foreign Affairs representative who was assisting me in Tokyo. I had Mr. Kon's address as president of the foundation and assumed he would wish to meet anyone whom his foundation was sponsoring.

I also placed a request to meet him with the foundation

office in Tokyo, all of whose officers I found very cooperative. These gentlemen all agreed that they would arrange a meeting for me with Mr. Kon sometime in the future.

During our first weeks in Tokyo we discovered that it was very difficult to locate a person unless you had his telephone number. Nevertheless, in spite of address limitations and obstacles we and our foundation friends managed to get in touch with most of the Japanese whose names I had on my list as persons of special interest to meet, either because of their accomplishments and viewpoints or because they were old friends. Although no appointment solidified with Mr. Kon I didn't worry because that meeting seemed obviously easy.

When we returned to Tokyo after our mind-and-body-blowing travels by train I went through my list of must-meets again and found Mr. Kon was the only one not accounted for. The others had either been seen or lined up for future appointments or classified as dead. Now Mr. Kon became number one priority. Again I referred his name to Foreign Affairs and to my foundation friends and reminded them that I was anxious to meet him before I left Japan. Again we all agreed that this was a simple matter and it would be arranged. I went through this same process several more times until ultimately I began to see that meeting Mr. Kon was not simple and that it probably would not be arranged. By then I didn't so much mind not meeting him as I wondered *why* I couldn't.

Did I lack the proper high status go-betweens? This couldn't be so, I thought, with my foundation friends. Or had these friends whom I had asked to make an appointment for me for some subtle reason beyond my understanding never intended to do so? Or had Mr. Kon suddenly developed an ulcer and disappeared into a hospital? Or did Mr. Kon really exist? Or did I?

I am even beginning to wonder if Sachiko was a figment of my imagination. This sincere, out-going, beautiful young woman was very much a part of our island travels. I shall never be able to recall our mad train rushes, frantic taxi rides, devoted Mount Fuji viewing, delectable Japanese meals, group therapy with the Kanazawa wives, agricultural forays, and quiet laughs at private jokes, without seeing dignified, lovely Sachiko beside us. Maybe smiling, maybe disapproving or questioning or maybe mutely expressionless — but always a force to rely on far beyond her physical strength.

It had never occurred to me that we wouldn't see her again in Tokyo. I still don't understand it. Perhaps contacts and human responses are impossible to predict. Our feelings say things for us that we think confirm our words — yet may deny them to a person of another culture.

I wish I could be born a second time on a different continent and see things from the inside looking out . . . from a body with another flesh color but with the memory of being white. Then I might really know what now I only sense — and perhaps wrongly.

Jiro came to tell us goodbye last evening. He is still having problems with Ineko who now says she wishes to start a dress shop business. Jiro, despite having diagnosed himself so thoroughly as a modern man, is behaving like any other young Japanese husband whose wife has diagnosed herself as a modern woman. He is frightened! Not that he's afraid of losing her — it is almost impossible for a wife to get a divorce in Japan without her husband's agreement, but he's afraid of being seen to be out-generaled, surpassed, in his own home.

After we had talked about his personal problem, we drifted into a discussion about race and racism in general. I asked him how the Japanese regarded themselves racially as compared to Caucasians. Did they feel superior to Caucasians . . . equal to . . . inferior?

"We are equal to the Caucasians," he said, "but we believe that other Asians — and I include Koreans — and Africans are not equal to us Japanese."

"You don't like the Koreans, I know."

"No, and we don't treat them well. They are the low wage workers here, and most crimes are blamed on them. We treat them the way you people treat the blacks in the states — or did until recently."

"What about the *Eta*?" I said, remembering Lewis Bush's description of them as being discriminated against.

"That word *Eta* is now forbidden. We call them *burakumin* because they live segregated lives in the *buraku* . . . the ghetto slums or hamlets which are inhabited almost exclusively by this group. They are actually a caste, although the caste system is now illegal."

"How did their segregation start? *Why* are they taboo?"

"The theory is that many years ago . . . in the sixteenth century, I think it was . . . their tribe was defeated in war and outlawed, cast out. In order to exist at all the survivors were forced to do all the dirty work in the tabooed occupations . . . slaughtering animals, skinning them, tanning hides, burying dead criminals, cleaning streets, collecting garbage . . . in fact any work that the Buddhists and Shintoists considered menial and unclean. In that way the *Eta* caste came to be looked down on as defiled, and now for generations they have been forced for the sake of their own protection to live together in segregation from everybody else, in the slums of the cities. Although discrimination against them is now forbidden by law it still continues in hidden ways."

"Such as?"

"For instance, a *burakumin* may now get a job on the strength of his ability, but he still must go home at night to his *burakumin* dwelling place if he wishes any security. Any outsider who marries a *burakumin* will be disgraced if the marriage is uncovered. This has caused some real tragedies. Of course our young Japanese are less prejudiced about this, and some mixed marriages take place among them. But this would never happen in an arranged marriage where the parentage of the young couple has been investigated on both sides. However, the *burakumin* now have formed a Liberation League which is getting more civil rights for them, more housing and schooling. So today they may have better jobs — but no better social position."

"About how many *burakumin* are there in Japan?"

"I believe there may be as many as three million. But they are literally uncountable and untouchable. You see, they are all Japanese in physical characteristics and they speak Japanese. Only their ghetto address distinguishes them, that and the curse of being considered unclean. The most encouraging thing I can say about it is that most of us are conscious now of the evil of the *burakumin* situation."

Before Jiro said goodnight we returned to the subject of Ineko and her determination to do something on her own.

"Could she finance a dress shop?" I asked.

Jiro looked decidedly annoyed as he answered, "My father has offered to help her."

"Your father! You said he was conservative and very traditional."

"He is . . . but he says that as Ineko has a good business head and *I* don't, she had better use it. He says that being in the import-export business himself he has many contacts that could help her. I think he wants to make us feel his influence. Well . . . ever since I came home from the States he has wanted me to take over the business. But I want to enter a law firm . . . that's what I studied for . . . and I'm not at all interested in business. Ineko is and he admires her for it. She gets on very well with him. Perhaps he thinks that if she makes a go of the dress shop . . . well, I don't know exactly *what* he thinks . . . maybe helping her is a way of rebuking me for not taking over from him. He's a wily old man, and not easy to outguess . . ."

"Why don't you let Ineko try it? If it would make her happy and your father, too."

"And me? I'd no longer be master in my own house!"

When we shook hands to say goodbye I felt that I knew this strange young man, whom we had met quite by accident only a few weeks before and would probably never see again . . . that I knew him more personally and intimately than anyone else in this enigmatic land. He had kept up no pretenses with us. As he had reminded us before, face-saving was not necessary with an absentee audience.

I see now quite plainly that the most vital difference between the Japan of 1934 and that of 1974 is not so much economic as it is the difference in the relationship between men and women. It is the battle of the sexes just beginning here . . . a battle never won, never lost and never ended.

Which reminds me of a note I read in the *Japan Times* the other day about forty Japanese women's lib. ladies who demonstrated against a tour of Japanese men organized to go to Seoul, South Korea. The tour was for the sole object of taking tired businessmen on a prolonged *Kisaeng*, or geisha party in Seoul. The protesters, one of whose husbands was on the tour, set off firecrackers and burned insecticide bombs in the JAL tour lounge where the gentlemen were assembled waiting to go. The ladies ended up in jail, and the gentlemen in Seoul.

32

~∞

THE DAY AFTER TOMORROW we leave Japan. Every time I spread out my maps of this city which bewitches me, I submerge in a wave of depression to think I shall probably never come back. I am saying goodbye to this monstrous, magical mixture of antiquity and the GNP, veiled in its modern smog. I am saying goodbye to its vital, youthful crowds, its hoards of slender hustlers who don't mind work, its snappy, round-faced, flower-cheeked girls with firm little legs and bobbling breasts, and its supple, sleek-haired boys who race toward subways, trains, examinations, universities, promotions, riches, success . . . and love.

I put love last because Japanese life is and always has been regulated by a code of duties and responsibilities owed to others, and in this code the least important of man's obligations is to a member of the female sex.

To most Japanese, their jobs are their lives, in contrast to us in the West whose lives exist outside our jobs and to which the jobs are incidental. They inherently value the group more than the individual, and they are the greatest patriots in the whole world at a time in history when patriotism is less vital to existence than global loyalty.

Now as I leave Japan I ask myself, How can I know the truth about a people whom I love . . . and do not fully trust? . . . Who contradict themselves, who are emotionally extravagant, who are unsurpassed for energy, and who can face an ugly death gracefully, but cannot always face life?

Here is a people who despite their high intelligence continue to be controlled by *giri ninjo*, the code of human obligations which so seriously encumbers them and programs their entire lifetimes. *Giri ninjo* is a term which to explain satisfactorily would require a whole volume. The dictionary attempts to do so by defining *giri* as justice; duty; obligation; (a sense of) honor; courtesy. It defines *giri ninjo* as duty and humanity. Yet *giri* is so specifically and completely Japanese that most Japanese will agree that it has no equivalent in any other country or other language, and no English word can satisfactorily describe it. One basic and seldom ignored tenet of that code is that the feeling of obligation is stronger and deeper than that of human affection. I think this sets the Japanese people apart from us, and perhaps it is one reason why Japanese-American marriages present special problems.

We are just leaving our room at the Okura, and have a car ordered for four o'clock to take us to Haneda Airport. Mr. Honma has not turned up. Unfortunately he functions under superior orders which assume his ability to be in two different places at the same identical time. He really tries to do this but so far the metaphysical realities of life have defeated him.

Later . . . They defeated him again. He did not turn up at four and we waited until four-forty, at which time we loaded the bags in the car and were about to leave when Mr. Honma arrived, out of breath and filled with apologies. It seems that the ambassador to Japan from the People's Republic of China, the first Chinese representative to come to Japan since before the war, had arrived at three-thirty at the airport in the first official Chinese plane to land there. This event was tremendously important diplomatically, and all Japanese Foreign Office personnel were on hand at the airport. Mr. Honma was there and he had been given new orders for work to do and so could not escort us to the airport. However, at some inconvenience to himself he had come to say goodbye. The change in plans did not surprise us. No one here says "No" to a superior. This may be a contributing factor to the monstrous growth of the GNP.

Just before we entered the isolated duty-free section of the airport terminal whom should we see waiting for us at the entry gate but Jiro and Ineko. They looked young, luminous, healthy, happy and prosperous. I think they looked to us as we may have looked to others years ago.

"We know that you don't like people hanging around to say goodbye," Jiro explained to Harry, "but we are still Japanese and we do this for people we respect and like."

"We aren't going to stay," Ineko filled in. "We remember that Mr. Keith always likes to be early for trains and planes. We just came to tell you that we are glad you returned again to our country . . . and that this time *we* met you." She handed me a single deeply scented red carnation.

"We're glad we came, too," I said, "for many reasons . . . but especially because of you two people." We shook hands all around, then stood a moment without words. Then suddenly the two young people dipped down in bows then lifted their heads and smiled and said, "Sayonara, Sayonara." Swiftly they turned and left. We waved after them but they were already engulfed in the hurrying crowds.

"Jiro says that love isn't important in a Japanese marriage," I said. "I wonder?"

"Do you think Ineko will win the dress shop battle?" asked Harry.

"I'm sure she will."

We had a long wait inside the air terminal as our plane was delayed in arriving from Hong Kong, and I had time to think.

Had I accomplished what I came for, I wondered? Had I at last made a whole man out of my conflicting concepts of what is a Japanese? Could I now reconcile the shock troops that had landed at Sandakan; the tough young guards at our prison; the controversial camp commandant, Colonel Suga; the brutal lieutenants, the decent doctor, kindly Mr. Hamasaki who hated it all . . . could I reconcile them with the friends I had made this spring almost thirty years later in Japan? With Sachiko, Tomoko, Chiyo, Isoko, little Mr. Honma, Su Ogino, Mr. Nishiberi, the clever, industrious young ladies at Kanazawa, the many-generation farming family of Inui in Inaawa, Taizo Kato, Shintaro Ishihara, Shoji Terayama, Mr. Soda, and all the friends of the Japan Foundation including Miss Nagina; Jiro and Ineko . . . and even Mr. Kimura of the travel agency who had so conveniently delivered us to the wrong hotel? What was a Japanese? One thing these people all had in common was that each one was different from the other. And by now they had all ceased to be people I had willed myself to like and were just likable people.

There was one meeting I recalled with complete satisfaction, our reunion with Kimpei Shiba. A journalist diplomat all his life, now at seventy-four he was still one of the most vivid and vital men I had ever met.

Of them all, the people who were most alive to me at this moment were Jiro and Ineko. I think you can learn more about an entire people from one good friend than from a na-

298

tion of mere acquaintances. Jiro and Ineko were completely credible to me because they were male and female first, and Japanese second. They could function understandably in two worlds, the Orient and the Occident.

Mr. Nishiberi I would never forget, brilliant, ambitious, charming, pursued by too many duties and too little time, his nicotine-stained fingers never empty, his brown eyes always questioning . . . and his mind seething with plans.

I knew I was glad to see Japan so prosperous. I was glad not to be sorry for her . . . or for myself. After all we were both survivors, as individuals and as nations. When life is so sweet, to survive is a great deal.

"You're looking rather melancholy," said Harry. "What's on your mind?"

"I was thinking about the people we met in Japan this time. There wasn't a single one who wasn't nice and kind to us."

"Why shouldn't they be?"

"They should . . . but they haven't always been. It still surprises me. I'm glad I can remember them this way . . . healthy, handsome, intelligent, likable people."

"Now don't be too exuberant. Prosperity agrees with most of us. Just wait till the pinch comes again. They tell me our plane won't be in for another half hour. Why don't you go over to the duty-free shop and spend our surplus yen? I'll watch the bags."

I walked over to the hot, lighted, sparkling showcases filled with glittering souvenirs. Nothing attracted me. Spiritually I was already on the way home. I returned to Harry and sat down and looked at our hand luggage piled around us. The only extra piece was a huge Japanese paper shopping bag now completely packed with Japanese paperbacks in English translation. How different this was from my first trip to Japan when I had come away with all my bags bulging with treasures from the Orient which I was taking home. This time it was the essence of Japan I was searching for and not its material treasures.

"There's just one thing I wish had been different about this trip," I said. "I wish we could have met Colonel Suga's son."

"We did everything we could. Anything more had to be up to him . . . if he still exists."

"I know. Before we left Canada it seemed terribly important to me to meet him . . . and I failed. But now I think it doesn't matter very much. My point of view has changed since being here this time. We saw Hiroshima and Nagasaki. The results of war never disappear . . . they are painful and horrible, and they hurt on both sides and always will and we who lived through it are lucky to be alive. But to those born afterwards it is just history. Perhaps better so. As the young folks say, 'We have forgotten.'"

33

♀

I REMEMBER the young countrywomen we saw with round, heavy faces, rosy cheeks and strong, vital hands; and the middle-aged mothers who were thin, with tired, lined, loving faces. I remember the ancients with faces like parchment-covered skulls, and hands like talons with veins like blue ropes. They seemed to have lost any racial distinction, and were just old women of any country, any place.

The upper-class women were different; the young ones were finely boned, with almond-shaped faces and well proportioned bodies. They had fragile, deft hands, and delicately lovely, sun-tinted faces. The middle-aged matrons were well preserved, their emotions always cloaked by pleasant expressions. Even the old ladies retained their fine facial structure with wrinkled distinction, and never lost their regal mien.

But all were women, and all Japanese. All are now being affected, consciously or otherwise, by the new awareness in Japan that women, as well as wives, are here to stay.

Shortly after we had left Tokyo for Canada some of my unanswered questions about the female sex were posed at a seminar in Tokyo by the Japanese Association of University Women, held in order to reexamine the status of women. That such a seminar should be held at all was a triumph over the past. Many questions were answered statistically — if not always satisfactorily, I felt.

It was discovered (with surprise?) that the vast majority of women feel that they are not treated as the equal of men, although the law proclaims their right to legal equality. Young women especially feel that as workers they are both alienated and discriminated against. It is interesting to note that more older men agreed with the women about this than did younger men, who seemed to be on the financial defensive.

Almost one half of the total Japanese labor force is female, and one half of the female workers are married. The feminine half is mostly employed in factory work and as unskilled labor. The wage rate for women is only one half that for men, and promotion in all jobs is much slower.

It was noted that all golf caddies are girls.

The traditional idea of shared labors in Japan has been that the husband goes out to work while the wife manages and rules over the home. When asked to comment on the justice of this arrangement, 80 percent of those questioned supported it. Only about 10 percent felt that if the wife went out to work, the husband should share in her household duties.

It was generally agreed that both husband and wife must share in the responsibility of making decisions for their children. And it was generally admitted that the wife had to implement these decisions.

The complicated subject of property division and shared tax responsibility for husband and wife was discussed. The financial plight of wives who were left without any source of income after being divorced or widowed was considered — but left unsolved. I was told by a number of women during our stay in

Japan that a woman had little or no chance of obtaining a divorce against her husband's wishes, no matter what grievances she may have had. And that in any case, the children would remain in the father's custody if he so wished.

Shortly before this seminar was held the prime minister's office had conducted a public opinion survey. A number of women in city housing complexes were asked if they would like to be born again as women. About half of them said yes. Others said that they believed that they could "develop their talents better" if they were men. (No doubt the government expressed regrets that it could do nothing about this.)

All agreed that women control the household budget and hold the family purse. One out of every four city housewives is a part-time worker and contributes regularly to the budget. Three out of every four wives in rural areas work at some sort of job. Many women have personal savings accounts, and a considerable number of older women make their own speculative investments. Probably padding the household accounts is a universal female practice. The great majority of housewives in farming areas said they were satisfied with their lives, and seemed more content than were city wives who had more material comforts.

Another recent survey showed that the average monthly income of a salaried male worker in 1974 was about $550 (Y165,219).

The first Japan Population Conference (privately sponsored) ever to be held here urged the "nuclear family" as being the ideal family unit, this unit being father, mother and two children, or *less*. Nevertheless, Japan does not permit free use of "the pill." The conference also commented on the alarming increase in juvenile delinquency in the last few years.

Another survey in a search for the causes of youthful suicides elicited the disturbing statistic that better educated fathers were more likely to have offspring who kill themselves.

Some time before this I had read a statement by the counselor to the Japanese Manufacturers Trade Association: "For us Japanese, work is a virtue. We have no welfare state so we must work and save for our old age. We are not ashamed of obeying orders." A loyal worker said: "We are loyal to our firm. When people work harder, then productivity rises, profits improve, wages increase, and everybody is better off. Why waste energy by striking?"

Shortly afterwards an Education Ministry survey showed that one-fifth of all college graduates now *choose* to be unemployed. According to the Japanese social system there is something extremely peculiar if after a student graduates he does not go forth to his chosen work (or that for which he is chosen) on April first. Yet one out of every five graduates in 1974 chose *not* to work. Unfortunately the survey failed to uncover the most pertinent fact — the reasons that lay behind this alien decision. Why, in this country which so values education and where a degree has long been the gateway to success, why does this important proportion of its youth suddenly renege on its agreement with society? What happens next?

According to a reliable newspaper report, more than half the urban marriages today are so-called love matches — or to be more realistic, propinquity matings. The fact is that on the job in office or factory is the most likely way for girls to meet

304

men without the services of a go-between. Both single and married quarters are provided by some companies, and some companies go so far as to facilitate marriages between their employees. The go-between would seem to be reserved nowadays for the upper classes and those without the need to work.

Today the retirement age for men is fifty-five years. This age is based on the now outdated statistic that the average death age for men in Japan was fifty years. With the years of life now stretched for men to seventy-three, and seventy-five for women, a "retired" man may have eighteen unemployed, unproductive, and unpaid years in which to disintegrate and rot away. In fairness it should be added that some retired males find either full or part-time work. Uusually, however, a man is relegated to some depressing and dilapidated home for the aged which itself is literally rotting away; often without running water or bathing facilities, usually without proper nursing care, and almost always without adequate food. The combination of increased longevity, lack of sound welfare programs, and insufficient housing facilities owing to overpopulation of city areas makes life hell for those whom modern methods force to survive. Although in Japan old age was once a time of respect, now it seems a time of apologetic neglect and guilty abandonment. The young are triumphant, the middle-aged can make do, but the old are superfluous — unless they are rich or fortunate.

The situation of aged women is slightly better than that of men, if only because as females they are accustomed to second-class treatment, and they can still find useful work to do in the homes of their children — whereas, nobody wants an unemployed old man drooling in the kitchen. Of the Japanese with whom I talked, almost all exhibited sincere distress over the fate of so many in the aged sector of their population, and assured me it was not by choice that so many people now had no accommodation in their homes for their parents. A changed way of life, they said, a Western way, was sweeping the Japanese islands. Did they like it? Well . . . they followed it.

But there was a vital difference in Japan, I suggested. In the United States we had functioning welfare programs and assured Social Security payments. Although subject to criticism, these were far ahead of any Japanese provisions for the aged.

Did they observe Mother's Day in Japan? I asked. They did — sometimes with flowers, or even with a single red carnation — which costs about sixty-five cents. This reminded me of Mother's Day at home, with its once-a-year recognition of Mom.

Another statistical study indicated that the average Japanese woman watches television for about five hours daily, listens to the radio for one hour, reads newspapers for an hour, reads magazines for half an hour and books for twenty minutes. This didn't sound right to me, as the women I talked with also liked to do dressmaking from Western patterns, knitting, art work — and, naturally, *ikebana*, flower arrangement.

A man, so statistics said, spent much less time on all these diversions. In theory this gave women eight hours daily of home entertainment — to offset their husband's office parties, I assumed!

Telephone communication was used most often and at greatest length by young people who, as in our own culture, avoid writing letters. Newspapers were universally read, and most assiduously so by people in their twenties.

A conclusion from my own experiences, and my avid newspaper reading, is that the Japanese are an extremely self-disciplined people (until they explode!), and that they complain much less about the high cost of living in their country than do the foreigners there.

34

JAPAN IS HERE to stay as a major world power. Her people are homogeneous and monolithic, a tribe as well as a nation, and they are strong. Bound together by a single rigid code of behavior, yet each person incredibly maintains his own individuality. They are brilliant thinkers, tireless workers, skillful craftsmen, shrewd traders, ambivalent friends and relentless foes. They will achieve international greatness. But given the world — they will still choose Japan.

They are devoted lovers of peace. And they are the world's most fanatic patriots. Lieutenant Onoda returned from the Philippine Islands after fighting the Second World War there for twenty-nine years after peace had come. During those years he was hiding out in the jungle in Lubang Island as an enemy guerrilla, and he managed to knock off a number of Filipino citizens who to him were still the enemy. This year a young Japanese hippie tourist happened on Onoda and talked with him, and later reported his whereabouts to the Japanese government. Search parties were sent out to "rescue" the fifty-one-year-old lieutenant, and pamphlets were dropped to persuade him to surrender and promise him immunity. When Onoda finally emerged from the jungle to talk with his would-be rescuers, they asked him why he had continued to fight for twenty-nine years after peace had come.

He answered that his last order from his commanding officer had been to fight on for the honor of the emperor. This he had done. Before he would surrender now his commanding officer must order him to do so.

Fortunately his C.O., a former Imperial Japanese Army major, was still alive. He was brought to Lubang Island where he ordered the surrender of the lieutenant. The president of the Philippines then pardoned Onoda for any crimes he had committed against the Filipinos, and he was taken back to Japan where he was made an official hero. He accepted this heroism gracefully, but said he did not think he could adjust to the "social changes" in Japan. To the Japanese, those twenty-nine years of "heroism" need no explanation.

It is a commentary on man's adaptability that Mr. Onoda has since put his experiences into a book whose sale he toured the United States to promote. He was last photographed with a pretty girl sitting on his knee. But the ultimate judgment on our civilization was pronounced by Mr. Onoda at the conclusion of his book sales promotion tour, when he said with a sigh, "I would rather go back to the jungle!"

The population of Japan is 108 million people. Seven-eighths of her land space is uninhabitable mountains, and level land commands a high price. A scrap of land in the center of Tokyo sold recently for $37,500 per *tsubo*, a *tsubo* being 3.3 square meters.

The Japanese are nonviolent. They hate the Bomb. Every government since the Second World War has refused to expand its military power, or to enter the nuclear arms race. The left wing groups adopt this stand as their symbol.

Those who chronicle these wind-torn, sea-battered islands say they are barren soil for Marxism. The family solidarity of the people, their code of behavior, their vertical structure of relationships, and their natural impulses are all against it. Yet the contradictory reality remains that there are many different Marxist organizations here, and Communist cells exist in all the Japanese prefectures. The Communist party is the third largest in the Diet Lower House, with a membership of about 300,000. Organizations affiliated with it number about 350,000 members.

Our friend Shintaro Ishihara is a member of the Diet Upper House, or House of Councillors. He founded the small, extreme *Seirankai* right-wing faction of the young Liberal Democrats, the LDP being the dominant party, and that of the former prime minister, Kakuei Tanaka, who has just resigned. It is rumored that Ishihara at age forty will be offered the Liberal Democrats' nomination for mayor of Tokyo. Recently he has called for Japan to have "at least one nuclear bomb, so that she may be listened to in the world."

The student generation gives its support (temporarily at least) to various Red groups which do not belong to the Communist party. There is the *Rengo Sekigun,* or United Red Army, which claims responsibility for the brutal Lod Airport massacre. The *Kakumaruha,* the Student Revolutionary Faction, admits that four of its youthful members were killed this year in fighting with the *Chukakuha,* the Middle Core Faction. The *Hanteigakuhyo,* or Anti-imperialist Student League, is another of many which all go in for strident, noisy action. These student and youth groups are all excessively violent and well-armed when they fight each other — sometimes without knowing for what they are fighting. It was the Red Army terrorists who seized the French embassy in Holland and forced the release of a young Japanese terrorist, Yoshiaki Yamada (who loved rock music!) from a French prison, and collected $300,000 in ransom. They had demanded a million dollars. All these young Red groups have two things in common; they relish violence, and they are ruthless. They seem to me to be a projection of the senseless brutality shown by the teenagers of the *Taiyozoku*, the Sun Tribe, in *Season of Violence*. They do not represent the average Japanese youth.

Yet if you add up the membership totals (in hundreds, only) of all these violent Red groups, and place their total opposite the 108 million people of Japan, you will think there is little to worry about. *Until* you recall what happened to the Chinese in China, who also lived by a strong family solidarity rule, and had iron-clad traditional values to armor them against Marxism — but not against liquidation.

In the spring of 1973 the Japanese unions won a 31 percent wage increase. The same year there was a 23 percent rise in the consumer price index. While foreigners complained, this left 8 percent for the frugal Japanese housewife to save or invest. And believe me, she did.

It is forecast by the Boston Consulting Group, commissioned by the British government to make an economic study of Japan in the coming decade, that Japan will sustain a growth rate of around 10 percent throughout the 1980s. This is the latest prediction in the guessing game of Japan's future, but these guesses are based on some very solid facts. (1) The Japanese consistently pursue a clockwork management policy in industry. (2) They understand the efficient use of a first-class, well-paid labor force, with wages on a par with European countries, although about one-half the United States level. Strikes are gentlemanly and usually very short. Unions exist inside the companies and are closely associated with management. (3) Government and big business work together in profitable collusion for growth and quality. (4) Massive over-seas investments insure access to raw materials. (5) Japan plans to offer in the near future high quality education, and to solve the pollution crisis before other countries do.

Even the worms are enlisted to help. In the production of paper pulp, of chemicals and man-made fibers, the disposal of factory wastes without pollution is a serious problem. It was reported recently that in Japan certain worms will eat through the entire waste products coming from such factories, and ex-crete half of what they eat in droppings. The droppings are then sold as fertilizer. The worms are now being propagated.

The Japanese have faced many problems cheerfully. In 1971 President Nixon ignored the long-standing alliance of the United States with Japan, and without consultation precipi-tately opened a bilateral China diplomacy which wounded Japanese self-respect. Shortly afterward the United States trade diplomacy (or lack of it) overnight ceased to be frank and friendly, and became almost as belligerent as if to an enemy. Japan sank sadly back and asked herself what she had done to offend? What? except to become prosperous!

In 1973 a general transport strike with more than three million workers out affected one out of every four Japanese. The revaluation upward of the yen raised the price of Japanese goods in export markets and made them less competitive. But when the yen sank downward, so did spirits. Meanwhile, do-mestic inflation rushed upward like the mercury in a boiling thermometer, only stopping momentarily at 20 percent, the highest inflation in the industrial world.

Most catastrophic of all was the energy crisis. Japan imports 99 percent of its oil needs, and the price of oil quadrupled when the Arab world discovered its own deadly strength. Col-lapse was everywhere predicted for Japan's envied prosperity, a prosperity in which the Western nations had never completely believed. Without oil, they said smugly, even hopefully, this prosperity had to collapse.

It didn't collapse. Japan understands discipline. The government imposed controls; the people are accustomed to controls and they accepted them. They are now being planned for (even as I was by Foreign Affairs), and they are no doubt finding that government knows best.

Whatever Japan has to say — or pay — in order to get oil, she will say or pay. Although in the past Japan has felt kinship with the Jews as a minority, when her oil was cut off she quickly discovered mitigating circumstances in the attitude of the Arab world to Israel. The Arab world in return soon uncovered hidden wells of friendly feelings for Japan.

The Japanese want raw materials from Canada; Canada prefers to give them her manufactured goods, and she dislikes being treated like an undeveloped nation. So Japan will now accept manufactured goods — *if* accompanied by raw materials. Japan will trade for and work for what she needs. It's not a magic formula; it's brains plus work plus sacrifice.

Our faith should not be in their high GNP, but in the Japanese. We would be crazy to denigrate their stable, stubborn, peaceful strength. There are language barriers, but these are being broken by the tremendous, flourishing language-teaching industry in Japan. A more difficult barrier than language, between them and us, is a different manner of thought. The Japanese communicate much to each other beyond their spoken words. Based on mutually understood standards, these "gut" communications commit the nonspeaker as much as do verbal promises. Yet the average foreigner hears only spoken words, yes, no, good, bad, with perhaps delicate gestures and careful glances which he cannot interpret.

One way to help Americans comprehend the Japanese is by devoted reading of their excellent newspapers in English translation. These give you, not only the spoken statements of the people, but the committed actions — which are probably the ultimate word in "gut" communication.

The Japanese, in their desire to understand the Western world, now translate into their own language yearly a tremendous number of foreign books. *Jonathan the Seagull* (the title as translated into Japanese), *The Exorcist*, and *How to Be Your Own Best Friend* are recent publications in Tokyo and very popular. One wonders which elements in these books contribute toward a better understanding of us.

In comparison, very few Japanese books in English translation are published in the West, although the writing is generally on a high cultural and artistic level. Although the slow pace of such literature is one reason publishers avoid it, I think basically there isn't a demand for these books. Our desire to understand the Japanese is not nearly so intense or persistent as their desire to understand, and be understood by, us.

Toward this end the Mitsubishi Corporation recently gave a one million dollar grant to Harvard University to encourage Japanese studies; Sumitomo Shoji Kaisha Limited donated two million dollars to Yale University with the same objective; and the Japan Foundation gave ten million dollars to promote Japanese studies in ten American universities.

A good image is fast becoming an important factor in conducting favorable world trade. There is a great deal written by Japanese themselves about Japanese tourists and traveling men in Europe, Asia and North America, who by their crude behavior upset the sensibilities of the people in whose countries they travel. I can only say that nothing could surpass the discourtesy and insensitivity I have seen exhibited by some Western tourists while sight-seeing in the Orient. I have cringed to acknowledge our racial kinship, though I may have offended sometimes myself.

But knowing the Japanese as I do, I cannot believe that they become ogres when traveling abroad. Rather, they are over-sensitive to their own failings, and sometimes too willing to correct whatever they fear is being criticized — to the extent that they are said to be copying. They do not possess the bland self-confidence which makes us Americans determined to imprint "The American Way" on the Oriental scene. Although theoretically this may be a nice idea, it doesn't make us more lovable.

But the frustrated tourist is only one image of the Japanese. I have some different, very personal images of them. We have in our home a fragile porcelain bowl with the delicate grain-of-rice design. This was given to me by my first real Japanese friend, the gentle Mr. Hamasaki, when we saw him for the last time. He was dying of cancer then, a condition that had been aggravated by war starvation. He asked us to take the lovely blue and white bowl to our home to remind us of the days when we had been friends.

I remember a nightmare journey on a small steamer in the tropical South China Sea. Below decks, the ship was crowded with Japanese troops. On the open top deck forty-seven women and fifteen children, prisoners of the Japanese, lived for ten days, lying unprotected in the blazing sun, the flooding rain, the salt spray and the vomit, shaking with malaria and seasickness and hunger — and cursing the Japanese. Into this hell one night crept a young Japanese soldier. Silently, se-cretly, not daring to be seen by his comrades, he handed me a ten dollar bill and a scrawled note which said, "Please buy some food for the children. I do not need money. I do not expect to live."

I remember a young Japanese who came to Sandakan, North Borneo, shortly after the war, to search for the ashes of his soldier father, one of thousands of unidentified war dead there. There were more corpses in the cemeteries of that little South China Sea town than there were living inhabitants in its homes. Thousands of bundles of unsorted bones had been collected by the War Graves Commission to go to the various mourning countries — but with nothing in the bones to distinguish friend from foe. When Harry told him that his search was hopeless, the young man said sadly, "I understand. But I must do this for my mother who greatly mourns for my father. He was a good man."

I remember Tomoko, my new young friend from Vassar, when she answered my question, "Are you as free as your brothers are?" She said thoughtfully, "I am more free than the eldest son. He has the authority to command and be obeyed — but he has the responsibility for all family mistakes. He is never free. I am really sorry for our young men."

And I hear Kimpei Shiba's voice saying, "We have too much now in this country. Japan is growing soft. People need to suffer. You must tell us the truth. We have not all forgotten the war . . ."

These are images I have of the Japanese — not as nationals but as human companions in the long, long history of man.

Some last-minute realities as quoted from the Japanese press and radio, December, 1974:

Cost of living up by 49 percent.

Taxi fares up 32 percent.

Train fares up 25 percent.

Sirloin steak quoted at $10 a pound.

Kobe beef (beer and wine fed) quoted at $40 a pound.

The consumer price for rationed rice has been increased by 32 percent.

Relief payment to needy families (four-member household) has been increased to Y65,295 a month (about $217 per month based on an exchange rate of Y300 to the dollar). This is the third increase in relief payments to needy families during the year 1974.

Some students rioted in protest against the visit, in November, of President Ford of the United States. The students were outnumbered by the police at about one to four and failed to reach the airport.

Prime Minister Kakuei Tanaka resigned as prime minister and leader of the Liberal Democratic party. The LDP remains the governing party.

Index

322

Tokyo: Keiths' arrival in 3–5; Keiths' 1955 visit, 4; in World War II, 19; dynamism, 45; costs, 81; as Edo, 87, 175; Ginza, 92–93; classes in, 189–190, 192; slums, 189; suburbs, 190, 192

Tokyo University, 279

Tomoko, 235, 298, 315; in Tokyo, 179–183; at Ishihara interview, 216, 217; at Terayama interview, 238

Torii, 46–47, 101, 158, 196

Tourists: Japanese as, 118–119, 172, 196–197, 204, 313–314; in Kyoto, 168; at Imperial Palace, 196–197

Traffic, 45, 157, 159, 227

Train travel, 91, 102–105, 143–144, 147–149, 164–165; go-slow strike, 149, 165, 210

Tsubaki, Sadao, 79

Tsubo, 308

Tsurugaoka Hachiman Shrine, 231

Tsuruoka, Masao, 31

Uemura, Kazuo, 241, 280

Ukiyo-e erotica, 282

Unique Ballet Theater, 231–234

United Red Army, 124, 244, 246–247, 309; Lod Airport massacre, 27–28, 246, 309

University of California, 278

Uno Port, 147

Utamaro, Kitagawa, 268

Victoria (Canada), 286

Vietnam, 20, 36, 203, 217, 233–234

Views From Here (Mitaro), 289

Violence, 215–216; young radicals, 27–28, 259, 309–310, 316

War, Keiths' opposition to, 19–20, 152–153, 154–155, 300

Warner, Langdon, 167

Waseda University, 279; violence at, 28, 36, 124

Water Police Headquarters, 17

Western influence, 111, 165; dress, 50, 56; prosperity, 202; entertainment, 281

Wine, Japanese, 54, 76

Wisteria Maiden dance, 224

Women, 305–306; traditional role, 14, 15, 35, 191–192; western dress, 50, 56 improved position, 67, 127–128, 181, 187–188, 235, 261 301–303; housewives interviewed, 125–134; wives' role, 35, 129–130, 190, 191, 264–266; in Kyoto, 170; liberation movement, 210–211, 261, 294

Work, attitudes toward, 62–63

Workers: loyalty to employers, 88–89; demonstrations, 88–89 (*see also* Strikes); benefits, 138–139, 303, 310; goals, 202; women, 302, 303; education and, 304

World War II, 16–18, 19; effect on youth, 29, 214; effect on Japanese generally, 42, 44, 69–70, 152, 234, 268; Hiroshima, 155–156, 161, 163; Kyoto and, 167; role of emperor in surrender, 199; puritanism of military, 282

Yamada, Yoshiaki, 309–310

Yamasaki, Minoru, 39

Yamatane Museum, 32

Yasakuni Shrine, 46–48, 195–196

Yashima Plateau, 145

Yen, inflation and, 32, 311

Yodo River, 136, 138

Yokohama, 10, 17